RELIGIOUS LIBERTY ON TRIAL

Hanserd Knollys.

RELIGIOUS LIBERTY ON TRIAL

Hanserd Knollys—Early Baptist Hero

Muriel James

PROVIDENCE HOUSE PUBLISHERS
Franklin, Tennessee

Printed in the United States of America

01   00   99   98   97   5   4   3   2   1

Library of Congress Catalog Card Number: 97–68658

ISBN: 1–57736–048–6

Cover by Bozeman Design; cover photo adapted from Thomas Armitage, A History of the Baptists *(New York: Bryan, Taylor, & Co., 1887), 548.*

PROVIDENCE HOUSE PUBLISHERS
238 Seaboard Lane • Franklin, Tennessee 37067
800-321-5692

Contents

Acknowledgments

My appreciation first goes to those who wrote during the fifteenth and sixteenth centuries, and to those who wrote in the centuries since then. Much would have remained unknown had it not been for the staffs of numerous record offices and libraries. Especially useful for this book were the resources of the libraries of the British Museum, Cambridge and Oxford Universities, as well as Canterbury Archives and the Bodlein and Lambeth Palace Libraries.

Other valuable materials came from Dr. Williams's Library in London, Charterhouse School, and the State Papers of England and New England. The Lincolnshire Council and its Library and Archives, as well as Buckingham County Council and the Public Record Office were very helpful.

Individuals who have encouraged me in this project are numerous. In England, Hazel Webberly was unquestionably important. Her gracious hospitality and many days of driving me to libraries and parishes sustained and encouraged me. Tony Warren, Caty Mulcahy, and Roy Helham performed similar courtesies and I sincerely thank them.

Two others in England deserve special mention. Elaine Robson of the Lincolnshire Historical Society was most gracious with her time and expertise. Her skill in finding elusive records was most valuable. The same is true of Robert Kershaw, who also introduced me to some of the parishes in which Hanserd Knollys, the Baptist hero of this book, lived and worked.

Closer to home in California, I am indebted to the libraries at Stanford University, the University of California, and the Graduate Theological Union in Berkeley, as well as Sutro Library in San Francisco. Staffs of the New England Historical and Genealogical Society, the Baptist Historical Archives, and the Family History Library in Salt Lake City also provided assistance.

My thanks go to Betty Kot, a fine genealogist and teacher who first showed me the value of family history, and to Molly Gravell, who encouraged me in my original search. Sue Hughes is entitled to unlimited thanks for editing my numerous revisions, and, most important, for being genuinely interested in the subject and helping me find books that were hard to find.

My gratitude also goes to Betsy Fielding for reading an early draft of several chapters and urging me on because she thought this book would be useful in college and university history courses. Jamie Gaerlan, at the computer the first two years I tackled this research, was incredibly fine and also deserves thanks.

To Charles Deweese, director of Denominational and Academic Publishing of Providence House Publishers and a historian in his own right, my sincere gratitude for his enthusiasm and professional abilities. In the same publishing house, many thanks go to Trinda Cole for supervising and copyediting this project, and to Ann Rehmann for her public-relations skills.

As for my family and friends? They were wonderful and did not complain when I was discouraged about finding a crucial bit of documentation or needed to travel extensively to do so. They never interfered, but instead cheered me on and gave me the quiet and privacy I sometimes needed.

To those of you who are reading this, what can I say except that I hope it stimulates your own thinking. It is neither perfect nor complete. As the author, I alone am responsible for errors or omissions or opinions that may differ from others.

Naturally, I would enjoy hearing that this book has interested you and especially if it has added to your courage and faith.

Preface

History as Fragments

Billions of events occur simultaneously. Stars shoot across the sky, a bird swallows a grasshopper, an army destroys a town, a baby is born. When such events are remembered and spoken about, they become the branch of history called oral tradition. Stories from grandparents, great-grandparents, and other elders fall into the category of oral history. The details given and stories told may not be totally accurate, but they are valuable. They show particular perspectives that the storytellers want others to know about.

Another form of history is written. Some written history is based on what is remembered; some is based on recorded events such as vital statistics. Yet, like grandparents' stories, these too can have errors. Histories are always incomplete because all historians have limited information. They have only fragments of events, never the full story.

All historians decide what to include and what to ignore, what to emphasize and what to let die. Those who wrote during the 1600s, the major time frame of this book, and those who wrote after the 1600s each had a message to convey. Their messages were often contradictory because of their personal interests, the political and social agendas of the historian's own time, and fragmentary information. Many readers assume that published history is true when actually it may be partly true but incomplete. What is omitted can be as important as what is included.

Even direct information from diaries and autobiographies is incomplete and biased. Those writing about their own lives select what to include and what to omit depending upon their purposes and their expectations about who might read what they have written.

Daniel Boorstin, American historian and librarian of Congress for many years, defines the historian as "the scientist of hindsight." Boorstin claims that since historians know (or think they know) how it all turned out, they are preoccupied with the question: "'What chain of events made it come out that way?'"[1] Yet, the experiences of those who lived through the events, as well as their interpretations of such events, may be quite different from the "hindsight of the historian." Therefore, questions arise not only about what happened when, but also about the why and how and the what and where. Christopher Hill, a scholar and author of many books and articles about seventeenth-century English literature and history, and also a scholar in Marxism, refers to another problem. He says that for historians of the sixteenth and seventeenth centuries, there are not too few documents, but there are too many predecessors and therefore the process of sifting and criticizing others often leads to what he calls "an element of academic show off." Although great self-discipline is required for an academic critical style of writing, he also opens one of his many books with a quote by E. H. Carr, "Historians rarely know what they are up to."[2]

As always, the details are partial. This biography of Hanserd Knollys, an early Baptist hero who lived for almost the entire seventeenth century, is no exception. Although it reflects my deep interest in the chain of historical events that were related to his life and times, and although I have checked and rechecked, compared and analyzed hundreds of primary, secondary, and contemporary sources, this too is incomplete. Like archaeologists who dig and dig and finally have enough to estimate what an ancient city was like, historians put together bits and pieces of events. Hopefully the pieces I have put together reveal a dramatic pattern of a powerful seventeenth-century life that was lived with integrity because of a profound faith. Furthermore, studying him and his times lights up some important events regarding issues of freedom in political, social, and ecclesiastical history.

Barbara Tuchman, a fine historian, writes passionately about the importance of recognizing the relevance of the past in the experiences of today. "We can no more escape the past than we can our own genes," she writes. To her, historians are much like artists who perceive what they believe to be historical truths, gather evidence, and choose what to include. With language, they create a structure that conveys a picture.[3]

Hanserd Knollys, who became one of England's very first Baptists, was a man who would have agreed with Tuchman. He conveyed "pictures" with the use of powerful metaphors. On trial many times, stoned out of church, and banished, he seldom received fair judgment because the law of the land was ignored at times and unduly oppressive at other times. Yet, he went on preaching about the importance of religious freedom at a time when tolerance itself was on trial because it was considered by many to be a "sin."

My Initial Interest

I first became interested in this man when my niece, who wanted to join a particular historical society (Daughters of the American Revolution), asked me to help find some documents for researching the Knowles family who settled in Hampton, New Hampshire, in 1660. I agreed to do this. Having written my doctoral thesis in ancient history and another book on nineteenth-century history, I did not anticipate serious research problems. How very wrong I was!

Family history is a subcategory of history. It contains fragments of family stories, as well as fragments of written records from primary and secondary sources. I did not realize how difficult it would be to find some of the primary sources. Many were not available because they had been destroyed by fire or lost through carelessness or indifference. Also, secondary sources often contained errors that were repeated in book after book. In spite of that, each step of the way was interesting, often frustrating, and sometimes exhilarating.

One of my early discoveries was when I found a microfilm of an old parish record that showed a John Knowles was baptized by his father, the Rev. Hanserd Knollys, in Lincolnshire, England, and another record that showed John Knowles as a mariner who married Jamima Austin in Hampton, New Hampshire, in 1660.

A John Knowles with a father whose name was spelled *Knollys*? Yes, the *Knollys* and *Knowles* surnames were spelled in several different ways, even in the same original documents.

Knollys was spelled in different ways because most people in England, even those who were educated, were not taught spelling. The clergy, often called clerks, usually recorded what was reported to them orally and then wrote down what they heard, or thought they heard, spelling words phonetically. So *Knollys* was spelled *Knowles*, *Knolles*, *Knolies*, *Nowles*, and even *Noles* in England. However, writers of New England history most often show it as *Knowles*.

During this period in history, surnames were created for different reasons. Some names originally referred to occupation. For example, *Smith* was used for blacksmiths, *Taylors* tailored, *Brewsters* brewed, *Wheelwrights* wrought wheels. Some surnames referred to where a family lived. *Bridgeman* referred to a family living by a bridge. *Knollys* originally referred to a family living on a knoll, and *Knowles* was the later spelling of the name.

Other important records surfaced including land records that showed Hanserd Knollys had bought land in New England in 1638–1639 in an area that later became Portsmouth and that this land was confiscated by authorities when he was banished. Letters that Hanserd wrote to England, and to the then governor of Massachusetts, revealed more of his faith and his struggle of conscience against intolerance. I suddenly felt compelled to discover whether or not the John Knowles, who was in Hampton, New Hampshire, in 1660, was the same John who was born and baptized by his father Hanserd Knollys in Lincolnshire.

Certainly I am not the only one who has felt an inner compulsion to search for someone from the past. Many historians who write biographies feel a similar inner pull, as do the millions of people interested in genealogy and searching for family roots. They too get excited when they find a new piece that is part of one person's life or part of family history. The same thing happened to me. When I started on this search, I originally envisioned Hanserd Knollys as some very small part of a larger Knowles family exploration. Wrong again!

Researching his life and faith and visualizing it in the context of the history became a consuming interest. I began an intense study of church and state history as related to sixteenth- and seventeenth-century England. I could hardly believe what I discovered. How could the concerns of that period of time be so similar to those today? Why is it that so many people want the freedom to think as they choose, yet want to control what others think about civil government and matters of religion? These were only a few of the questions I asked myself. So, in many ways, this book is the result of my intense interest and my search for Hanserd Knollys, who, although dead for three hundred years, became so alive to me that I could not turn away.

Searching the Archives

In search of his manuscripts and other information, I went to England to look for primary records and to confirm or correct data in secondary sources. For example, several secondary references state he had only one child whereas primary documentation shows he had ten—seven sons and three daughters.

It was a deeply moving experience for me to sit in the famous archives of the Library of the British Museum in London and read Hanserd Knollys's very, very short autobiography, written twenty years before he died. A museum guard stood beside me to be sure that nothing happened to Hanserd Knollys's treasured writings. The print was fairly large, the page size was very small, only about four by five inches, and there were only forty-five pages about his incredibly active life that lasted ninety-three years.

Also interesting, though not part of this study, were his books in which he translated Hebrew, Greek, and Latin grammar into

English. They reflect that side of him that was always a scholar and teacher who wanted others to be able to read the Bible in the early languages. Other writings, such as his sermons, biblical expositions, and letters, reflected the depth of his religious faith, first as a priest in the Church of England, then as a nonconformist who became one of the first English Baptist ministers. In reading the few short things he wrote and studying his life, it is clear that the depth of his integrity will never be out-of-date.

Therefore, the focus of this historical biography is not so much on Hanserd Knollys's sermons and grammar books in four languages as it is on the whole context of his life as a man. He lived by faith throughout almost the entire seventeenth century when violence was very common against those who spoke in favor of religious freedom.

Using a broad historical context for understanding Hanserd Knollys has not been attempted by other historians. At first I wondered why it had not been done. Then, I realized the vast complexity of the task.

Fortunately, his little autobiography was a vital source for beginning to know him as a person. It revealed some of his theological struggles that led to his emerging commitment to religious freedom and faith. He never gave up this commitment. Even when exiled and imprisoned many times for believing as he did, he continued to teach and preach on the need for tolerance of others and religious freedom at a time when such beliefs were considered by many to be sinful.

Important as his memoir was, it was much too brief, and other short articles and books about him did not show his life in the wider context of history; so, I decided to study national and local history and search for civil as well as ecclesiastical documents to discover more about the chain of events that led to his extraordinary life. In the process, I searched early records in Lincolnshire, England, and finally found the will of his grandmother, Christobel Sutcliffe Hanserd Lacon. This was valuable documentation because Knollys was included as her grandson along with others who were beneficiaries. Family history can be important in historical biographies because it often indicates the effect of specific ancestors on later generations.

Parish records of births, marriages, and deaths were also invaluable. So were the poll and land taxes, customs and excise records, and other primary sources. Original records from schools and universities including Charterhouse and Cambridge provided further documentation of Hanserd Knollys.

However, it was the study of national and local history during the sixteenth and seventeenth centuries that provided much of the crucial context for this book. The *State Papers* of England and the *Provincial Papers* of New England documented several court trials Knollys endured. Some secondary and contemporary sources were very useful. Some were not if they only repeated what had already been written, including the errors, or if they were opinions masquerading as facts. Even so, occasional references, like spokes radiating out from the hub of a wheel, pointed in so many possible directions that life would be too short to explore every possibility. In my bibliography, I have included only those references that I found to be most accurate and useful.

Along with brief backgrounds of rulers, reformers, and church authorities of the sixteenth and seventeenth centuries, specific episodes are included about Hanserd Knollys in relationship to Charles I, Charles II, James II, and Oliver Cromwell (Lord Protector). There were also other powerful people in his life such as Bulstrode Whitelocke (Commissioner of the Great Seal), Sir Edward Hyde (Earl of Clarendon), Francis Willoughby (Baron of Parham), and Archbishop Laud.

Some of the less-known ones, but influential in different ways were William Kiffin, Vavasor Powell, John Bastwick, Benjamin Keach, William Legge, Venners Rifing, Anna Trapnel, Edward Montague, Henry Jessey, John Lilburne, Christian Ravis, and Katherine Sutton.

When he was in New England (1638–1641), some of those who are part of this biography include John Winthrop, John Cotton, John Underhill, George Burdett, Anne Hutchinson, and Thomas Larkham. They are included because of specific episodes that reflect turbulent times in the colonies when faith and religious freedom, tolerance and intolerance were again on trial.

For me, the years of researching Hanserd Knollys in a historical context and getting to know about the events of his time brought him to life in a way that is difficult to explain. It has greatly expanded my awareness of how one individual can affect local and national history and vice versa. Furthermore, writing this has challenged me more than writing any of my other books or articles.

This book is intended for students of any age who are interested in learning something new about history and implications of the past for current and future situtations. I am not using the academicians' style that compares all past and current writings that may be even remotely related to the subject. If I did that, the theme and intention of this book would be buried in an avalanche of paper.

However, I am including some previously unpublished information from primary records and newly published materials from books such as *Parliamentary Army Chaplains, 1642–51* by Anne Laurence. Her fresh research of army records gives lists with dates that show when Hanserd Knollys was chaplain in Parliament's army and under whom he served—a valuable addition to the few known facts of his life.

A Look Ahead

This book, RELIGIOUS LIBERTY ON TRIAL: HANSERD KNOLLYS— EARLY BAPTIST HERO, is organized into eight chapters. The first chapter is "Rulers, Reformers, and Discontent."

Discontent under totalitarian rule is as old as time, but when the Reformation emerged from the Renaissance, when those who translated the Bible in new ways were branded as heretics, when the intolerant rulers of church and state created acts of supremacy and demands for uniformity, then discontent and protest became widespread. People began to demand religious and political freedom, partly due to the influence of scholars such as Wycliffe, Tyndale, Erasmus, Luther, Zwingli, Calvin, and Knox. The second chapter, "Rebellion and Family History," has the focus on the county of Lincolnshire where conformity was demanded by law, but obedience to conformity could not be ensured. Hanserd Knollys's ancestors were from Lincolnshire County where people did not hesitate to rebel against repressive rule. Although in 1536 a rebellion there against Henry VIII was quickly suppressed, the feelings were not. They still ran high toward the end of the reign of Elizabeth I when Hanserd was born.

"Cambridge and Conversion" includes a significant event during Hanserd Knollys's childhood when he fought with his brother. Later, as a student at Cambridge, he defined himself as a sinner because of his occasional failure to keep his promises.

Ordained in the Church of England, after two years of doubt about some of the rituals, he renounced his ordination. However, as an itinerant preacher and lecturer, Hanserd remained in spiritual agony.

The next chapter discusses "The Elect and Elected in Colonial New England" and provides background for understanding some of the freedom-seekers who migrated to the American colonies in hopes of religious freedom and yet found much less than expected. Even the Pilgrims and Puritans disagreed with each other.

The civil and religious authorities in Boston, Massachusetts, considered themselves to be "elected" by God and banished people who did not agree with them.

The "Escapes and Banishments" of Hanserd Knollys began in 1638 when he talked his way out of jail in England and fled to Massachusetts with his wife. Then life became even rougher.

He was banished from Boston, Dover, and Strawbery Banke (now Portsmouth) for criticizing the authorities, and in 1641, Hanserd Knollys returned to England destitute.

"War without Wisdom" followed and Hanserd Knollys enlisted as a chaplain. However, he became so disillusioned that he resigned. He joined an Independent church but left because of disagreements about infant baptism. In 1646, he formed one of the earliest Baptist churches in England.

Then came "Trials and More Trials." Hanserd Knollys was stoned out of a church for preaching about the need for tolerance and religious freedom. He was put on trial before the Committee for Plundered Ministers.

However, he was imprisoned many other times, once because the authorities erroneously associated him with the Fifth Monarchists, a radical religious group who believed they would and should rule the world. After being released, in 1660, he fled from England to Holland and Germany. There he wrote books on Latin, Greek, and Hebrew grammar to assist people in studying the Scriptures in ancient languages. He also wrote introductions and recommendations to controversial books written by others.

In the last chapter, Hanserd Knollys faces death with the desire "To Owe Nothing but Love." After returning from Germany, he had been imprisoned for breaking the Conventical Act, an act which forbade nonconformers to worship in groups larger than five persons, and he also had another problem. His house and school had been illegally taken by the army in the name of Charles II. What could he do? Never afraid to do what he believed was right, Hanserd sued in 1670 and won the case years later.

When James II became king, Knollys, then eighty-four years old, was imprisoned for the last time because he refused to use his great influence with the Baptists to convince them to agree with some changes King James wanted. He refused because these changes would give special favors to some groups and deny these favors to others. A brilliant man, a true hero, and a defender of religious freedom, Hanserd Knollys remained a student and teacher, working and writing until he was ninety-three years old. His bones lie in Bunhill Fields, the only cemetery in England that would accept the bodies of nonconformers.

That Old Disciple

When Hanserd Knollys wrote his tiny autobiography in 1672, he was seventy-four years old. He had been ill and close to death, and many in his family had died the year before, including his wife, whom he dearly loved and cherished. Yet, he continued to work.

At his death in 1691, his longtime friend and colleague William Kiffin added to the tiny twenty-year-old autobiography the last letter Hanserd Knollys wrote to his church just a few days before dying. The book was published in 1692, and references to it in this book are cited as *Life and Death*.

Knollys wrote at a time when the letter "s" was often written as we currently write "f." Instead of modernizing it, I am leaving some passages in the old style, as this seems to add a rich flavor for today's reader who is interested in the past. Another interesting custom during the seventeenth century was the frequent use of paragraph-long summaries which were put on the covers of many books. On the cover of Hanserd's was the statement created either by William Kiffin or by the publisher:

> The Life and Death of That Old Difciple of Jefus Chrift, the Eminent Minifter of the Gospel, Mr. Hanferd Knollys, who died in the Ninety Third Year of his Age written with his own Hand to the year 1672, and continued in General, in a Epiftle by Mr. VVilliam Kiffin. To which is added, His laft Legacy to the Church.

And Then I Wonder

While researching and writing RELIGIOUS LIBERTY ON TRIAL, I often wondered why I was so excited about this man. Would he interest anyone except me? Then I recalled John Bunyan, author of *Pilgrim's Progress,* whose life paralleled Hanserd Knollys's and who ended up in the same cemetery. Bunyan, too, was imprisoned several times and wrote his famous allegory during a long stay in prison. Published in 1678, it was immediately popular as it reflected the trials and tribulations of the time. In his author's apology at the beginning of the book, Bunyan shared his uncertainty, "Some said, John, print it; others said, Not so; Some said, It might do good; others said, No."

I resonate with Bunyan's statement and ruminate about my own pilgrimage and wonder if others will be interested in this early Baptist hero Hanserd Knollys, born during the reign of Elizabeth I, an independent thinker who lived almost three hundred years ago, and who was put on trial time after time for believing in the power of love and the need for religious freedom.

I hope you find his life and work, and the history of his times, to be interesting and inspirational. As for me, Hanserd Knollys captured my admiration, and whether he is one of my ancestors or not, I am grateful for a kinship of spirit.

FELTER.

1

Rulers, Reformers, and Discontent

*Furthermore, every man runs his own risk in
believing as he does, and he must see to it himself that
he believes rightly. As nobody else can go to heaven or
hell for me, so nobody else can believe or disbelieve for
me.*
— *Martin Luther, 1483–1546*

From Renaissance to Reformation

Religious freedom was on trial during the sixteenth and seventeenth centuries. In England, anyone who disagreed with the authorities was severely punished—branded, tortured, burned, or hung. Yet, it was not unusual for the same intolerant authorities to also be punished—tried by Parliament and banished or executed.

This is a biography about a specific man in the wider context of social, cultural, and political history. It is about his successes and failures, his challenges and his choices, his personal integrity, and his commitment to freedom. Hanserd Knollys (1598–1691) was a dissenter and a nonconformist who was influential in both the political and ecclesiastical currents of his time. He recognized no other authority except what he believed to be the will of God, yet he was tolerant toward those who held other beliefs. It was his faith and toleration, in a time when church and state were often intolerant, which deserve attention and respect. In many ways, he was like a classic hero, a defender of religious freedom.

In understanding the overwhelming conflicts of the seventeenth century during which Hanserd Knollys lived, it is necessary to briefly refer back to the Middle Ages, the Renaissance, and the Reformation and how issues of religious freedom were played out with prejudice and violence.

The period of the Middle Ages existed between antiquity and the Renaissance. It began in the fifth century with the fall of Roman political control in western Europe and continued until about 1300 with the papacy in political, as well as ecclesiastical, control. During this period, law was systematized, secular universities were established, and international trade flourished. Feudal structures broke down as Spain, France, and England emerged as national monarchies.

Social conflict also emerged, partly due to the spiritual search for a direct relationship with God through inner mystical experiences or personal study of the Bible. Thomas Aquinas (1224–1274) was one of the most influential thinkers of the late Middle Ages. An Italian philosopher and theologian, he also studied and taught in France. He believed that reason was possible within the context of faith—that some truths were known through revelation, others through sensory experience, and that God was known through both. Based on the writings of Aristotle and the early church fathers, his argument was that, in religion, the help of revelation was needed along with sensory experience. To Thomas Aquinas, the two were compatible. Not everyone agreed.

The desire to be free of intolerant rule and to be self-determined began as a recognizable movement in the Middle Ages when social mobility was severely restricted. People were born into a particular class, and it was nearly impossible for them to change their situation. Few outside the clergy and nobility could read. Except for rulers, people were expected to obey, not think. It was not until the cultural and intellectual change known as the Renaissance, from the French word *renaistre* meaning "rebirth" or "to be born again," that upward mobility from one class to another became more common.

The Renaissance began in Italy about A.D. 1300 with a revival of classical art, literature, and learning. However, the Renaissance did not take the same form throughout Europe. In Germany, claims historian Will Durant, the Renaissance was more like a revival of early Christianity than a flowering of classical letters and philosophy.[1] During the Renaissance, which lasted almost two hundred years, a new humanism emerged. People began to think in new ways, and what they were thinking was often contrary to what the political and ecclesiastical authorities claimed to be true. Both church and state became increasingly intolerant of individual conscience, and their use of power was often unbearably restrictive. Slow-burning resentment against authorities flared up from time to time and became a conflagration fueled by desperation.

When these independent thinkers began to act on what they believed instead of only obeying those in power, they were clearly declaring that they valued personal freedom even more than life itself. They also began to see that society needed to be reformed if individual freedom would be possible.

The Reformation, a political and religious movement of the sixteenth century, overlapped the Renaissance and was greatly empowered by it. Generally believed to have been a middle- and lower-class movement, scholars have defined the Reformation by emphasizing the individuals who fought for freedom from church and state. They have also focused on people's anger against the absolute authority and abuses of the Church and the clergy—the Church was selling absolution of sin for a high price and equating the sale with the forgiveness of God. Such misuse of authority caused some people to decide that *nobody* should have that much power.

However, historian H. G. Wells disagreed with this narrow perspective. He understood the Reformation to be driven by three distinct groups: the rulers who wanted to strengthen themselves by stopping the flow of money and power to Rome; the people who were so outraged by the unrighteousness of the Church that they wanted to start over with a new Church purified from the corruption of the rich and powerful; and those within the Church who wanted to restore its rightful goodness and power.[2] These were not class distinctions as much as they were differences in motivation.

Translators as Heretics

Yet even before the Reformation, there were individuals and groups who "protested" against the authoritarian position taken by both the papacy and the rulers. These protesters were called "heretics" and were beaten or killed, excommunicated or banished. One of these was John Wycliffe.

John Wycliffe.

John Wycliffe (c. 1310–1384) was an Englishman who studied and taught theology at Oxford, and in 1360, was master of Balliol College. He was a prolific writer who promoted the doctrine of predestination. This was the belief that God predestines, before birth, those to be lost or saved in eternity. Those to be saved were the "elect" and could be identified by their good works.

Both Parliament and King Edward III consulted him about whether or not England should make payments to finance Rome's building programs, and Wycliffe wrote pamphlets refuting the pope's claims on England's livelihood. He also wrote against many beliefs of the established Church.[3] However, his opposition to war and serfdom made him unpopular with many of the rich and powerful. His vitriolic attack against the pope and clergy who preached poverty to others but lived in luxury themselves was, understandably, also resented.[4]

Wycliffe believed in a direct relationship with God without the necessity for priestly mediation. He also claimed that all people, not just the clergy, needed direct access to the word of God as found in the Bible. Because he believed this, he initiated two translations of the Bible from Latin into English, one being more idiomatic than the other. This was considered heresy because the Church considered itself to be the only authority. The pope declared Wycliffe a heretic; to others, he was a reformer.

Although Christianity had arrived in England in the third century, by the fourteenth century only a few passages of the Bible had been translated from Latin into English. The Old Testament was originally written in Hebrew, with the Books of Daniel and Ezra in Aramaic. It was a Semitic language from the sixth century B.C. and was the official language of the Persian Empire. In contrast, most of the New Testament was first written in Greek with parts of it in Aramaic. It is thought that Jesus and his disciples spoke Aramaic.

Latin was originally a Roman dialect, influenced by the Celts of northern Italy and Greece. Gradually, it became the basis of the modern Romance languages and the official language of the Catholic Church. In contrast, in the English courts of law, French was used until anti-French sentiment became strong during the Hundred Years' War (1337–1453). This war was a series of battles fought intermittently between France and England over territorial limits, including English attempts to take over part of France and French support of Scotland's efforts to be independent of England. The two countries also fought over England's claim to the French throne through the mother of Edward III. The battles went on and on, but the turning point came when the British army was attacked by forces successfully led by Joan of Arc.

After these wars, the use of English became more common, and the first translation of the complete Bible from Latin into English was by John Wycliffe. It helped spur the Reformation and, by 1450, there were thirty-three different translations. Perhaps an even more important factor was the development of the printing press by Johann Gutenberg in Germany in 1450. The first book printed by moveable type was in Latin, in 1455, and became known as the Gutenberg Bible. Until then, the Bible and other written works were only available in manuscript form and not readily accessible in England outside the monasteries. When the printing press arrived in England twenty years after it had been created, it gave new impetus to the spread of education.

William Tyndale (1492–1536), another reformer, was a scholar at both Oxford and Cambridge. As Wycliffe had already translated the Bible from Latin into English, Tyndale went back to earlier sources. In 1525, he translated the New Testament from Greek into English and parts of the Old Testament from Hebrew into English. However, publishing his translations was forbidden in England. He went to Germany, met with Martin Luther, and many copies of his translations were smuggled back into England. Unfortunately he disagreed with the humanist Chancellor Sir Thomas More and, in 1536, was imprisoned, strangled, and burned at the stake. Joan Boucher received the same sentence in 1550 for distributing Tyndale's translation, visiting prisoners, and refusing to apologize for doing so.

The movement against educating the public to read the Bible had begun in 1543. All of Tyndale's translations were ordered destroyed. The law was that no women, except gentlewomen, no artificers, no journeymen, no husbandmen, nor laborers were to read the Bible to themselves nor to anyone else on pain of a month's incarceration in prison.

Subsequent English translations, including the King James Authorized Version of 1611 and the Standard Version of 1946–1952, were greatly influenced by Tyndale's style with its beauty and simplicity. This availability of the Bible to the laity, as well as to the clergy, had an enormous impact. People gained new freedom to read and interpret the Scriptures for themselves. It made possible "the priesthood of all believers," the concept that the priesthood was a shared role and not the exclusive possession of the official clergy. Many other translations followed including one by Miles Coverdale ten years after Tyndale's. His was the first complete English Bible to be printed. Coverdale based his translation on German and Latin as well as on Tyndale's version.

Yet, scholarship was not only related to the Bible. Desiderius Erasmus (c. 1466–1536) was born near Rotterdam, lived at the same time as Tyndale, and was the greatest humanistic scholar in northern Europe at that time. Humanism emphasized the dignity and worth of the individual based on the belief that people are rational beings with the potential for goodness and truth. Erasmus believed that early Christian ethics were more important than trying to reform the Church. Restless in mind and body, he was strongly against ignorance because it so often led to superstition.[5] With this point of view, Erasmus's writings also helped fuel the Reformation.

The author of many books, witty and elegant in style, Erasmus was best known for his book *Praise of Folly*, which he wrote while a lecturer at Oxford and Cambridge and while staying with Sir Thomas More. More was also a humanist as well as a statesman and chancellor of England. Erasmus described his friend in glowing terms as a "man for all seasons." However, when More refused to attend the wedding of Anne Boleyn to Henry VIII, he was accused of failing to approve of the king as head of the Church of England. For this he was beheaded. Much later he was declared a saint.[6]

When *Praise of Folly* was published in 1511, it immediately became popular at Cambridge as a satire against church officials. Naturally, it infuriated them. Yet, Erasmus continued to write, and his first edition of the New Testament was published in 1516. It contained the Greek text and his own Latin translation along with his commentary. Later, when Erasmus's *Colloquia* was published, Erasmus was accused of trying to influence Martin Luther. A literary battle raged between the two of them as they disagreed on interpretations of the New Testament and the nature and function of the clergy. In fact, Luther forbade his sons to read Erasmus. Luther claimed the Bible to be the most important authority, not the Church or state. He took the Bible literally in contrast to Erasmus (and later Hanserd Knollys) who interpreted parts of it as allegorical.

Tolerant and Intolerant Reformers

Three of the most important early reformers in Germany and Switzerland, Martin Luther, Huldrych Zwingli, and John Calvin, were stimulated by Wycliffe's English translation of the Bible and shared his opposition to the papacy's great power. Each of the three believed he was right, and each was intolerant of the views of the other two.

Martin Luther (1483–1546), often called the "Father of the Protestant Reformation," was a professor in biblical theology at the University of Wittenberg in Germany. In 1517, he posted his theses,

"Disputation for Clarification of the Power of Indulgences," on the door of the church. With the publication of his Ninety-five Theses in German, he became very controversial because, among other things, he criticized the Church's practice of selling forgiveness for money. He also refused to submit to Church authority and urged that individual faith be based on Bible study. (Perhaps his anger against authority was partly a result of the harsh schooling he had received as a child. For example, one day at school he was flogged fifteen times.)

When condemned and excommunicated, Luther would not recant his beliefs but continued to teach and preach while he translated the Bible from the original Hebrew and Greek into German. This became the official Bible for German Protestants. Known as a lusty man, Luther ruled his wife and loved his six children and eleven other children who were orphaned nieces and nephews. He also enjoyed food and wine, feasting and dancing, and jokes. Yet, he often exploded in anger. Courageous and dogmatic, he claimed he was unable to pray unless at the same time he was cursing the papists:

> Many think I am too fierce against popery; on the contrary I complain that I am, alas, too mild; I wish I could breathe out lightening [*sic*] against pope and popedom.[7]

Luther also maintained that what a man believes or disbelieves is a matter of his own conscience. Furthermore, since this took nothing away from the temporal authority, the authority should be content to attend to its own affairs, let men believe this or that as they are able and willing, and constrain no one by force.

Another leader of the Reformation was Huldrych (sometimes spelled *Ulrich*) Zwingli (1484–1531), a priest in the Great Cathedral in Zurich, Switzerland. He studied Latin in school, the classics in the University of Vienna, and taught himself Greek so he could read the New Testament in its original language.

Like Luther, he opposed the sale of indulgences and other practices including the adoration of saints and the worship of images. Unlike Luther, he was deeply influenced by liberal humanism and greatly admired Erasmus.[8] After he studied a Latin translation of the New Testament, Zwingli, like Luther, came to believe in biblical authority over any other kind. He then persuaded the Zurich legislature to forbid religious teaching unless it was based on the Bible.

Zurich became a theocracy under Zwingli, who began to act somewhat like a dictator and taught that neither the pope nor Church was necessary to devout Christians. Zwingli's power was challenged from two directions—by the more radical Anabaptists and by conservative Roman Catholics. The Anabaptists were believers in adult rebaptism and were also against Luther whom they accused of retaining too much of the Roman Catholic ritual. (Later, the term Anabaptist was used as an accusation against any who were thought to be carrying Protestant beliefs too far.) Also opposing Zwingli were the conservative Catholics who did not want change. This disagreement became so intense that it escalated into a civil war. Much to the horror of Erasmus, Zwingli encouraged the fighting and was killed in battle. To restore peace, each canton in Switzerland was given the freedom to choose its own religion.

John Calvin.

John Calvin (1509–1564) was a French theologian who was forced to flee France because of his humanistic theological writings. He then made Geneva his home, and like Luther and Zwingli, Calvin also stressed the importance of the Bible and God's sovereignty. To him, God's sovereignty was absolute—God preordained all things, including the salvation or damnation of each person, and salvation was due only to God's grace, not to personal merit. The virtues of piety, thrift, and hard work were signs that a person was "elected" to a state of grace and, of course, the "elect" were church members. Calvin also preached that financial success was evidence of God's grace. In America, Calvin's values became known as the Puritan Ethic, and his concept of the "elect" became a major issue in early Massachusetts, as will be seen in a later chapter.

Although the reformers Luther, Zwingli, and Calvin often disagreed on details of doctrine and practice, they strongly agreed on the importance of the Bible and the rejection of papal authority. Because of this agreement, their followers were sometimes accepting of each other. But not always. For example, Luther, already intolerant of Erasmus, was against any book that disagreed with his own position; so, Luther had Zwingli's books prohibited in Wittenberg.[9]

Calvin's intolerance was expressed in an even more direct way against Michael Servetus (1511–1553), the physician who discovered the circulation of the blood through the lungs. Servetus thought the trinitarian doctrine was wrong, that it denied the concept of one God, and wrote about it. He furthermore believed that only adults should be baptized. Servetus also edited a Latin translation of the Bible. This took years to do, and some of his interpretations infuriated the Catholics and the growing number of Protestants. When Calvin accused him, Servetus was sentenced for rejecting trinitarianism in favor of unitarianism and for rejecting infant baptism. Although burned at the stake, to the end he denied he was a heretic.[10]

Calvin's theological beliefs were widely popularized in Scotland through the religious reformer John Knox (1505–1572). Originally a Roman Catholic priest, Knox was the founder of Presbyterianism. When Mary I had became queen, Knox fled for his life to Geneva and studied there with John Calvin. He agreed with Calvin's concept of predestination of the "elect."

It was while he was in Geneva that Knox wrote his treatise against women in government titled, *The First Blast of the Trumpet against the Monstrous Regiment of Women.* This was primarily against Mary of Guise, who was the Roman Catholic regent of Scotland for her daughter, Mary, Queen of Scots. Knox was also against any other women rulers. Elizabeth I became queen the year it was published, and, understandably, resented the treatise and Knox. Yet, she managed to tolerate it because it was politically expedient to do so.

In 1559, Knox returned to Scotland after an exile of almost twelve years. The French, who had been in control in Scotland, were driven out. Then a three-way conflict developed among the Roman Catholic Church, the Church of England, and the emerging Protestant groups. As a result, Roman Catholicism was abolished in Scotland; and on August 1, 1560, John Knox and some of his followers drew up the Confession of Faith, which is still the official statement of the Presbyterian Church of Scotland.

Like Knox, Hanserd Knollys was a strong Calvinist and focused on the importance of the Bible. He was also one of the few dissenters who tolerated others holding different opinions. Although he believed in the salvation of the "elect," he was not a supremacist, and he did not insist that others agree with him. Whereas Luther had attacked the Church and papacy with fury, Erasmus advocated peaceful compromise that could lead to a reformed Church. Knollys was more in tune with this humanistic melody.

Supremacy and the Throne

The supremacy of the throne and uniformity in religious belief were major issues in England and subsequently in the colonies. John Calvin's ideas became most influential in the English Protestant movement, including his belief that the state should be subject to the Church and that the Church was to be the final authority. Calvin was a contemporary of John Knox and the rebellious and authoritarian Henry VIII (1491–1547).

Rulers of England in the
Sixteenth and Seventeenth Centuries

Henry VIII	1509—1547
Edward VI	1547—1553
Jane Grey	1553
Mary I	1553—1558
Elizabeth I	1558—1603
James I (VI of Scotland)	1603—1625
Charles I	1625—1649
Commonwealth Declared	
Oliver Cromwell, Lord Protector	1653—1658
Richard Cromwell, Lord Protector	1658—1659
Restoration of the Monarchy	
Charles II	1660—1685
James II	1685—1688
William III	1689—1702
and Mary II	1689—1694

Athletic and well-educated, Henry became king at age eighteen. He was a Roman Catholic and wanted to remain one but would not tolerate the papacy dictating to him about his marriages. Henry wanted a male heir and demanded an annulment from his first wife, Catherine of Aragon. Although she had given birth to six children, only one daughter survived, the future Mary I. Henry's attraction to twenty-year-old Anne Boleyn gave him the impetus for seeking an annulment. When the pope refused to give him what he wanted, Henry took the situation into his own hands and ordered the English clergy to accept him as head of the Church of England. In this way, all payments to Rome could be cut off and he could arrange for his own annulments, marriages, divorces, and beheadings, including that of Anne Boleyn, his second wife.

The Act of Supremacy, initiated by Henry VIII, was passed by Parliament in 1534. This act declared that the supreme power of the Church of England was vested in the throne, not in the papacy of the Roman Catholic Church. Then there was the Treason Act, which prohibited anyone from worshiping except in the new Church of England. The Oath of Supremacy followed, and those who refused to take it were executed. Three years later, Henry authorized an English translation of the Bible and ordered that it be used in all churches. He also dissolved the monasteries and sold the land to gentry who sided with him.[11] Those who did not lost their property. This was the case of some in Lincolnshire where the Knollys family originated.

Edward VI was born in 1537, the son of Henry VIII and Jane Seymour, who was Henry's third wife. When Edward was ten years old, Henry died and Edward became king of both England and Ireland in 1547. A follower of Luther, he was a scholar of Latin, Greek, French, and Italian, played the flute, and enjoyed astronomy.[12] Delicate in health, Edward was controlled by the Council of Regency led by his uncle Edward Seymour, Duke of Somerset. Seymour influenced Parliament to repeal the treason and heresy acts. In addition, under the Act of Uniformity instigated in 1547, all churches were required to use Archbishop Thomas Cranmer's *Book of Common Prayer.*

Two years later, the unscrupulous John Dudley, Duke of Northumberland, plotted against Seymour and had him arrested on a charge of high treason and executed. Whereas both Seymour and Dudley had agreed with Edward's commitment to emerging Protestantism, they had done so for different reasons. Seymour recognized its intrinsic value; Dudley saw it as an avenue for gaining more personal power.

With Dudley in control, changes accelerated. The revised second *Book of Common Prayer* was published. The second Act of Uniformity was passed. It forbade confession to a priest and made Holy Communion an act of remembrance, rather than an act of transubstantiation. These changes were due to the strong influence of Luther and Calvin through those who had studied with them on the continent and returned to England.

Then other plots unfolded. John Dudley wanted his son, who was married to Lady Jane Grey, to have power. When the young King Edward was sick, Dudley influenced him to disown his half-sisters Mary and Elizabeth so they would not be in line for the throne and instead name Lady Jane Grey as next in line. Edward died of tuberculosis at age sixteen. Lady Jane Grey was crowned. Her reign lasted only nine days before she was overthrown by Mary Tudor. Lady Jane and Dudley were ordered executed.[13]

Two Marys and Their Deaths

Mary Tudor, born in 1516, ruled England and Ireland as Mary I for only five years from 1553 to 1558. She was the daughter of Henry VIII and his first wife, Catherine of Aragon, and half-sister to Edward VI. She was, in Catholic eyes, the only legitimate child of her father. To rid himself of Catherine, Henry claimed that Mary was illegitimate because she was the result of a union between himself and his own brother's widow. This, he said, must be incestuous. The pope was not swayed. He would neither dissolve the marriage nor declare Mary illegitimate.

Intelligent and well-educated, Mary took the throne at age thirty-seven after the death of Edward VI. He had made English mandatory for worship services instead of Latin. Mary believed his rule had been intolerable and thought it was her absolute duty to restore the country to Catholicism. When she married the Catholic Philip II of Spain, Parliament was irate.

Furthermore, because her religious policies caused so much bloodshed, she was soon dubbed "Bloody Mary." During her reign, over three hundred Protestants were executed, often tortured to death, in the name of the Church. Hated by many, Mary Tudor died in 1558, childless and seriously depressed. She was followed to the throne by her sister Elizabeth I.

The other Mary, who was also a Catholic queen, was Mary Stuart (1542–1587), Queen of the Scots. Great-niece to Henry VIII, she became queen of Scotland when she was only six days old when her father, James V of Scotland, died. In Scotland, as in England, there was bitter strife between the Catholics and

Protestants, so when Mary Stuart was still very young, her firmly Catholic mother, Mary of Guise, sent her to France.

At age sixteen, she married the heir to the French throne, Frances II. He died after only a year, leaving Mary a young Catholic widow at eighteen. She then returned to Scotland, more French than Scot, to rule a country that had become more Presbyterian than otherwise.

Beautiful but unwise, Mary married again, this time to her cousin, Henry Stuart, Earl of Darnley. He was vindictive, ambitious, and jealous of her male French secretary and, in 1566, arranged for him to be murdered in her presence. Mary Stuart then found solace with James Hepburn, Earl of Bothwell, and the next year her husband, Earl of Darnley, was mysteriously strangled. Bothwell was suspected of the murder when he divorced his wife and three months later married Mary.

This so aroused the wrath of the army that, in 1567, Mary, Queen of Scots, was forced to give up the throne in favor of her one-year-old son, James, who was to be raised a Protestant. Of him we will hear more later. Bothwell fled to Italy, and Mary fled to England to her cousin Elizabeth. There she had so many Catholic supporters that she was seen as a threat to the English throne, so Elizabeth imprisoned her for eighteen years. When a Catholic plot to assassinate Elizabeth was discovered, Mary was thought to be involved. She was tried in an English court and Elizabeth, somewhat reluctantly, had her beheaded in 1587 at the age of forty-four.

Elizabeth: Last of the Tudors

The movement away from Catholicism toward Protestantism accelerated when Mary I died and her half-sister, Elizabeth I, became queen and ruled from 1558 to 1603. The last of the Tudors to rule England, Elizabeth, when she took the throne, was determined to achieve an acceptable compromise for the religious turmoil that had so polarized the people.

Her compromise was to establish a National Church of England. Ten days after her coronation, she assembled her first parliament and let it be known that she desired one uniform order of religion. Like her father Henry VIII, Elizabeth was to be the final authority instead of the pope. To effect this, she immediately allowed Protestants into her council and excluded the Catholics. An Act of Supremacy was soon passed that reestablished the Crown as "supreme governor" of the Church.

Unlike her father, who remained Roman Catholic except for rejecting papal control, Queen Elizabeth demanded that the *Book of Common Prayer* be used in all churches. Added to that was the requirement that the Thirty-nine Articles, defining the teachings of the Church, be accepted as doctrine for the entire nation. Those who did not attend church on Sundays and feast days, or did not join in common prayer, were fined twelve pence. If they refused the sacraments and rites or openly rejected prayers, they were imprisoned for six months.

Elizabeth also insisted on uniformity in clerical vestments and in the use of the liturgy. When the Oath of Supremacy, giving her the right to head the new Church, was demanded of nine thousand clergymen, only 187 refused to take it.[14]

However, this nonconformist 2 percent had a powerful effect on subsequent developments. For example, Thomas Cartwright (1555–1603) was strongly against Church of England ritual and in favor of Presbyterianism. When he lost his position as a Cambridge professor and published an *Admonition to Parliament*, he had to flee from England.

The acts of Parliament and the fines imposed for disobedience did not resolve the issues surrounding the use of authority. Catholics were vehemently against Elizabeth's religious and political control. The Irish suffered both religious and economic oppression as well as the plundering of their ancient oaks which were used to build ships to fight the Spanish Armada. On the Protestant side, there were many who claimed her religious changes were nowhere near far-reaching enough. Although willing to accept an episcopal form of church government, with bishops and archbishops, they refused to use the revised *Book of Common Prayer* and because of this were labeled "nonconformists."

Some nonconformists were sarcastically called "Puritans" as they wanted to "purify" the Church from everything Roman Catholic

and, instead, establish a more representative form of church government. Many members in the House of Commons were in favor of the
Puritans.

Other nonconformists become "Separatists." Originally called
"Brownists" after Robert Browne (1550–1633), they wanted total
separation of church and state and a congregational form of church
government. The Pilgrims were early Separatists.

In general, groups that were not Roman Catholic became
collectively known as Protestants, and smaller groups within
the movement were eventually called denominations. Thus, we
have the Anglicans, Presbyterians, Congregationalists, Baptists,
Methodists, and many others.

In spite of religious dissension, Elizabeth was able to keep
England together while she was alive. After her death in 1603, the
country began to flounder. Since Elizabeth died childless, England
turned to the Scottish throne for an heir. Scotland was firmly
Presbyterian and had been so for fifty years. Although the
Presbyterians were a branch of the larger Puritan movement, the
Puritans were a very diverse group. Sometimes this diversity
fostered tolerance between them; other times it fostered intolerance.

James of Scotland and England

James VI, son of Mary, Queen of Scots and Darnley, became
James I of England in 1603.[15] His firm Presbyterian upbringing led
the Puritans to hope he would favor them. The Catholics hoped he
would also be tolerant of them for the sake of his Catholic mother.
The hopes of both factions were dashed. In spite of his upbringing,
James gradually came to see Presbyterian doctrine and rule in a
very different light. When he gained the English throne and the
role of supreme leader of the Church of England, he decided its
hierarchy and uniformity firmly supported what he believed to be
his "divine right" to rule the national church as well as the country.
James even wrote books on the subject.

He saw the dissenting Presbyterians as a threat to his determi-
nation to rule absolutely.[16] At the Hampton Court in 1604, the year
after he became James I of England, he presented his argument

against Presbyterianism as incompatible with his divine right. "Presbyterians," he said, "agreeth with a monarchy as God and the Devil. Then Jack and Tom and Will and Dick shall meet, and at their pleasures censure me and my councel."[17] Unfortunately, James lacked Elizabeth's political skills, and his vision of his royal power was grandiose.

At the same Hampton Court Conference of 1604, eight hundred Puritan clergy asked James to help reform the Church of England. They were opposed to some rituals such as the use of the cross in baptism (as none had been used in Christ's baptism). They wanted greater emphasis on preaching and asked for a fresh translation of the Bible. James agreed only with the last. He authorized a new version of the English Bible, now known as the King James Version. Based on the earlier translation by William Tyndale, it became one of the greatest pieces of English literature and was widely accepted.

The *Book of Common Prayer* was another issue. When the House of Commons began to assert itself against its enforced use, a few revisions were made, but not enough. The new Puritan groups did not like prayers to be read from any book; they preferred spontaneous prayers. Under pressure, Parliament abolished the required use of the *Book of Common Prayer* but later reversed itself.

Like kings and queens, popes and archbishops, Parliament insisted on its authority being recognized. Sometimes it used its power to raise armies to control rebellion. Sometimes its power was either for or against reforming the Church. Still other times it was used to support or attack the throne. It even attacked the army when it withheld wages that were long overdue.

The growth of Parliament's power started very early in England's history. The word *parliament* came from the French word *parler* meaning "to talk." Parliament sessions were called irregularly by the ruling king or queen, usually to settle disputes or raise money. It became three houses: the king and his council, the House of Lords, which included the bishops of the Church of England and hereditary and life peers appointed by the Crown, and the House of Commons, which was mostly landed gentry, knights, and privy councillors who were not lords and were elected by districts. The early parliaments were supposed to assist the king; later, they became more controlling.

Gradually, procedures were developed for use during parliamentary meetings. In 1581, during Elizabeth's reign, it was decided that the chairman must always call for a negative vote and that no personal attacks or "revelling or nipping works or impertinent speeches" would be allowed. Later, this was reversed and members of Parliament were free to say what they wanted to say without fear of imprisonment.

By tradition, parliaments were often given nicknames. One of the first was the "Model Parliament." In 1295 it was called into session by Edward I to raise money for war. It came to be nicknamed "model" because it was the first to include representatives elected by cities and boroughs, not just ecclesiastical authorities and others appointed by the king. In 1388 the "Merciless Parliament" earned its name because of the severity of punishments given to some supporters of the king. The "Unlearned Parliament" of 1404 was called to raise taxes to avoid bankruptcy and gained its name because lawyers were not allowed to be members of it.[18]

Still another interesting nickname was the "Addled Parliament," which met for two months in 1614 when Hanserd Knollys was growing up. It was called "addled" because James I of England (James VI of Scotland) ruled England with such a lack of diplomacy that Parliament would not support his requests.

The Winter of Discontent

The immortal line, "Now is the winter of our discontent" was first crafted in 1592 during Elizabeth's reign by Shakespeare for his play *Richard III*. Although this play is set in the late fifteenth century, it spoke to the discontents of Elizabeth's age.

At that time, the theater was a powerful tool for showing contrasts of vices and virtues from a humanistic position. Inexpensive and popular with the laboring classes as well as the court, the plays were not only performed in London. They were also taken on tour throughout the countryside.

Richard III, one of Shakespeare's great tragedies, was about a villainous king, sometimes called "Crouchback" because of his deformed spine. The historical background for this play is that before becoming king, Richard III, as Duke of Gloucester, had been loyal to his brother, Edward IV. However, when his brother died, Richard became protector of two of Edward's sons. One was Edward V, who was then age twelve, and the other was the Duke of York. Declaring them illegitimate, Richard had his nephews imprisoned in the Tower of London, had himself crowned and his young nephews murdered. Richard reigned for only two years, 1483–1485, before he died in battle and was followed by Henry VII, the first of the Tudor rulers.

When Shakespeare's play was published over a hundred years after Richard III reigned, the audience could understand its double meaning because discontent due to the intoleration of the Crown and Church had continued and, in fact, was increasing. The word *discontent* meant something quite different at that time than it does today. Now it is used to refer to a mild form of unhappiness with the status quo. Then, it referred to much stronger feelings. When people were described as discontented, it usually implied a rebellion was brewing, so much so that in treason trials those who had the reputation of being discontented lost their cases automatically, even before the jury retired.[19]

At the time Shakespeare's play was written, the discontent of Roman Catholics was especially high. They resented the fact that Elizabeth had her cousin, Mary, Queen of Scots, beheaded because she was Catholic and therefore a threat. James's subjects were also discontented—some of them enough to leave for America. Their discontent was rooted not only in his authoritarian rule. His recurring wars with Spain, France, and Holland were continuing problems. The heavy taxation required to finance them only intensified the king's domestic troubles.

James tried, as had Elizabeth I before him, to impose the English Reformation upon the Irish. The Irish resisted James as best they could; to them, his "divine right" was all wrong. Discontent in Ireland finally erupted in 1609 when James took over the six northern counties from the Irish chiefs and lords, divided the land into parcels, and rented it to English and Scottish settlers, thus increasing his income. This was prime agricultural land. Having such valuable land pleased the new settlers but not the Irish. They were not only discontented; they were ready for rebellion.

Then there was England's long-standing conflict with Spain over religion and trade. Although the Spanish Armada had been defeated during Elizabeth's reign, friction continued between Spain and England. It grew worse. The Irish revolted against England's attempt to replace Catholicism with the Church of England, and Spain supported the Irish. Desperately, James tried to defuse conflict with Spain by arranging a marriage between his son and the Spanish Infanta, but he had to withdraw his offer because the English people were so angered at the thought of a potential Catholic heir. In 1624, James felt forced to declare war on Spain to placate his people.

Wars cost money. The king often quarreled with Parliament and flatly refused to ask its approval of new taxes. Instead, he declared new taxes on his own authority and this greatly increased animosity against him. Seacoast towns were particularly bitter against a new "ship tax" because they already provided ships in exchange for protection in the case of invasion. They thought this was enough. The king did not agree.

Another of James's fund-raisers was the creation of the Order of Baronets. All men with an income of forty pounds or more were "invited" to buy knighthoods for a suitably hefty fee. And if this "generous opportunity" for knighthood was refused, an even higher penalty was levied. In a sense, it was an enforced tax, and it was resented. This was all in addition to the personal property taxes that had existed since the twelfth century.[20] About the only things that escaped taxation were private thoughts. It is not surprising that many wanted to escape James's oppressive rule.

Gradually, the voices of protest could be heard in unison in three parts of England. One group developed in the eastern part of the country, another one in London. A third and even stronger voice came from the north of London in the counties of Nottingham, York, and Lincolnshire, where Hanserd Knollys's grandparents and parents lived during the reigns of Elizabeth and James.

Hanserd Knollys was born in 1598 in Lincolnshire and was five years old when Elizabeth died. Protests against her Acts of Uniformity and Conformity were rising, and Knollys protested them throughout his life.

In 1603, about the time when James I took the throne in England, Hanserd and his family moved from his birthplace in Cawkwell, near Louth, the seat of the famed rebellion of 1536, to the city of Great Grimsby and then to nearby Scartho. His father served as rector in both Grimsby and Scartho.

Hanserd grew up during the rule of James I and the persecutions of James's son, Charles I, who became king in 1625. Intolerance so intensified under the rule of Charles that in 1628 Parliament issued a Petition of Rights. The king could no longer assess taxes without Parliament's consent nor could he arbitrarily imprison anyone. Using military courts to collect mandatory "loans" and conducting trials without juries were forbidden and so was the coercive billeting of the militia in private homes.

At the time this Petition of Rights was written, Hanserd Knollys was a student in Cambridge University, struggling with theology as it applied to church and state, dealing with his self-image and purpose in life, trying to understand why tolerance was so often on trial, and considering what lay ahead in his own life. Yet, the university and rulers and reformers were not the only forces in his life. His family and the political events in Lincolnshire County, where he grew up and lived as a young man, also had an impact on him. Discontent was so high that rebellion was inevitable.

2

Rebellion and Family History

It is good to be well-descended
But the glory belongs to our ancestors.
                    —*Plutarch of Greece, ca.* A.D. *46–120*

The Louth Rebellion of 1536

Henry VIII wanted religious freedom from the Church of Rome but did not want others to have any freedom contrary to his dictates. Shortly before Christmas in 1536, the king's council made four intolerable demands of the people which triggered a rebellion in Lincolnshire where Hanserd Knollys's family lived.

There were obvious reasons for the rebellion. Henry was dissolving all the small monasteries. With the passing of the Acts of Succession and Supremacy, he had become head of the Church of England. Money that had once gone to the pope was now available for his use, and those who would not pledge loyalty to him were imprisoned or executed. Every man was required to take his gold to the Tower of London to support the wars. Parish churches were required to forfeit all jewels and ornaments. What is more, for the second time in twelve years, every parson and vicar was to be examined to determine whether or not his learning was sufficient for the cure of souls.

Both clergy and laypeople resented the authoritarian intolerance of these orders. They still harbored resentment because, a dozen years earlier, Henry VIII had dissolved the local monasteries and had the clergy examined for their loyalty to him. Furthermore, some people lost their churches when small parishes were consolidated and only one parish church was allowed in a six- or seven-mile radius.

The Lincolnshire Rebellion of 1536 began when Thomas Kendall, vicar of Louth, advised his parishioners to consider the implications of Henry's use of power. Louth was an important town in a valley at the foot of the Wolds, the hill country of Lincolnshire where sheep and cattle provided considerable wealth to their owners.

People took sides for and against each other and for and against the king. Riots broke out; books were burned. Sixty-three protesters were sentenced, and thirty-four leaders were condemned to death including priests and laymen from Louth, Scartho, and Biscathorpe. The last two were villages where some of Hanserd Knollys's ancestors lived and where he grew up.

Sir William Parre intervened for the condemned protesters and pleaded with the king that the people were sorry. Henry relented just a little. The number of those to be tortured to death was reduced. Instead of the original thirty-four, only twelve were condemned to be hung at Tyburn, cut down alive, disemboweled, and their entrails burned while they were still alive.[1] The rebellion lasted merely two weeks, but the cruelty of the executions did not stop the movement toward nonconformity that grew out of the spirit of dissent.

Henry continued his inquisition. On October 1, 1538, he ordered Archbishop Cranmer and eight others to go aggressively against those who were rejecting infant baptism, which he insisted upon. Their books and letters were to be confiscated. Those suspect were to recant or be put to the flames.[2] The next year, he issued a proclamation of mercy which provided some leniency. But still worried about those who disagreed with him on the need for infant baptism, Henry excluded them from his general pardon in July 1540.

The Debate on Baptism

Until the rule of Henry VIII, the pope had been the highest authority in England, exercising his power in both church and state matters and arguments over who should be baptized, where, when, and how. In apostolic days, rivers, pools, and baths were used, and by the third century A.D. outdoor baptisteries were built. By the sixth century, they began to appear inside some churches, and in England baptisteries as well as rivers were used. Based on the writings of the Venerable Bede, who died in A.D. 735, historian Thomas Armitage wrote briefly of baptisms of some notable people. He also noted the custom among border countries which left the right hand of male children out of the water during baptism "in order that they might with this unsanctified hand deal the more deadly blows upon their foes."[3]

Total immersion in water was considered biblically based and necessary. Immersion was often called "dipping." It was required that a person be dipped three times under water to indicate the death of Christ and raised from the water indicating the resurrection with Christ. However, throughout the centuries there were different interpretations of the meaning of baptism and how it should be done. Some thought baptism was an entry into the Church, others that it was purely symbolic, and still others that it was a means of grace in which God entered in.[4]

By the third century at least, the baptism of infants was by immersion. This became a subject of great dispute during the sixteenth and seventeenth centuries. Tragedies were not unheard of. Infants sometimes drowned or died later as a result of being dipped in cold water.

Another argument against dipping was that the river Jordan had been acceptable for baptism in the time of Christ because it flowed through a country that was so hot. But, the argument went, Christ in his love and kindness would surely not want people to face death in the cold Thames. Warm water for men was acceptable by the fourteenth century, and in the cases of impending death, Pope Stephan allowed baptism in wine. In Ireland, several children were immersed in milk, perhaps still warm from a cow.[5]

Under Edward and Elizabeth the three-time dipping was reduced to one. Instead of immersion, water could be poured or sprinkled over an infant's head. Since Edward VI died at age fifteen of consumption, one wonders if his ill health contributed to his ruling that immersion could be by dipping once instead of three times.

Some people considered baptism by pouring or sprinkling to be invalid. Still others thought infants should not be baptized at all until they were old enough to confess their faith as "believers." This became Hanserd Knollys's conviction, perhaps rooted in his personal experience. It was surely what he advocated in 1645 when he was lecturing on the subject publicly and arguing about it in an Independent church.[6] Rulers and clergy, religious groups and individuals often took strong positions for and against particular ideology and practices, and more than two hundred books and pamphlets were written on the subject of baptism by immersion. Gradually, sprinkling became more common.

However, the issue of who should be baptized was also a flaming torch. This often centered around the Anabaptists. They rebaptized those who had already been baptized as infants. On one side, the debaters claimed that rebaptizing ignored the validity of infant baptism. On the opposite side, supporters said that infant baptism was not valid in the first place. Therefore, to baptize a "believer" was not a rebaptism.

These issues of baptism were not only debated in the Church. They also were argued in Parliament. In 1646, five years after Hanserd Knollys had returned from New England and gathered his own church in London, Walter Cradock encouraged Parliament not to judge by the amount of water used in baptism, whether by immersion, pouring, or sprinkling, but only to judge on a person's affirmation of faith. This was considered a radical position.

One of the reasons this subject is important in this book is because it helps establish the birth date of our Baptist hero. In the archives of Lincoln is the approval of the original presentation deed of Richard Knowles to Cawkwell on August 5, 1608. A Cawkwell parish record shows Richard married Rachell Pagett, a widow, on January 26, 1609. She was probably his second wife. If so, no records have been found of his first wife, Hanserd's mother.

Secondary writings claim Hanserd was born in Cawkwell, Lincolnshire County, in 1598. Parish records show he was not baptized until November 13, 1609. Civil birth records were not kept, and it would be easy to assume that the traditional date given for his birth is wrong, but that is not necessarily so. At the time of his birth, baptism issues were extremely controversial. In Lincolnshire a growing number were agreeing that baptism should be delayed until the person was old enough to understand its meaning and make a personal commitment.

This may have been what Hanserd's father thought. A well-educated vicar of two churches and a bit of a nonconformist, he may have decided that his son should be baptized as a boy who could understand the implications of baptism instead of as an infant who could not.

Henry VIII's Control through Wills

In addition to controlling rituals in the Church, Henry VIII had many other ways of controlling people, especially the landed ones. He did this through his regulation of wills. Wills often supply historical missing links impossible to find elsewhere. They can prove or disprove educated guesses and traditions, and the bequests that are made often reflect customs of the times and socioeconomic conditions. Wills frequently reveal names of unknown family members and other close associates. To discover more of Hanserd Knollys's background, it was necessary to search archives for baptisms, marriages, and wills. Some prominent families to whom Hanserd Knollys was related were Sutcliffe, Cheney, Hanserd, Lacon, Skipwith, Pagett, Goche, and Tyrwhit.

One of the most frustrating problems for historians interested in family connections is identifying people in wills who were listed by surname only. Several members of the Knollys family fall into this category. The duplication of names, generation after generation, is another problem, and some first names were overly popular. For example, in the fourteenth century, 64 percent of all the men in England had one of five first names—Henry, John, Richard, Robert, and William.[7]

The majority of wills were written by men who were in the middle or upper classes. In fact, during much of England's history, wills by women were seriously restricted or were not allowed at all. A married woman could not write a will without the consent of her husband. Widows and unmarried women over the age of twenty-one sometimes wrote them if they had sizable assets, but Henry VIII had instituted laws that often interfered with this. He seized the monasteries and sold their lands to businessmen from London, who thereby became the new gentry.[8] This replenished the royal treasury for a while, but when the money from the sale of monasteries was spent, Henry needed more land to sell. He was able to get it with his statute that read:

> Wills or testaments, made of any manors, lands, tenements, or other hereditaments, by any woman covert, or person within the age of one and twenty years, idiot, or by any person *de non sane memory*, shall not be taken to be good or effectual in the Law.[9]

The result of this statute was that Henry could claim property that was willed to others by women, by those who were under age, by those who were mentally ill, or by those whose memory was failing. This statute remained law until 1837. However, unless an heir or someone else objected, Henry's statutes were often ignored, and until 1750, many wills were not proven, thus avoiding court costs. Sometimes wills were kept in safety for possible disputes among heirs and were probated years later.

Ownership of land was of high importance, and marriages were often arranged not for love but for the acquisition of land. At the time of marriage, a woman's personal property passed directly to the husband. Other property, such as leaseholds, also went to him. Then there was freehold property. This was a form of land tenure. It was land that was held in the family because of service as a knight or some other kind of service. After marriage, this land belonged to both the wife and her husband.

Land was normally inherited under the law of primogeniture by which the oldest son was the heir to all the land, and daughters and younger sons usually received only a share of the personal estate such as jewelry and clothes. In some parts of England, "gavelkind" was the custom instead of primogeniture. Gavelkind was the tenure of rent (gavel) instead of service. This allowed the land to be split among several heirs. The trouble with dividing land was that over several generations the parcels of land could become too small to support those who inherited them or too small to be economically useful.

The statutes about what could or could not be willed were controversial and inconsistent. The Lincolnshire Rebellion of 1536 was, in part, a protest against taxes, against new laws that required parish registration of births, deaths, and marriages, and also against the laws which did not allow landowners to bequeath their land to whomever they chose.

Debates about women's wills continued for hundreds of years. As late as 1837, Queen Victoria forbade the making of a will by anyone under twenty-one. Wills by married women of any age were legally valid only if the wills had been recorded before 1837. A woman was not even supposed to will her personal belongings as she chose (although she often did); they belonged to her husband or father. It was not until 1882 that women were allowed to keep property they had owned before marriage or acquired later.

Elizabeth and Raleigh

Hanserd Knollys's grandparents were alive during the Lincolnshire Rebellion against Henry VIII in 1536. Since the rebellion took place only a few miles from where they lived, it was probably still being discussed when Hanserd Knollys was a child and Henry's daughter Elizabeth I ruled.

Elizabeth became queen in 1558 at the age of twenty-five and ruled for forty-five years, until 1603.[10] She was queen when Hanserd was a young child, during much of his parents' lives, and even during part of his grandparents' lives. Hanserd Knollys came from a long line of clergy. During Elizabeth's reign, Bishop Cooper's records show that in 1560 all the bishops in Lincolnshire were married. Thirteen out of sixty-one cathedral clergy were also married, as were twelve of the sixty-one parish clergy. The number may have been much higher. Records do not have further information except that the number of married clergy rose so quickly

Queen Elizabeth I.

that they were cautioned to be careful and not select undesirable wives.[11]

During Queen Elizabeth I's rule Protestantism was firmly established in England greatly due to the influence of William Cecil, her advisor as secretary of state for fourteen years and lord treasurer for the next twenty-six. Cecil was astute, thoughtful, and tolerant of nonconformists, and he admired Elizabeth's political skills and education. Fluent in French, Italian, and Latin, Queen Elizabeth I could speak directly to ambassadors. She also read Greek and studied history daily. One of her less-known interests was knitted silk stockings. She wore the first pair in England in 1561.[12] She was better known for her greediness, especially for jewels and land, and her manipulations to get land sometimes contributed to dissent.

As for religion, Elizabeth preferred Catholic ceremony but feared Catholic foreign power. Like her father, Henry VIII, she wanted Catholicism minus the papacy. The Church of England provided her with some of this and suited her political purposes. Even Pope Sixtus V (1585–1590) admired her in a way. He once wrote, "If she were not a heretic, she would be worth the whole world."[13]

During her reign, the use of a Latin liturgy in worship was no longer required. Yet, clergy were expected to know it and also to have a New Testament in both Latin and English as well as the New Testament paraphrases of Erasmus. Occasionally the clergy were examined for their knowledge and continuing study. About one-half were considered inadequate in Latin, but Hanserd Knollys was not one of these. When a young boy, he was able to read the New Testament in Latin to his father and later wrote an English-Latin grammar book to assist those who were studying languages.

One of Elizabeth's well-known relationships was with Sir Walter Raleigh, whom she admired because he was a brilliant soldier, explorer, diplomat, and as the historian A. L. Rowse notes, "a most welcome and flamboyant companion."[14] For this she gave him vast estates and other privileges. Yet, Elizabeth was jealous when Raleigh secretly married one of her maids of honor, Elizabeth Throgmorton, and had a son by her, who became as flamboyant as his father.

After Elizabeth's death, James I accused Raleigh of plotting against him. Raleigh was condemned to die and imprisoned in the Tower for years. During this time, he experimented with chemistry and wrote poems, letters, and his *History of the World*. James released him temporarily in 1616 when Raleigh promised that he would sail to South America and bring back gold from legendary mines. Raleigh was unsuccessful. He lost his son in the attack on Santo Tomas and returned to England, where he was executed in 1618.[15]

For years after this, Hanserd no doubt heard Raleigh and his writings being discussed. In fact, when Hanserd escaped custody and fled to New England, his personal library was inventoried by his captors. Along with his theological books was a copy of Sir Walter Raleigh's *Advice to His Son*, and having this was considered to be suspicious.[16] Why Hanserd had it, or why it was considered suspicious, is not known. Perhaps it was only because of King James's enmity against Raleigh.

Wills and Visitations

Against this historical background, the ancestors of Hanserd Knollys became more than names and dates. But the clear identification of historical figures' names is important, and the challenge related to Hanserd's name was to discover its origin and to conclude, beyond reasonable doubt, that it came from combining the surnames of two of his grandparents, Hanserd and Knollys.

When A. R. Maddison, priest-vicar of Lincoln Cathedral, compiled his two volumes of *Lincolnshire Wills* in 1888 and 1891, he had many records available for the fifteenth and sixteenth centuries but did not use them all. In making his selection, he stated that he focused only on country families who, according to him, "were of undoubted gentle birth and good standing in the

County."[17]As priest-vicar, perhaps he did not approve and therefore did not include those who leaned toward nonconformity.

At the end of some wills that Maddison copied in full or in excerpts, he added brief notes. For example, he stated that one of Hanserd Knollys's grandmothers was Christobel (Sutcliffe) Lacon whose first husband was Richard Hanserd Jr. of Biscathorpe and that his father was Richard Hanserd Sr., mayor of Grimsby. One of her grandsons was also a Richard Hanserd, so sorting them out was not easy. Maddison commented that Christobel was the daughter of Matthew Sutcliffe of Grimsby. Although Maddison did not give his sources, his note seems reasonable. Her brother was John Sutcliffe, one of her beneficiaries.

Other sources Maddison used to determine which families to include in his books were the lists of Heraldic Visitations of 1562 and 1592. On these are the names of families who survived the much-earlier Wars of the Roses (1455–1485), fought between the houses of Lancaster and York for the throne, and some of these families were still there during a visitation one hundred years later.

Visitations were official inspections made by bishops or their deputies to record all church ornaments such as utensils, vestments, and books and to record what needed replacement or repair. During the visitations, worship services were also observed to see if they were conducted properly.[18] During Elizabeth's reign, the visitations were somewhat relaxed because of her toleration, but later, during the reign of Charles I when Archbishop Laud had so much power, religious freedom was not allowed and the visitations often led to fines, imprisonments, or executions.

In his research, Maddison also used the list of Lincolnshire gentry who had contributed to the defense fund against the Spanish Armada in 1588. The Spanish Armada was a fleet of 130 ships with twenty-five thousand sailors and soldiers who were sent to invade England and restore it to Catholicism after Elizabeth had Mary, Queen of Scots, executed. However, the much smaller and faster English fleet and the weather defeated the Armada and only one-third of the Spanish ships returned home. Many of those who financially supported the queen in this endeavor were well-established families in Lincolnshire.

Gifts of a Grandmother

By the time Christobel Lacon wrote her will, Elizabeth I had died and James VI of Scotland had become James I of England. He was alienating his subjects with his arbitrary taxation and autocratic rule of the Church. The court was scandalous as well, at least to the Puritans, partly because his favorite, the Duke of Buckingham, sold peerages and titles to any who would pay for them. This was offensive to those who had previously earned them by loyal service.

Christobel Lacon's will, probated in Lincoln, Lincolnshire County, on January 12, 1611, opened up a treasure chest of information as she was a grandmother of Hanserd Knollys. He was still a boy when he became a beneficiary of her will.

Christobel's father was Matthew Sutcliffe and his father was the founder of Chelsea College and dean of Exeter.[19] Christobel's mother was Anne, daughter of John Bradley of Louth, as proved by her husband's will.[20] Christobel was first married to Richard Hanserd Jr. of Biscathorpe, whose will was administered May 3, 1597, and her father-in-law was Richard Hanserd Sr., mayor of Grimsby.

Christobel's second husband was Harbert Lacon (gent.) of Humberstone, whose will was proven in 1602. The dates of these two wills establish her second marriage as between 1597 when Richard Hanserd died and 1602 when Harbert Lacon died. Clearly, their family history was rooted in the wider history of the time when religious freedom was on trial. Her will is included because it gives so much data about family ties in Humberstone, the village where Hanserd Knollys was first assigned to a church after he was ordained.

Researchers today who examine wills of old England have several problems. Paragraph breaks were seldom used, so two have been added in the following copy of her will to make it easier to identify family groups. Another problem was that later compilers often spelled *Knollys* and *Hanserd* in different ways, sometimes in the same document. Most often *Knollys* was spelled *Knowles* or *Knolles*, even in the early colonial records. The third challenge was that some beneficiaries were identified by one name only, while others were listed with two names. The fourth challenge was that the words used then for relationships do not always mean the same as today. For example, *sister* was often used when *sister-in-law* would be more accurate. And, of course, there are ongoing problems with spelling. The spelling used in the following is that used by Maddison.[21]

> I Christobel Lacon of Biskerthorp within the Countie of Lincolne, wydowe, late wyfe of Herbert Lacon late of Humberston in the Countie aforesaid, gent., deceased, sick in bodie but whole in mynde etc. First and principallie I comend and betake my soul into the hands of our Lord, the eternal and almightie God, through the passion and deathe of whose onely sonne Jesus Christ our saviour and Redeemer I beleeve cleare remission of all my sinnes. My bodie to the earthe to be buried in the Churche of Biskerthorp. To Mr. Edward Skipwith, my sonne in lawe, one goulde Ringe, and to my daughter, his wife, another goulde Ringe, being the better of them. To Edward Skipwith, sonne of the said Edward, one Frenche crowne. To Mary Skipwith, his sister, my best gowne, my best kirtle, and the bodies belonging unto it. To Elizabeth, her sister, my best petti-coate. To Gibert, Rikhard, Elizabeth and Marie Hanserd, my granchildren, ijs. vjd. apiece. To William Pagett, Hanserd Knowles and Zacharie Knowles, my grandchildren, ijs. vjd. apiece. To William Hanserd, my grandchild, xls. To Mr. John Suttliffe, my brother xs. To my cosin Mr. William Hanserd my best napkyn, and to my cosin Marie, his daughter, ijs. vjd. To my sister Hanserd my best smocke. To my sister Goche my best Camebrick bend. To my dawghter Knowles my cloth gowne, my burrato kirtle, my pillyon seate, and pillion clothe, my truncke, and some of my lynnen which I used to weare. My will is that my sonne Knowles shall have all my arable land and leas belonging to my farme at Gayton this yeare, to sowe or other-wyse to dispose of as he shall thinke best. I give to Mrs. Leeche my best Cambrick bend save one, and my black rashe kirtle. To Mr. Leeche vs. To my cosin Marie, wyfe of Humfrey Needham,

mine old stuff gown, my hat that is new dressed, and one new smock. To good wife Stele one course Cambric bend. To widow Compote one smock, to Michael Smith his wife one smock. To the wife of John Stevenson one petticoate. To either of the maides in the house xijd.

Whereas I bought certainet thinges of my grandchilde William Pagett which are yet unpayd for, viz., iiij silver spoones, one plate cupboard, one chest, one blankett, one coverlet, one paire of bellowes and one fyre shovell, my will and desyre is that he have them all again in full satisfaction and payment for them. Residue to Sir William Hanserd my son whom I make sole executor. Witnesses. Henry Leech, clerk, George Stele. Prob. at Lincoln. 12 Jan. 1611 by Ex.[22]

The way Christobel wrote her will, giving the use of her farm at Gayton to "my sonne Knolles" to sow or dispose of (he was actually her son-in-law), indicates her farm was income-producing but not necessarily where he was living. Her farm was six miles from Alford, the home of the famous nonconformist Anne Hutchinson, whom we will meet in a later chapter. In fact, the homes of several other early dissenters who fled the country for safety were close by. As the law prevented land being willed directly from mother to daughter, Christobel, by leaving it to her son-in-law, indirectly provided protection for her "dawghter Knowles" as well as her grandchildren.

Christobel Lacon gifted three different William Hanserds. One was her son Sir William Hanserd and another was her grandson also named William Hanserd. The third was William Hanserd her "cosin," one of her husband's relatives.

All of Christobel's children were by Richard Hanserd Jr. The number and names of all their children are not proven. John, one of their sons, lived in Biscathorpe but died before his mother so he was not in her will. His will was proven April 2, 1591. Another son, knighted as Sir William Hanserd, lived at Gayton-le-Wold, which was only six miles west of Louth, the seat of the 1536 rebellion. He was an uncle to Hanserd Knollys and an executor of Christobel's

will, and received the residue of her estate after many other
bequests were made.

Two sons-in-law were also in her will. Edward Skipwith was
one, and "my sonne Knowles" (meaning her son-in-law) was
another. "My sonne Knowles" was Richard Knollys/Knowles,
father of Hanserd. It was to him Christobel left "land and leas
belonging to my farme at Gayton." Christobel's eleven grandchildren were also beneficiaries: Hanserd and Zacharie Knollys,
William Pagett, Edward, Mary, and Elizabeth Skipwith, and
William, Gibert, Rikhard, Elizabeth, and Marie Hanserd. She also
left gifts to a number of seemingly unrelated persons, probably
servants or tenants.

One-Name Problems in Family History

In addition to repeating names generation after generation, by
the sixteenth century many female surnames became hereditary
Christian names and were given to the firstborn male of each
generation. This was done to recognize the fact that the eldest son
would inherit family property, or to differentiate one branch of the
family from another, or to indicate illegitimacy.[23] Dotted lines
between generations were sometimes used on old genealogical
charts to indicate illegitimacy.

Even more complicated for the family historian is that
surnames in wills were sometimes used without first names. One
of the puzzles of Christobel's will is identifying "dawghter
Knowles" and "sonne Knowles," both of whom she makes important beneficiaries. The phrase *in-law* was occasionally used, but
just as often it was not. A sister-in-law was simply called "sister"
and the word *son* could refer to an actual son or to a son-in-law. No
doubt her daughter married Richard Knollys and, by custom,
Christobel called him son. The identity of her "sisters" was also
difficult to determine as Christobel also listed them only by their
surnames, "Goche" and "Hanserd." They could have been her
natural sisters, her half-sisters, or her sisters-in-law. If they were
her natural sisters, they would have also had Matthew Sutcliffe as
their father and married into the Goche and Hanserd families. If
sisters-in-law, they could have originally belonged to the Goche

and Hanserd families and carried on their family names.

Fortunately, she gave the full names of her grandchildren. Three of them, William Pagett, Hanserd Knowles, and Zacharie Knowles, were grouped together in her will, so probably one of her daughters first married William Pagett and had a child by him. Then this daughter was probably widowed and married a Knowles/Knollys and gave birth to at least two children, Hanserd and Zachariah ("Zacharie"). On the other hand, her "dawghter Knowles" might have really been Christobel's daughter-in-law whose maiden name, or name through a previous marriage, was Pagett and who carried on her surname through one of Christobel's sons. Clearly, Hanserd Knowles and Zacharie Knowles were children of Christobel's son-in-law whom she called "sonne Knowles" and whose first name was Richard.

Searching for the Hanserd Family

Other ancestral lines of Hanserd Knollys were even more difficult to sort out. On the paternal side, one of his great-great-grandfathers was Thomas Hanserd of Wickenby whose wife's name is not known.

The other great-grandfather on the paternal side was Thomas St. Poll (sometimes spelled *St. Paul*) who married Faith Grantham, also from a prominent family. They had eight children, but only four survived infancy. He was an ardent Protestant, a member of Parliament for Grimsby, and sheriff of Lincolnshire. According to the carving on his elaborate monument in St. Lawrence Church in Snarford, he died in 1582, owning vast estates near Grimsby.

Ellen St. Poll, one of his daughters, married Richard Hanserd Sr., who became mayor of Grimsby in 1569.[24] Another daughter, Faith, married Sir Edward Tyrwhitt, one of the prominent leaders of the 1636 rebellion.[25] The Tyrwhits were one of the major families involved in the Louth Rebellion. Hanserd was a descendant from this line.

Richard Hanserd Sr. (Hanserd's great-grandfather) became mayor of Grimsby in 1559.[26] One of his sons Richard Hanserd Jr. married Christobel Sutcliffe and they had three daughters. One of their daughters (whose first name is not known) married Richard

Knollys and thus became Hanserd's mother. Another daughter married Edward Skipwith, and still another married Richard Pagett.

Richard Hanserd Jr. and Christobel Sutcliffe also had three sons. One was Hammon (also spelled *Hamon*), who had the same name as his uncle Hammon Hanserd and like him, became the vicar of Scartho. A second son was John Hanserd of Gayton-le-Wold, whose will was dated March 1, 1587/88, and proven April 2, 1591. Gayton-le-Wold still exists as a lovely farm on a hill, and the will reflects a way of living.

After willing his son Thomas the best bed and bedding, John divided the residue of the household equally between wife Elizabeth and Thomas. He also left his wife some cattle, oxen, a brown mare, three calves, sheep, five swine, and some poultry. The second son, Edward, received a "chaldron of good barley." His next son, Henry, received three cows, two oxen, four mares, and "all his debts remitted to his father." After these gifts, John Hanserd again listed his children and gave them more farm animals. His land and tenements at East Barkwith and elsewhere in Lincolnshire were bequeathed to his son Henry and his heirs with the proviso that if Henry's issues died, his share would go to Edward, and if both died as well as their heirs, it would go to John's brother William Hanserd. The executives of the will were to be his son Henry and his brother William.

Elizabeth Jackson of Gayton-le-Wold was the widow of John Hanserd. In her will dated March 17, 1590, and proven September 28, 1591, Elizabeth left her assets to three children, Margaret, Edward, and Marie, and made her father, John Jackson of Asterly, the executor. Her brother Thomas was named supervisor.

Sir William Hanserd, first son of Christobel and Richard Hanserd, also lived in Gayton-le-Wold. An uncle to Hanserd Knollys, he was first married to Anne Fane, daughter of Richard Fane of Pickham, Kent County; his second marriage was to Anne Goche, daughter of Barnaby Goche of Alvingham. The "sister Goche" listed in Christobel's will may have been the mother of this Anne.

The most important source in the search for the Hanserd family was photocopies of original wills from Lincolnshire and references from the Acts of Administration (1631–1648) of the Prerogative Court of Canterbury. Other sources used in this search for the Knollys/Hanserd family connections were *Lincoln Wills,* as compiled by C. W. Foster, and the previously mentioned *Lincolnshire Wills* and *Lincolnshire Pedigrees,* compiled by A. R. Maddison.

Maddison's compilation included three families in Lincolnshire with the surname Hanserd. They were Hanserd of Binbrook, Hanserd of Cuxwold and Usselby, and Hanserd of Biscathorpe, Gayton-le-Wold, and Humberstone.

It was the Hanserds who lived in Humberstone, Biscathorpe, and Gayton-le-Wold who were Hanserd Knollys's immediate relatives. Gayton and Biscathorpe were so close that people of Gayton were listed in Biscathorpe parish records. Richard Hanserd Jr. and his wife Christobel Sutcliffe were two of Hanserd Knollys's grandparents.

Richard Hanserd Jr. and Christobel bought a manor in Gayton in 1578. A manor was more than a house. A manor was a piece of land, usually in two parts. One part was the demesne, which was kept by the owner for his own use, the other part was for tenants, who either paid rent for its use or gave service. Some manors were so large they included several towns. Sometimes a town was split, part of the town was in one manor and part was in a different manor.

Records of the Consistory Court of Lincoln show the will of Hansert Hanserd in 1583 in Biscathorpe.[27] (The inconsistency with the way *Hanserd* was spelled in various records and even in the same record was as common as with the name *Knollys.*) Wills were sometimes written many years before death, but it would often take years before the land could be settled and the estate closed. Another interesting record is that of 1590 when Hamon Hanshart (perhaps meaning Hansert Hanserd or perhaps his son, with his name spelled slightly different) is one of those listed in the Subsidy of Armour, "a Qua."

Four years later, the *Liber Cleri* of 1594 shows him as Sir Hamon Hanshart, rector of St. Giles of Scartho, and in his will, dated February 23, 1595, he requests burial in the churchyard of Scartho.

The same *Liber Cleri* of 1594 shows a Sir Richard Knowles as vicar of St. James in Grimsby and a Richard Knowles as vicar in

Scartho. There could have been two vicars by the same name or one vicar serving two churches. Grimsby, Scartho, and Biscathorpe were within a few miles of each other, and Hamon Hanshart and Richard Knowles/Knollys were in some way related. It would be interesting to know more details about how they both served the church in Scartho and also how both became "Sir."

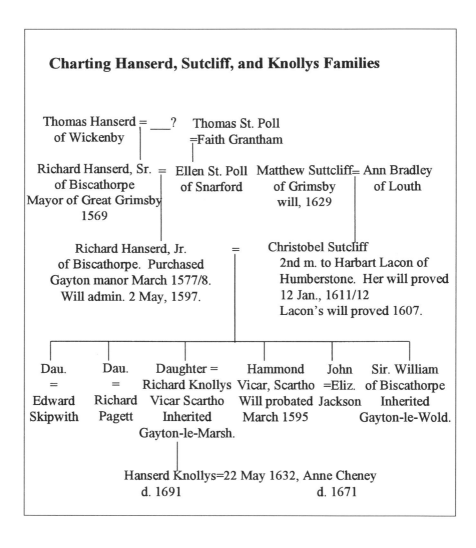

Charting Hanserd, Sutcliff, and Knollys Families

Thomas Hanserd = ___?   Thomas St. Poll
   of Wickenby   =Faith Grantham

Richard Hanserd, Sr. = Ellen St. Poll   Matthew Suttcliff= Ann Bradley
   of Biscathorpe   of Snarford   of Grimsby   of Louth
Mayor of Great Grimsby   will, 1629
        1569

         Richard Hanserd, Jr.   =   Christobel Sutcliff
      of Biscathorpe. Purchased   2nd m. to Harbart Lacon of
     Gayton manor March 1577/8.   Humberstone. Her will proved
     Will admin. 2 May, 1597.   12 Jan., 1611/12
                                             Lacon's will proved 1607.

Dau.   Dau.   Daughter =   Hammond   John   Sir. William
  =   =   Richard Knollys Vicar, Scartho =Eliz. of Biscathorpe
Edward   Richard   Vicar Scartho Will probated Jackson   Inherited
Skipwith Pagett   Inherited   March 1595   Gayton-le-Wold.
                   Gayton-le-Marsh.

         Hanserd Knollys=22 May 1632, Anne Cheney
              d. 1691   d. 1671

Early Dissenters and Separatists

Although Lincolnshire wills give no indication of the turbulent times in which the writers lived, dissent and discontent had been ongoing for decades. When Mary Tudor became queen in 1553, many clergy were angry that she forbid them to either minister to a congregation or say mass if they were married. Having been allowed these privileges under Edward's rule, they resented the change. Some conformed, or pretended to conform. Others resigned. Still, others fled to the continent.

Scholars have debated whether this movement to the continent was a migration or a flight. They do not agree, but the issues have been well-explored by historian Christina Garrett. Using non-English as well as English archives, she gives a census of those who left England during Mary's rule including 166 gentry and 67 clergy, with brief sketches of many.[28]

John Knox was one who fled to Geneva during the reign of Mary I. Another who tried to escape her wrath was John Foxe (1516–1587) writer of *The Book of Martyrs*, which is about the persecution of English Protestants in the sixteenth century. He and his followers sent printed protests against Mary to be distributed liberally on the streets of London. Still, other Separatists went to Zurich and Frankfort, Basle and Strasbourg.

Dissent continued under Queen Elizabeth, especially when, in 1564, she insisted on uniformity in worship. However, the term *dissenters* does not seem to have been used until the Westminster Assembly in 1643. The term *nonconformist* was not used until 1660 with the Act of Uniformity when Charles II was restored to the throne. Then, in England and Wales, all who dissented from the established Church of England were generally called nonconformists. In Scotland, the word was used differently; the nonconformists were those who were not Presbyterians.

Although the beliefs of dissenters and nonconformists had roots in earlier concepts held by Separatists, they were not the same. The Pilgrims were Separatists early in their history. In contrast, the Puritans were more often dissenters or nonconformists who did not want to separate and did so only after a long struggle of conscience.

The Brownists were one of the earliest Separatist groups named after Robert Browne, who, in 1581, formed a congregation in Gainsborough, Lincolnshire County. Although six years later he left for the Netherlands, his influence remained. Twenty years later, when Hanserd was teaching in Gainsborough, he visited with an elderly Brownist and wrote that he learned much from her.

A similar Separatist group was the Ancient Church of London. The members fled London in 1593, settled in Amsterdam, and were often without trained clergy. When Elizabeth died and James I became king in 1604, the Ancient Church asked to become the favored one, but James rejected it in favor of the Church of England.

Shortly after this, a John Smyth who attended Christ's Church, Cambridge, and was ordained in 1594, renounced his ordination in the Church of England. Then, like Robert Browne, Smyth organized a church in Gainsborough, basically following the same covenant as the Ancient Church of London.[29] Most of the members of Smyth's church were educated, including women who signed their names in church records and came to hear him from towns as far away as fifteen miles. Smyth believed that Scripture should be read from the pulpit only in Hebrew and Greek and encouraged his followers to study these ancient languages.[30] However, he got into a dispute with the local authorities for lecturing, preaching, and practicing medicine without a license. So, in 1608, Smyth and some of his followers sailed for the Netherlands.

John Smyth.

Smyth was against the Calvinist belief of predestination and, when studying the New Testament, decided that infants should not be baptized, that baptism was only for believers. He then baptized himself and others thereby founding the first Baptist congregation in human history.[31]

John Robinson formed another Separatist group in Scrooby, Nottinghamshire, a county adjacent to Gainsborough. They sailed to Amsterdam the year after Smyth.

However, Robinson and his followers were so dissatisfied with Smyth's church and also with the transplanted Ancient Church of London that they left Amsterdam for Leiden in 1609. There, the church grew to three hundred members. In 1620, some of them left Leiden on the *Speedwell*, returned to England, and sailed on the *Mayflower* to New England. Robinson encouraged them to go, preaching, "I am very confident that the Lord hath more truth and light yet to break forth out of His holy word."[32] This group went down in history as the Pilgrims; one member was William Bradford, who became governor of the Plymouth Colony in Massachusetts.[33]

In these early Separatist congregations, intense debates over baptism were frequent. The debates were influenced by English Baptists, including Hanserd Knollys, who was one of the first.

Except for his student years at Cambridge, his growing up years were in Lincolnshire, the home county of so many early dissenters. As a young man, he also taught in the city of Gainsborough, which had some of the earliest dissenters and some of the earliest dissenting churches. Unquestionably, the values of religious freedom, and the events of those times left a mark on Hanserd Knollys, as well as on his parents and grandparents. The widespread early dissension must have contributed to the spiritual anguish he experienced in childhood, the anguish he knew as a student in Cambridge, and the even greater agony that became his after being ordained, serving churches close to his childhood home and disagreeing with the established Church.

As we will see later, Hanserd Knollys was not the first Knollys who disagreed with authorities. His father Richard was also accused of nonconformity and taken to court. Even better known was another Knollys—Sir Francis Knollys (1514–1596). A leader in the House of Commons beginning in 1542, he was willing to speak out for what he believed. Married to Catherine Carey, daughter of Anne Boleyn's elder sister Mary and first cousin of Queen Elizabeth, he was very outspoken in favor of the Puritans and well-liked by Edward VI and Elizabeth, although at one time she wrote to him that he needed to moderate himself. In 1551, Francis Knollys met in conference with Catholics and Protestants at the home of Sir William Cecil. He came to be vice-chamberlain of the household, and his wife belonged to Elizabeth's privy chamber.

However, when Mary took the throne on July 19, 1553, a strict Catholic rule was enforced. Hundreds of Protestants were burned at the stake or fled to the continent. They were known as the Marian exiles and included John Knox, although the movement had started much earlier. Sir Francis Knollys was suspect because of his beliefs in religious freedom. Apparently he went to Geneva secretly with his wife and five of his fourteen children, perhaps as an envoy from Sir William Cecil to John Calvin to ask permission to establish a colony of immigrants there. Evidence for this is Calvin's complimentary memo written about Knollys and his son Henry. Sir Francis also went to Basle. A list from the University of Basle archives shows he was there in 1556, and this list is now in the Bodleian Library.

Until his death in 1593, Sir Frances Knollys was a leader in the House of Commons. Time and time again he challenged the concept of the episcopacy being instituted by Christ and therefore divine.[34] Although he has often been defined as a Puritan, he was not against the Church of England but was strongly against the way the bishops used their authority. He accused the bishops of undermining the queen's supremacy. At court, he was a principal supporter of the Puritans and pleaded for religious freedom with the archbishop:

> Open the mouths of all zealous preachers, that be sound in doctrine, howsoever otherwise they refuse to subscribe to any tradition of man, in order that they might withstand the armies of the Pope, to draw us into his pompous, glittering kingdom of strong delusions.[35]

When Archbishop Whitgift began to attack the clergy in 1584, Sir Francis Knollys counterattacked. Many of his papers and letters of protest to Lord William Cecil Burghley are now in the British Museum. He accused the bishops of undermining the queen's supremacy and became so vehement in his campaign against the bishops that Elizabeth asked him to stop. He was creating too much turmoil when she was trying to calm factional strife.[36]

There is no evidence that Hanserd Knollys, the Baptist hero of this book, was related to Sir Francis Knollys. However, Sir Francis was so close to the queen and so well-known for his belief in religious freedom and support of the Puritans that he could easily have been a significant model for the Knollys family of Lincolnshire.

3

Cambridge and Conversion

If a man will begin with certainties, he shall end up in doubt; but if he will be content to begin with doubts, he shall end up in certainties.
—Frances Bacon, 1561–1626

The Land in Lincolnshire

Lincolnshire, on the east coast of England, is one of England's largest counties, almost surrounded by great rivers and the sea. In the seventeenth century, flooding was frequent in the lowlands. Vast areas of salt marshes required ongoing drainage programs with seawalls for protection. Only the southern border of Lincolnshire was open to travelers by foot and by horse.

Lincolnshire consisted of three divisions, Lindsey (the largest), Kesteven, and Holland. Subdivisions in some northern counties, once under Norse domination, were called "wapentakes." This was equivalent to the term "hundred" in other counties. The unit was probably based on the size of one hundred hides. Originally, a *hide* meant the amount of land that could support a family who had 90 to 120 acres that an eight-ox plough team could cultivate. Later, *hide* was used in tax records.[1]

Lincolnshire had three kinds of agricultural areas. The wolds were gentle undulating hills grazed by sheep and cattle. Living in the parish called Gayton-le-Wold were Sir William Hanserd and his brother John. They were Hanserd Knollys's uncles, sons of Christobel Lacon and her first husband, Richard Hanserd Jr.

The marshland was land that had been drained to be used for farming with the sea held back by seawalls. In her will, Christobel had given to Hanserd's father, Richard, her son-in-law, her marsh-land: "all my arable land and leas belonging to my farme at Gayton this yeare . . . or otherwyse to dispose of as he shall thinke best."

The third kind of land also found in Lincolnshire was known as the "fens." The fens were lowlands originally covered, wholly or in part, with fresh, shallow water. Later, they too were drained. The fens had peat-based soil, richer than marshland because so much soil and fresh water once drained into them from the hills. In contrast, the marshland had once been covered by salty seawater.

Ever since the Middle Ages, Lincolnshire's thriving agriculture attracted a large population. One of its most important products was wool because the land was fine for grazing the big, slow-moving sheep that grew long, lustrous, curly fleece valued all over Europe. In fact, most of the ransom for Richard the Lionhearted had been paid in wool. When the export sales fell off in the sixteenth century, wool was so important to England's economy that a law was passed that everyone must be buried in wool shrouds. If not, a substantial fine was levied against the estate or the survivors. The country was also famous for its coach- and riding-horses, as some could trot as fast as sixteen miles an hour.[2]

Lincolnshire was also attractive to people because it had a port with busy international trade. The river Trent was a major waterway flowing to the sea and was widely used. The early Romans, Anglo-Saxons, and Danes had recognized its value and established villages such as Lincoln and Stamford. Many abbeys, monasteries, and large churches dotted the rural landscape.

It was from the city of Boston in Lincolnshire (about fifty miles from Scrooby) that the Pilgrims had first tried to leave for Holland in 1607 and 1608. At that time, Hanserd would have been ten years old and no doubt heard discussions about these early Separatists.

Early Childhood of Hanserd Knollys

Hanserd Knollys grew up in several towns within a mile or two of each other. According to tradition, he was born in Cawkwell, a very small town in the wapentake of Gartree in Lindsey, in the county of Lincolnshire. Cawkwell was on the road to Horncastle, six miles from Louth where the rebellion of 1536 had been fought.

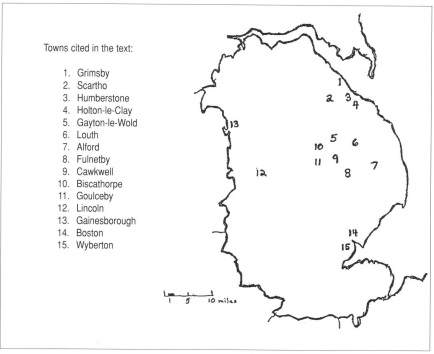

Towns cited in the text:

1. Grimsby
2. Scartho
3. Humberstone
4. Holton-le-Clay
5. Gayton-le-Wold
6. Louth
7. Alford
8. Fulnetby
9. Cawkwell
10. Biscathorpe
11. Goulceby
12. Lincoln
13. Gainesborough
14. Boston
15. Wyberton

Map of Lincolnshire.

According to the Diocesan Return taken in 1563 and now located in the British Museum, Cawkwell had only three houses at that time. Evidently, people came to the church from the surrounding farm area. Almost three hundred years later, the town had four more houses.[3] The "living" was a discharged vicarage in the archdeaconry and diocese of Lincoln. It was rated in the king's books at £4.8.6 1/2, endowed with £600 royal bounty, and in the patronage of the Crown. The church itself was dedicated to St. Peter.

The value of any church was estimated in terms of the "living," a phrase found in many old records. Clergymen were assigned to their churches by their bishops and made their "living" from tithes that were mandatory, through farm products and rental fees of church land, and sometimes by teaching. Probably Hanserd's father's income came from each of these sources. An income was not always predictable nor was life itself.

A traumatic childhood event occurred when Hanserd almost drowned at age six, probably because of his natural curiosity:

> I, *Hanferd Knollys*, was born in *Cawkwell*, near *Louth* in *Lincolnshire* and was removed thense with my Parents to *Schartho* near *Market Grymsky* in the fame Country. About the fixth Year of my Age I fell into a great Pond, and was preferved from being drowned by the water bearing up my Coat till my Father came, leaped in, and pulled me out.[4]

Although tides sometimes flooded the area, the great pool into which Hanserd fell must have been one of the "Blow Wells"—deep circular pits where underground water rose but seldom overflowed. If it had not been for Hanserd's coat keeping him afloat until his father rescued him, this biography would have ended abruptly.

Aside from almost drowning, Hanserd's childhood was evidently typical for clergy's children of the times. His father, Richard Knollys, was vicar of two churches, one in Grimsby and the other in Scartho two miles away. The bishop sometimes allowed well-educated clergy to serve several small churches at the same time, and Scartho was only a little larger than Cawkwell. Two generations of clergy with the surname Hanserd served the church in Scartho, as did three generations of Knollys.

One reference to Richard Knollys is confusing. According to historian G. Lipscomb, before going to Grimsby and Scartho, Hanserd's father, Richard, was inducted as vicar of Mentmore in August 1597.[5] Lipscomb also states that a Thomas Noke was inducted as vicar at Mentmore in August 1597. It is not likely that two vicars would be inducted the same month, but another reference clarifies what probably happened. It says that in September 1597, Richard Knowles, vicar of Mentmore, was elected one of the proctors for convocation for the Mursley Deanery.[6] Therefore, Richard served the church in Mentmore only very briefly as Hanserd was born in Cawkwell near Louth the following year.

Grimsby in the Past

Hanserd had tutors at home for much of his childhood, but for a time he went to school in Grimsby where his grandmother

Christobel had lived as a child. Grimsby was a borough, seaport, market town, and parish located 35 miles from Lincoln and 161 miles north of London.

Supposedly, it was at Grimsby that the Danes first landed when they invaded Britain at the end of the eighth century. The town was founded about 1185, was the home of Benedictine nuns, and had a priory of Augustine canons during the reign of Henry I.

Episodes of violence, homelessness, and rebellion were also part of Grimsby's history and still traceable through existing letters. In one letter to the mayor of Grimsby written by Henry VII, who reigned from 1485 to 1509, Henry tells the mayor to stop those people who were acting violently against the Augustine friars.[7] Another letter is against "vagaboundes" who refuse to "labor and travail for their lyving, but being rooted in idelness doo wander in all parts." Then, there are letters about Grimsby's representatives in Parliament and about an insurrection led by a Lord Hussey, which involved twenty thousand men and led to his beheading.

The city's charter, given by James II, organized the town as a corporation with exclusive fishing and fowling rights in the manors of Grimsby and Clee. One of England's largest fishing ports, Grimsby was also permitted to lay claim to all shipwrecks thrown upon the coast and could collect fees from ships that were driven ashore in gales of wind though not actually wrecked.

Some of these storms caused great damage. Thomas Allen's *History of the County of Lincoln* tells of the great storm of October in 1571 during Elizabeth's reign. Three score ships were lost. Houses were washed away with people clinging to the roofs. Some twenty thousand horses, cattle, and sheep drowned and, near to where Hanserd's parents and grandparents lived, on a farm between Humberstone and Grimsby, an unusual tragedy occurred. During one of the storms, a shepherd returned home for lunch and asked his wife to serve it. Instead, she looked out the window and saw sheep in the marshes with waves breaking over them, so she accused him of being a poor shepherd because he was not out "laying down his life for the sheep." When he went out to care for them, he and eleven hundred sheep were drowned and his body was found upright, stuck in mud in a ditch.[8] Storms were not the only natural catastrophes. In 1587 there was a great drought that led to famine due to the scarcity of corn. The next year a plague hit, another in 1603, and still another in 1625.

Grimsby was also visited by King Henry VIII and his then wife, Catherine Howard. They stayed at the mansion of a Mr. Kingstone, who also owned land in Humberstone, one of the villages involved in the rebellion of 1536 and where Christobel Lacon lived with her second husband Harbert Lacon. In his will, probated May 26, 1617, John Kingstone requested burial in the parish church of Great Grimsby, a much larger church than the one in Humberstone, and Richard Knollys and Charles Garth were listed as clerk (meaning clergy) and supervisor. Each one was bequeathed "a xjs piece of gold in remembrance of my love."[9] The phrase "in remembrance of my love" indicates a family relationship between John Kingstone and Richard Knollys.

Many old documents used the word *clerk* after a man's name. The meaning of the word in those days was not the same as it is now. Now, it refers to someone engaged in office work; at that time, such a person was called a "writer." Then, the title *clerk* was used in two ways. Sometimes it meant "clerk of peace"—a legal officer of the Quarter Sessions which were assemblies of justices of the peace who dealt with specific problems. Most often, however, *clerk* meant "one who was ceremonially tonsured by the bishop," that is, a clergyman. In such a case, *clerk* was an abbreviation for "clerk in holy orders."

Attending church in Grimsby was not always voluntary; it was required, and even the kind of clothing that could be worn to church was prescribed. In 1595, an ordinance was passed that required the mayor and other members of the city corporation to sit in the chancel on Sunday and holidays in "decent apparel" or pay a fine of three shillings and fourpence. Wives were required to do the same. Forty years later, attendance was still required, and in 1636 if an alderman did not attend church, he was fined one shilling. Others who did not attend were considered derelict in their duty and fined sixpence each.[10]

With Tutors and School

The life of the clergy usually involved more than serving a church. Educated clergy often taught school or tutored children privately. In their early years, Hanserd and his brother had a tutor who lived with them, but whether or not their tutor was ordained is not known. When the tutor left for a better-paying position, the boys attended Great Grimsby Grammar School.[11]

The school had a long history. Its charter was issued during the reign of Edward VI, son of Henry VIII. King Edward reigned only six years, from age nine to fifteen (1547–1553). Because of his youth and bad health, he had a lord protector, Edward Seymour. Seymour encouraged education and religious toleration and no doubt was instrumental in obtaining the school charter which established the goals for the school:

> Know ye that we out of the zeal and love which we bear towards the subjects of our town of Grimsby and the adjacent country, and that the youth of tender years there may be instructed and endued as well in good manners and polite literature as to the advantage of our kingdom, etc., etc., to the intent that a free Grammar School may there be instituted for boys and young men to be instructed in grammatical knowledge by a master and sub-master to be appointed by the Mayor and Burgesses, and with power to remove either or both of them at their own will and pleasure, and to appoint others in their room, etc.[12]

The property for the school had been donated by a chantry priest, Thomas Tomlinson, and by Sir Christopher Ayscough. At the time Hanserd was growing up, education was taken seriously. Although details of the curriculum are not known, Latin grammar was the major focus. Boys were taught to speak and write Latin at an advanced level. Two forms of Latin were taught in England. One was the old medieval Latin, used by lawyers in legal documents, manorial accounts, and court rolls. The other was Latin as written by the great writers in antiquity. Martin Luther had thought Latin was almost as important as the Bible. Latin dictionaries were used in the schools from the beginning of the seventeenth century.[13] In addition to Latin, it can be assumed that the curriculum at the grammar school in Grimsby was much like that in Caistor, a small market town on the side of a hill twelve miles from Grimsby. Caistor's grammar school was founded in 1630. Greek, Latin, English, writing, and arithmetic were taught, and the school was open to all boys because of an endowment made by William Hanserd, Esq., who was Christobel's son and Hanserd Knollys's uncle.

Boys often started school at age five. Girls did not go to school; those who were educated (and many were) were tutored at home. The school day began at six or seven o'clock in the morning and lasted until five. One day, walking through a field on their way to school, Hanserd and his brother Zachariah got into a quarrel. Suddenly, they remembered that they had been taught by both their father and tutor that quarreling was sinful. Evidently they felt deeply guilty. Years later, Hanserd recorded the event and its effect:

> We both kneeled down upon the plowed Land, and I prayed, wept and made supplication to God, as well as I could and found so great assurance from God at the time, that I never used any set prayer afterward; which done, we both kissed each other and went to school.[14]

That decision Hanserd made as a young boy, to pray spontaneously from his heart and not a set prayer from a book, later conflicted with the Church of England's demand that the clergy use only the *Book of Common Prayer* with its established ritual.

Meanwhile, Richard Knollys took seriously the education of his sons. Once when ten-year-old Hanserd was reading to him in Latin from the thirty-fifth chapter of Jeremiah, they came upon the story of a certain Jonadab telling his sons not to drink wine and Jonadab's sons obeyed. Hanserd's father took this opportunity to teach him the dangers of drunkenness and to elicit a pledge not to drink alcohol. Additionally, he cautioned him not to make a sacred vow unless he understood it because breaking a vow would be a sin. Hanserd promised and did not drink anything stronger than water for the next eleven years. He also continued to study languages, and some fifty years later wrote grammar books translating Latin, Greek, and Hebrew into English so that people could read the Bible in its original form.

Meanwhile, Richard Knollys hired another tutor for Hanserd and Zachariah. Like their first tutor, he lived with them and, in the process of preparing them for the university, stressed the sinfulness of disobedience to parents and Sabbath-breaking.

The Sabbath continued to be widely debated in communities and universities. In 1618, King James ordered all clergy to read from the pulpit his *Book of Sports*. In this book, James prescribed many kinds of entertainment and games that could be played on Sundays, including archery, leaping and vaulting, the setting up of maypoles, and dancing. He did not permit the brutal bear-and-bull baiting on that day although such "sports" were allowed at other times. However, the Puritans were so opposed to Sunday amusements that James felt compelled to withdraw his order. Then in 1633, his son Charles I insisted once more on the clergy reading the *Book of Sports* from the pulpit. Ten years later, when many in Parliament were Protestants, sports and games on Sunday were again prohibited and not allowed until Charles II came to the throne in 1660.

Hanserd Knollys was still a boy when his grandmother Christobel wrote her will which was probated a month later in January 1611/12. Hanserd was one of her beneficiaries, and it would be interesting to know what he did with the money he received. However, records of his life between this time and when he went to Cambridge are missing. A year after Christobel's death, his father, vicar in Grimsby at that time, was also installed as vicar of Scartho. The family may have moved there or stayed where they were as the two churches were only a few miles apart.

Hanserd's childhood must have been more than just study. No doubt he watched sheep being herded and sheared, grain being sown and cut, and people going about the various tasks of everyday life in Cawkwell, where he lived when he was a child, in Scartho and Grimsby, where he lived during his teens, and in Biscathorpe, when he visited his grandparents, Christobel and Richard Hanserd. Probably, he also spent time at Gayton-le-Wold, which was willed to his uncle Sir William Hanserd, and at Gayton-le-Marsh, which was willed to his father, Richard Knollys.

Life at Cambridge University

Hanserd, his son Cheney, and his father, Richard, all attended Cambridge, and each became vicar of St. Giles at Scartho. The *Alumni Cantabrigienses* lists Scartho as Richard's and Hanserd's hometown and states that Richard was "probably" the father of Hanserd. Other evidence in this book, however, reveals that this Richard Knollys was definitely Hanserd's father.

Oxford and Cambridge were originally founded for men who intended to become clerics. Gradually, both universities changed, and it became popular for men with other goals to seek a more liberal arts education than previously offered, or to receive a degree.[15] It was during the earlier rise of humanism, greatly stimulated by Erasmus, that a liberal element began to be expressed in the universities. However, as early as 1571, an unknown Puritan writer criticized both the casual style and high style of students and teachers:

> [They] go very disorderly in Cambridge, wearing for the most part their hats, and continually very unseemly ruffs at their hands, and great galligaskins and barrelled hose stuffed with horse tails, scabilonians and knit nether socks, too fine for scholars.[16]

Cambridge had been founded in 1209 by students from Oxford, including Franciscans and Dominicans. It gradually became a system of independent colleges, and some of the greatest figures of the Reformation came from Cambridge. However, it did not become a major university until Henry VIII founded Trinity College there in 1546. When the Church of England was confirmed during the reign of Elizabeth I and she was excommunicated by the pope in retaliation, Catholics were excluded from the universities until the end of the nineteenth century. Small wonder there was so much animosity.

The rules were strict. Students were required to use Latin, Greek, or Hebrew in their conversations unless they were in their own rooms. Furthermore, they were not allowed to read "irreligious" books, have pets, or play cards or dice except at Christmas. Women were not admitted as students and, in 1625, a rule was passed that women could not be employed in any of the colleges.

Hanserd's father, Richard Knollys, matriculated at Trinity College in 1581, migrated to Peterhouse in December 1582, and received his B.A. from Cambridge in 1585–1586. At that time, there were various categories of students, quite different than today. Using references from several sources, the historians Henry and Morton Dexter clarified the categories:

> . . . there were *fellows,* who lived from the revenues of the college; *fellow-commoners*, who sat at the table and enjoyed the conversation of the fellows; *scholars,* or students partly supported from the funds of the institution; *Bible-clerks,* whose duty it was to read the Scriptures aloud at meals; *pensioners,* who paid a *pension*, or rent, for lodging in the college; and *sizars,* or poor students, who performed menial, or semi-menial, services.[17]

According to an important and previously unknown primary source—the college's annual audit accounts—Hanserd Knollys was a pensioner while he was a student, meaning he paid for his own room and board.[18] He matriculated at St. Catherine's College on Michaelmas of 1627. St. Catherine's College was originally founded in 1473 for postgraduate secular clergy and was, at that time, named St. Catherine's Hall because the buildings they used were called houses or halls. In the early days, it was a small college with a master, six fellows, and twenty to thirty students at most. Currently it has over six hundred students.[19]

Students were carefully monitored at night, at least twice a week, to see that they were not feasting, playing cards, or "indulging in idle conversation."[20] The well-known White Horse Inn lay between King's and St. Catherine's Colleges, and Lutheran texts from Germany, as well as banned books and pamphlets, were often debated and exchanged there. If discovered by authorities, they were confiscated and burned.[21]

One focus of the curriculum was on the form of the church and its relationship to civil government. Another focus was on theology, especially the nature of God and the relationship of God to nature and man. And still another argument involved "good works" as a means to salvation versus the experience of the indwelling Holy Spirit. These same issues concerned Hanserd throughout his life.

Other university records show he matriculated at Cambridge two years later, the Easter term of 1629. While a student at Cambridge, Hanserd had a religious conversion. In conversion, a person experiences guilt, sorrow, and repentance, which is turning away from something and turning to God. It is a form of self-judgment for "sins of the flesh" or evil thoughts or failure to love enough or being too self-centered or self-indulgent.

At age ten, Hanserd had promised his father he would not drink anything stronger than water and had kept the promise, but, while listening to a sermon at Cambridge, he decided that he had often broken the Sabbath, disobeyed his parents, and told untruths. This troubled him greatly, which was no doubt the purpose of the sermon. Later in the day, he went to another church service and became even more convinced of his sinfulness and that he was "a child of wrath."

This conversion experience was so overwhelming that Hanserd changed his behavior and became more studious. About this time, he became acquainted with "gracious Christians, then called Puritans." With them he fasted and prayed, begged pardon, and was as angry at himself for his own sins as he was at others for theirs.

Teaching in Gainsborough

Hanserd Knollys was also master of Gainsborough Free School in Lincolnshire. Queen Elizabeth had founded the school and allowed any of her liege subjects to endow it with land or other property as long as the gift was not over thirty pounds per year.[22] Why she would not allow larger gifts is not known. Perhaps it was a tax-deduction issue, or perhaps it was to avoid very large gifts that might place the giver in a position to control the school.

Gainsborough, on the east bank of the river Trent, was an ancient city where King Alfred had been married and Canute proclaimed king. Henry VIII held court in the Old Hall in Gainsborough, which was built in the fifteenth century and still stands. In 1596, William Hickman bought the manor at Gainsborough and entertained people such as John Knox, the Scottish reformer. Increasingly, the city became a center of the separatist movement from the Church of England, and the Pilgrims held meetings in the Old Hall.

The trend toward separation was further fueled with the arrival of John Smyth in Gainsborough in 1603. He had been a fellow at Christ's Church, Cambridge, from 1594 to 1598 and had preached in the city of Lincoln from 1600 to 1602. He then renounced the Church of England and left London to go to

Gainsborough to preach to other Separatists. Strongly noncon-formist, John Smyth's influence was still felt in Gainsborough when Hanserd Knollys was there teaching school, but the school records were destroyed during England's civil wars.

Robert Browne's influence was also strong. He did not urge separation from the Church of England but wanted to change the church structure. Robert Browne vehemently opposed having bishops and a church hierarchy. He claimed that the Church should be regulated *for* the people and *by* the people. His followers were called Brownists. Gradually, they too began to urge separation from the Church of England. Some became Independents, later called Congregationalists.[23]

Hanserd Knollys wrote that he occasionally visited a Brownist who was privately teaching his own family about prayer and the Bible. Although Hanserd did not agree with the Brownists, who wanted to change the structure of the Church, or with the Independents, who urged separation from the Church of England, no doubt these visits were thought-provoking and affected some of his later decisions.

Ministry in Humberstone

On June 29, 1629, Hanserd was ordained deacon and the next day was ordained presbyter by the bishop of Peterborough. Before Hanserd's ordination, it was required that he preach sixteen sermons to show that he would be a good preacher. He passed the test with flying colors, and later his powerful preaching attracted large crowds.

After the ordination, the bishop of Lincoln, John Williams, assigned Knollys to a small church at Humberstone. It was four miles from Great Grimsby, on the banks of the river Humber, and located on flat pasture land. Knollys sometimes preached four times a day—in Scartho where his father was vicar, in the nearby village of Holton-le-Clay, and twice a day in his church in Humberstone and where his grandmother Christobel lived when he was a boy.

It was not uncommon for clergy to serve several churches if they were "qualified" to do so. Being qualified meant that they were licensed to preach instead of just read the service. There were not enough clergy who could preach well. Out of four hundred clergy in Lincolnshire, only seventy-four were licensed to preach. Hamon Hanserte had been so qualified, as were Richard and Hanserd Knollys. In the growing Puritan movement, preaching was highly desired. But more of this in a later chapter, including the fact that both Hanserd and his father were taken to court for nonconformity.

One time, when Hanserd was ministering to a parishioner in Humberstone, an important healing took place. The doctor, family, and friends of a dying widow had given up hope that she might live. She asked Hanserd to stay with her during the day as "a protector against Satan" until she died or got well. The woman became worse, almost speechless, and unable to eat for several days. Hanserd had begun to prepare her funeral sermon when he decided to pray more intensely for her life. Suddenly, she sat up in bed and said, "The Lord hath healed me. I am restored to health." Her kinswomen and servants were amazed. She asked for food and they gave it to her. The next day she could walk.[24]

On May 22, 1632, three years after his ordination, Hanserd Knollys married Anne Cheney in Wyberton, which was near Boston, in Lincolnshire. Anne's father was John Cheney (sometimes spelled *Cheaney*), Esq., of Bennington.

The Search for the Cheney Family

The search for the parents and grandparents of Anne Cheney has been more than challenging. A. R. Maddison, vicar of Lincoln who edited the two-volume set of *Lincolnshire Wills,* also edited a book titled *Lincolnshire Pedigrees.*[25] In Maddison's preface to this last-named book, he stated that the pedigrees were originally collected by Arthur Larken, who was fascinated with genealogy and made extracts from many parish registers.

A problem for Maddison was that when Arthur Larken was preparing his work for publication, he had several of his children copy his notes because he knew he was not going to live long enough to finish all the work alone. His children were not always careful, and Larken himself stated that their copies were imperfect.

Most genealogists make similar disclaimers, but when Mr. Larken died and Mr. Maddison was asked to organize his notes for publication, he discovered they were in four or five different handwritings, some almost impossible to read. On the basis of his own research, Maddison then made some corrections and additions to the earlier work. Generally, he did not include information that was available in other printed sources such as Edmund Burke's *Landed Gentry*. So, like similar books, *Lincolnshire Pedigrees* is neither perfect nor complete. However, when the information it contains is analyzed along with details from Frances Cheney's will, which is discussed in this chapter, some of the gaps and inaccuracies disappear.

It is indeed fortunate that Frances Cheney wrote a will. Without her will, it would have been more difficult to identify the family and ancestors of Anne Cheney, who married Hanserd Knollys and went with him willingly whenever he was banished or self-exiled.

Cheney was the surname of Anne's grandparents on both sides of her family. Frances Cheney's father was Sir Thomas Cheney, the Lord Warden of the Cinque Ports. The original Cinque Ports from the eleventh century were Dover, Hastings, Hythe, New Romney, and Sandwich. They provided ships and men for the king. Over the centuries, other towns were added, but the sea tides so undermined the land that eventually the Cinque Ports lost their importance.

Sir Thomas Cheney lived in Kyrton in the section of Lincolnshire County then known as Holland.[26] He married Frances, a distant cousin with the same surname. One of their daughters was also named Frances Cheney. She was the grandmother of Anne Cheney, who married Hanserd Knollys, and wrote her will November 25, 1604. It was probated in Boston, Lincolnshire County, August 4, 1608. In it, she requested that she be buried in the church in Boston as near as possible to the body of her "late husband, William Cheney" whose father was William Cheney of Thorngumbald.

In this will, Frances Cheney left to her son Christopher a "scale of armes, also all my harnes armes and artilleries." To another son John Cheney she gave two hundred pounds. To John Cheney's daughter, her granddaughter, also named "Frances," she gave one hundred pounds. Thus, there were three Frances Cheneys in four generations.

Along with this, she issued a grandmotherly proviso that her own daughter Anne would use the money during her lifetime to bring up and supervise the education of the youngest Frances. Leaving money for her granddaughter's education and assigning the supervision of it to her own daughter indicates the trust she had in her daughter and the importance she placed on education.

Frances Cheney then bequeathed gifts to another daughter Elizabeth, to Elizabeth's husband, John Killingworth, to cousins, and to William Skepper, a godson. To John Morton, her old servant, she gave five pounds and instructed her son Christopher to give him "that cottage which his father Mr Cheney gave unto him the said John on his death bed." Her will ended with:

> Item to Anne Cheney my daughter my little rounde coffer bounde with barres of iron which was my mother's as it stands with all therein fast locked. Residue to Anne Cheney my daughter whom I make full executrix.[27]

It is interesting that Frances made her daughter the executrix instead of either of her sons, John and Christopher, as was common at the time. Shortly after Frances died, her son John Cheney had a second daughter, born 1608, whom he named after his sister. It was this second Anne Cheney who married Hanserd Knollys in 1632 in Wyberton, Lincolnshire. As her grandmother died before she was born, Anne was not in her grandmother's will.

A different will, written in 1635 and probated 1639–1640, was by Jane, a daughter of the first Anne Cheney, who married a William Field. In her will, Jane gives a gift to Anne her niece who she says is "married to Hanserd Knolles, clergy of Fulnetby." This was a small chapel about six miles from Biscathorpe, and the will is further documentation of Hanserd's marriage and his closeness to Scartho where he had lived when a boy.

The following chart is not intended to show all the Cheney family members. It includes those mentioned in Frances Cheney's will. She was the grandmother of Anne Cheney. Anne married Hanserd Knollys in 1632 and with him had ten children.

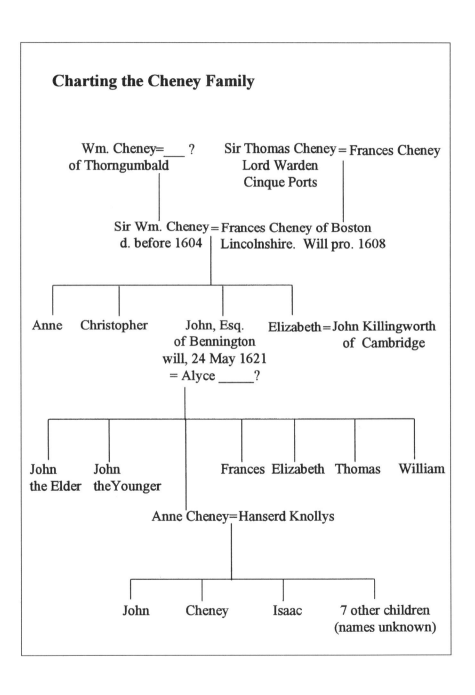

Charting the Cheney Family

Wm. Cheney=___ ?
of Thorngumbald

Sir Thomas Cheney = Frances Cheney
Lord Warden
Cinque Ports

Sir Wm. Cheney = Frances Cheney of Boston
d. before 1604 | Lincolnshire. Will pro. 1608

Anne   Christopher   John, Esq.   Elizabeth = John Killingworth
of Bennington   of Cambridge
will, 24 May 1621
= Alyce _____ ?

John   John   Frances Elizabeth Thomas   William
the Elder   theYounger

Anne Cheney = Hanserd Knollys

John   Cheney   Isaac   7 other children
(names unknown)

Clergy at Scartho

Queen Elizabeth had been very concerned over the adequacy of the clergy. In 1559 her Act of Supremacy repealed all anti-Protestant rulings, and her Injunction required every parson, vicar, curate, and stipendiary priest to have copies of the New Testament in both Latin and English, with paraphrases of the same. Then in 1584, she insisted on information about their morals, education, and marital status. Statistics from the *Liber Cleri* of 1584 show that about one-third of the clergy were married.

Generally speaking, it was the clergy who were best educated. In their wills, they often left their books to a church or to specific persons. Some wives of clergy were highly literate but others seemed to resent their husbands' attention to the written word. The wife of Thomas Cooper, bishop of Lincoln from 1571 to 1584, was an example. Once, she got so angry that she tore up half of his *Thesaurus* and threw it into the fire.[28]

Bishop Cooper's records from the sixteenth century show that members of both the Hanserd and the Knollys families were clergy in St. Giles Church in Scartho and there was a series of eight vicars who were probably related. The first three were presented to the church by Richard Hanserd/Hanshert of Biscathorpe (gent). (Some records spell his name *Hanserd*; in others it is *Hanshert*, but it is obviously the same person.) On August 28, 1560, he sponsored Hamon Hanserd when the previous rector resigned. Hamon died in 1576, and Richard then sponsored a Francis Tompson who had been ordained in Lincoln in 1566 and lived in Scartho. Tompson, thirty-four years old and married, was described by the bishop as one who "performs the holy mysteries prescribed by public authority; is ignorant of Latin; moderately versed in sacred learning."[29]

After Francis Tompson, a Sir Hamon Hanshert was installed in August 1580. He had been required to sign the S. and S. clause, which meant he subscribed to the Articles of Religion and had taken an oath to acknowledge royal supremacy and renounce all foreign power.

Meanwhile, Richard Hanshert died, and his will was administered in 1597. The next rector to St. Giles was Maurice Gulson, B.A.,

St. Giles Church in Scartho, Lincolnshire, where Richard Knollys and later his son Hanserd Knollys and grandson Cheney Knollys served as vicars.

who died November 19, 1613. He was followed by Richard Knollys, Hanserd's father. At that time, it was common for a benefice to remain in a family and be passed down generation after generation. Therefore, it is probable that the wives of Francis Tompson and Maurice Gulson were either related to the Hanserds or to the Knollys.

According to the bishop's Certificates of Canterbury, Richard Knollys was presented to the St. Giles rectory at Scartho and instituted December 2, 1613. The *Liber Cleri* shows Richard was still there in 1634 at the time of Archbishop Laud's visitations, which were more like inquisitions. He was also still there in 1641 when he and Hanserd's brother Zachariah were required to sign the loyalty oath to the king, the Oath of Protestation. They may or may not have been hesitant to do this. This was a time of great political and ecclesiastical upheaval, and 1641 was the same year that Richard wrote to Hanserd asking him to return home from New England.

As for the continuing vicars in the church in Scartho, Hanserd Knollys was instituted to the rectory in 1648 when Charles I was a prisoner. By this time, he had fled to New England and returned. He had established a school in London, joined the Parliament's army as a chaplain and resigned, formed one of the first Baptist churches in London, been stoned out of a church, brought to court on several occasions, and was writing about what he believed in.

Hanserd Knollys and his family had moved twice from London to Lincolnshire and back again, so he must have divided his time between the London and Scartho churches and traveled by horseback or by horse and carriage for a 140-mile journey. When Hanserd fled to Wales, Holland, and Germany for safety, it was his son Cheney who became rector in Scartho, in the same church that had, for so long, been served by both the Hanserd and the Knollys families.

The Intolerance of Archbishop Laud

During Hanserd Knollys's young adulthood, religious and political unrest was continuous. In 1625, James I had died and his son

Charles I was crowned. Reared and well-educated in Scotland, Charles liked becoming head of the Church of England and depended upon the advice of William Laud (1573–1645), who rose in power to become archbishop of Canterbury in 1633. Laud was powerful and highly authoritarian. He sent his vicar-general to the dioceses to enforce conformity and to see that worship services were in keeping with what Laud believed to be correct. The churches were also examined to see if they were maintained properly.

King Charles I.

In 1635, Hanserd's father, Richard Knollys, came under suspicion for heretical teaching at the time when Archbishop Laud tolerated only total obedience. The *Calendar of State Papers* reads:

> On October 15, 1635, Richard Knowles, clerk, Rector of Scartho, co. Lincoln, appeared and took oath to answer articles, and was monished to answer before next court day. On Oct 22 he appeared and was ordered to be examined before next court day under pain of contempt. On the 29th if he be not examined by next court day he is to be attached. On Nov 12 he is examined. Proofs to be completed by the third session from the present.[30]

It is not known what Richard Knollys was accused of doing or not doing. Perhaps he was refusing to wear the surplice or kneel at communion. Perhaps the condition of the church did not please the investigators or maybe he had some forbidden books. Perhaps the investigation was launched because it was known that his son Hanserd disagreed with some of the practices of the Church. Perhaps the suspicion of Richard was related to the enormous conflict between Bishop John Williams and Archbishop Laud.

Archbishop Laud.

John Williams was a very powerful bishop who, in 1618, had gone to Scotland to be personal chaplain to James I. He was made bishop of Lincoln in 1621 and thus was bishop to both Hanserd and Richard. He also had a long-standing feud with Archbishop Laud whose strictness was interpreted by many as cooperation with Rome.

One of the disputes between Laud and Williams was related to the location and treatment of the altar. Laud believed the altar should always be at the east end of the church and never moved. Williams believed an altar should be moved according to the situation and wrote a pamphlet, *The Holy Tables Name and Thing*, which was an argument against Laud's ruling.

Another disagreement concerned bowing to the altar and also bowing at the name of Jesus. Church canon law required bowing at the name of Jesus but not bowing to the altar. To Laud, the more bowing the better, though not to Williams. In fact, one of the vicars in Williams's diocese once bowed so deeply that he fell on his face in the aisle to the great amusement of the parishioners. This occurred in the same church where a test case was made about theology in reference to the location of an altar.[31] In time, the argument became more intense and was even taken to Parliament.

Archbishop Laud's inflexibility led to the so-called Bishops' Wars (1639–1640), which occurred because Laud and Charles I tried to force Church of England structure and ritual on Scotland. When the English prayer book was introduced, the strongly Presbyterian Scots rioted; and when the Scots invaded England, England could not win. Opinion solidified against Laud's policies. Later, he was impeached and put in the Tower for almost four years. When he would not admit to having tried to undermine the fundamental laws of religion, he was taken to the scaffold and decapitated on June 10, 1645, in the middle of the civil war.

The Agony of Religious Doubt

Meanwhile, in 1636, one hundred years after the rebellion in Louth and the year after Richard Knollys's ordeal in court, Hanserd was feeling deeply discouraged. He wanted to resign from his parish in Humberstone because he knew of no conversions resulting from his service.

He thought a conversion experience was important, partly because of his own conversion when a student at Cambridge and also because others who claimed to have had similar experiences were either physically healed or able to redirect their lives in more positive ways. The case of one woman in his parish being physically healed as a result of his prayers was not enough for him.

Bishop Williams did not want Hanserd to resign. He believed Hanserd was a good preacher and offered him a better parish if he would remain in the Church. But Hanserd questioned some of the practices and ceremonies, such as wearing a surplice. He agreed with other dissenters that special robes implied clergy were special and "above" their congregations.

Williams then encouraged him to lecture in other parishes. Lecturers were usually Puritans and preachers who were supported by congregations. They were not required to read the established service from the *Book of Common Prayer.* Although Laud insisted that the clergy stay with the approved church services, clergy who believed in spontaneous prayer resisted his ruling and Williams permitted this.

In spite of Williams's encouragement, Hanserd remained racked with doubt about God's will for his life; he did not know what to do. He wrote that one day he went to the woods to pray and with loud cries and tears asked God for direction in his ministry. There was no answer. Later, while walking home at sunset and meditating along the way, he suddenly seemed to hear the words from within: "Go to Mr. Wheelwright, and he shall tell thee, and fhow thee how to glorife God in the Ministry."[32]

At that time Hanserd did not know Wheelwright personally, but he did know that Wheelwright was a silenced minister who had been instrumental in converting many souls. Determined to find him to discuss his agonizing doubt, Hanserd mounted his horse expecting to ride twenty-five miles to Lincoln, where he thought John Wheelwright was living. Fortunately, a neighbor came by and told him that Wheelwright had recently moved to Anderby, which was only three miles from where Hanserd lived.

They met and talked several times. Wheelwright was a persuasive debater and explained the Bible to him in new ways. He told Hanserd to stop focusing so much on "good works" and to trust God's "grace." As Hanserd began to do this, he understood God's grace to be central to what he personally believed.

Finally, after several intensive discussions and a great deal of prayer, Hanserd heard words that touched his heart. They were from Acts 26:16 and seemed to have been spoken to him through Wheelwright's spirit:

> I have appeared unto thee for this purpofe, to make thee a Minifter, and a Witnefs both of thofe things which thou haft feen, and of thofe things in which I will appear unto thee.[33]

This direction to be a minister and the promise of God's presence for the future freed Hanserd Knollys from his uncertainty. Until his death almost sixty years later, he ministered to others and turned confidently to prayer and Bible study even when banished or imprisoned for doing so. Willing to doubt what he had first been taught, he developed certainties that sustained him through hard times, when tolerance continued to be on trial and he felt the need to defend the cause of religious freedom.

4

The Elect and Elected in Colonial New England

Voted that the earth is the Lord's and the fullness thereof; Voted that the earth is given o the Saints; Voted that we are the Saints.[1]
—*1640 town records of Milford, Connecticut*

Pilgrims, Puritans, and the Great Migration

During the rule of Charles I, there was a migration from England to New England sometimes called the "Great Migration."[2] It occurred during a period of oppression in England, and it has been estimated that between 1625 and 1643 some twenty thousand immigrants arrived in New England. The migration was fueled by the 1614 report of Captain John Smith, who had explored the New England coast, Virginia, and the West Indies and went back to England to write about it. He did more than write about it; hoping to raise money for another expedition, he went from town to town distributing books and maps he had created. He wrote honestly and with enthusiasm, telling readers about the problems to expect and also about the potentials: "Who can desire more content that hath small meanes, or but onely his merit to advance his fortunes, then to tread and plant that ground he hath purchased by the hazard of his life."[3]

Six years after Smith's return home, in November 1620, the Pilgrims arrived on the *Mayflower* at Cape Cod, where they established Plymouth Colony, the first permanent settlement in New England. There were 101 men, women, and children. They were referred to as "saints" in an old manuscript by William Bradford, their first governor. Two hundred years later, Daniel Webster called them the "Pilgrim Fathers," and that term became common for the group.

The Pilgrims wanted separation from the Church of England and looked to the New World as a place of refuge with freedom to worship as they pleased. Their response to the intolerance they had experienced in England was to withdraw, and they had been in Holland for about twelve years before coming to the colonies.

In contrast, the Puritans did not want to separate from the Church and were intolerant of those who did. The Puritans wanted to "purify" the Church from within and believed they could do it.[4] Puritans also favored the middle-class party in Parliament which was striving to limit the power of the Stuarts, who believed in the divine rights of kings.

The Puritans, with a charter from the Massachusetts Bay Company, arrived only a few years after the Pilgrims. Led by John Endicott, some Puritans settled in Salem as early as 1628 and that was only the beginning. During the 1630s fifteen more ships landed with over a thousand Puritans. John Winthrop was a leading power among them. His dream was to put Puritan ideals into practice and build a "city upon a hill" that would be an example to others of how early Christians had once lived. Winthrop was a Puritan, not a Pilgrim, and there was a major difference between the two groups.

Generally, the Puritans of New England were not as worried over England's rule as they were with owning land, having enough to eat, and surviving wars with the Indians. Historian Samuel Drake claimed that only the Bostonians were deeply concerned with religious dissension and supremacy.[5]

New Forms of Supremacy

The influence of John Calvin, the French theologian of the Reformation who believed in limiting the rights of rulers, was as strong in New England as it was in the old country. Calvin had claimed that salvation was freely given by God. However, it was given only to the "elect," not to everyone. To Calvin, the "elect" were the saints who were predestined to have the closer relationship to God.

As evidenced by the opening quote for this chapter from the town records of Milford, some early settlers obviously considered themselves the "elect" and wanted to be thought of as saints. This quote is typical of the attitude held by many early colonists, regardless of their religious orientation. The tendency was to think of themselves as better than others, and they tried to elect to public office only those who subscribed to their particular theological and political beliefs. Whereas in England rulers claimed to rule by "divine right" as well as by inheritance, in colonial New England it was the governors and clergy who ruled. They believed they were "elected" by God, as well as by the people who voted for them. The concept of being chosen by God for specific tasks is found in most cultures since the beginning of history. Young and old have recited and recorded these kinds of beliefs, often on the basis of a conversion experience, such as Hanserd Knollys had when he was a student at Cambridge.

In this chapter, the spotlight is on specific early settlers who immigrated to New England from 1620 to 1640 during tumultuous times in England, including John Cotton, John Winthrop, John Wheelwright, Roger Williams, and Anne Marbury Hutchinson. Like Hanserd, each felt called by God. All had been educated at Cambridge except for Anne Hutchinson, who was also well-educated and able to debate with the best of them. Anne affected Hanserd indirectly, the men more directly.

Many other Puritans were highly educated intellectuals who, with their strong heritage from Cambridge, were committed to education. Harvard University, founded in 1636, was the first of a long line of colleges founded by Puritans. Interestingly enough, Harvard's first president, Henry Dunster, refused to have his infant child baptized in 1653 and was put on trial and publicly admonished for not doing so.

In early New England there was a total population of less than 25,000 people. Of this number, over 130 were university graduates from England, an average of one university-trained man to every forty or fifty families. Many other early settlers who were not university graduates had sound, classical educations from English grammar schools; although, neither mathematics nor science received as much attention in England as in Italy, Holland, and France. Subjects such as medicine and law were usually learned only through apprenticeships or were studied at continental universities.

In the colonies, it was the men who graduated from Cambridge who had the greatest political influence, and many of them were members of the clergy. Consequently, religious debates, which were a tradition in England, continued in the colonies and generated as much attention and animosity as presidential elections do today. Each group was intolerant of the other.

In Massachusetts, the Congregational Church was a state church established by the Puritans. It was a new form of supremacy. As a state church, it controlled community as well as religious life. Of great importance is the fact that only freemen could vote and hold office, only church members were freemen, and to become a church member, it was necessary to be approved by the clergy. They considered themselves to be saints elected by God. This exclusive right to vote lasted legally until 1691, and Congregationalists maintained a favored position in the colony for many years after that. A branch of the broader Puritan movement, Congregationalists were originally called "Independents" (and still are in Welsh-speaking communities). Each congregation made its own decisions and was independent of any higher human authority. As such, the churches emphasized a concept of the Reformation which was the "priesthood of all believers," meaning everyone had responsibility for the ongoing work of the church.

In England, the early Calvinist Baptists, also called "Particular Baptists," emerged from an Independent Congregational church. The two groups essentially agreed on independence in church government and sometimes disagreed on whether or not infants should be baptized. The Particular Baptists were firmly committed to the Bible and to Calvin's beliefs. They were compatible with Presbyterians in this way. Hanserd Knollys formed one of the earliest Particular Baptist churches. The Baptist movement in America paralleled the one in England but was not an offshoot of it.[6]

In the Church of England, authority was held by bishops in a hierarchical structure. This was different from Presbyterian church government, which was more representative but not as independent as the Baptists. Local Presbyterian congregations chose their own church officers and elected their representatives to presbyteries. These, in turn, elected representatives to regional synods that met together as a general assembly, which made doctrinal decisions and governed the Church as a whole.

At the time Hanserd Knollys came to New England in 1638, he was not a Baptist. The first General Baptist church in England had been founded by Thomas Helwys in London in 1611 or 1612. (Helwys would soon publish his famous work, *A Short Declaration of the Mistery of Iniquity*. Because of its attack on the Church of England and its vigorous defense of religious liberty, this work would land Helwys in Newgate Prison, where apparently he died in 1616.)

The first Particular or Calvinistic Baptist churches were not founded until some years later, after Hanserd's return to England. To understand his life as an early dissenter and founder of one of the first Baptist churches, it is necessary to know the conditions in New England before he went there in 1638 and during the three years he lived there.

John Winthrop's Rise to Power

Political independence and the right to worship according to one's conscience could not coexist in Massachusetts with John Winthrop's and John Cotton's authoritarianism in civil matters and matters of the church. Tolerant of those who agreed with them, they were strongly intolerant of those who did not.

John Winthrop (1588–1649), a Puritan and Congregationalist but not a Separatist, was born in West Suffolk, England, into the landed gentry because his lawyer father had purchased a five-hundred-acre estate in Groton from Henry VIII. John Winthrop attended Cambridge, studied law at Gray's Inn, London, and became a justice of peace. From 1627 to 1629 he was in the Court of Wards and Liveries but lost this highly paid position because of his

Governor John Winthrop.

growing Puritanism and the antagonism Charles I had for Puritans.

Strongly religious and believing himself to be among those definitely "elected" by God for leadership, Winthrop converted his estate into sound investments that would give him a regular income. He then joined the Massachusetts Bay Company in London and was chosen to govern a new colony in New England. This was during the time when Puritans in the House of Commons were protesting the loss of rights, including the livelihood of some ministers in Boston, Lincolnshire.

In 1630, Winthrop was forty-three years old when he sailed from Yarmouth on the *Arabella* to became governor of the Massachusetts Bay Colony. During the first winter, the weather was so bitter that many indentured servants who had emigrated with the early colonists were allowed to go free. Their masters could not feed them, so they released them from their contracts that they might be able to find their own food.

To the servants, this freedom was not paradise. They had to live in huts, and many died of scurvy. Some went to Plymouth where the Pilgrims had landed. Winthrop, who had fifteen servants of his own, wrote to Gov. William Bradford of Plymouth complaining that Plymouth was harboring the servants who belonged to the people of Boston and this harboring "inconvenienced" those who had paid twenty pounds to bring each servant to New England.[7]

The Plymouth Pilgrims so resented this letter that they denied Winthrop's people the opportunity to trade corn with the Indians of Cape Cod as they had done the year before. This was a more dire inconvenience to Winthrop than losing his servants, but eventually and with apologies on both sides, the issue was resolved.

The winter of 1631 was as dismal and cold as the year before, and there was still a great scarcity of food until, after a voyage of sixty-four days, a long-awaited ship arrived. It was the *Lyon* from Bristol, England, with about two hundred tons of food and goods and twenty passengers. Roger Williams and his wife were two of the twenty who landed.

John Winthrop was a very effective administrator who opposed the principles of democracy. He believed the many should be governed by a few and that he was destined to be their leader and governor. One of the difficulties in researching Winthrop's life and leadership is that much of the material about early Massachusetts was written only by Winthrop himself or by writers who used his journals as background for their own writing. As later historian Edmund Morgan points out, such writings reflect Winthrop's biases.[8]

In his *Journal,* written between 1630–1649, Winthrop defended his attempt in the Massachusetts Bay Colony to form a theocracy, a utopia based on biblical laws with God at its head. Although the word *utopia* comes from the Greek meaning "nowhere," Winthrop was able to develop a strong sense of community among settlers who agreed with his social values and religious beliefs. Like James I, he resented those who did not agree with his autocratic style, including those who wanted a representative assembly to be elected by all freeman. Independent thinkers such as Roger Williams, Anne Hutchinson, John Wheelwright, and Hanserd Knollys had no choice except to leave the colony.

John Cotton in England and New England

A very different kind of man, who also became authoritarian, was John Cotton (1584–1652). Cotton was installed as "teacher" in First Church, Boston, and thus became one of the most powerful Puritans in New England. Much of his power lay in his relationship with John Winthrop; between the two of them, they had a tight grip on Massachusetts. Competent and authoritative, each had his own sphere yet agreed that they should jointly control the beliefs and behaviors of their entire colony.

John Cotton.

John Cotton was born in Derby, England. His father was Rowland Cotton, a lawyer from a distinguished family. John Cotton was highly intelligent and supposedly entered Trinity College in 1598 at age twelve when most entering students were considerably older.

There was a long-running argument at Cambridge about which was the best form of church government—the system of bishops and archbishops or the Presbyterian system of local clergy and laity. The Puritans preferred a compromise. They wanted a church within a church; in other words, they wanted a local church within a theocracy. In the process of developing this structure, they had informal meetings between clergy and laity and discussed the Bible at length.

This kind of informal meeting had made John Cotton very popular in England. He was a strong, confident preacher, intelligent and well-educated, and he became an influential lecturer and dean of Emmanuel College, Cambridge. Cotton was also popular at the parish church of St. Botolph in Boston, Lincolnshire. He served for twenty-one years until his views began to change and he became more and more independent in his thinking.

Although Cotton was a charismatic preacher, his sermons were often so long that his listeners fell asleep. A visitation record written in 1614 makes the point:

> Mr. Chancellour and my selfe heard 3 of his sermons in 2 days, wch 3 were six howers long very near. This testimonie we are able to give of his sermons: good pains were bestowed in ye contriving of them . . . but that there was mors in olla, every sermon to o^r Judgments was poysoned with some errour or other. Theire afternoone worship as they use to term it, wil be 5 howers long, where to my observation there was as many sleepers as wakers.[9]

Reginald Dunning, in his history of Alford, interprets this quote as proving it was not the tyranny of the church or state that drove the Puritans from their homes but the fact that they were obsessed with intellectual subtleties and "sulked like spoiled children at the moderate reforms of Archbishop Laud."[10]

Opinions differed about Laud's so-called "moderate reforms." The general religious and political climate was certainly not moderate. When two Oxford scholars drank a toast with words that were derogatory of Charles I, they were overheard and censured in the Star Chamber. The Star Chamber was a court at Westminster Hall where offenders against the Crown were tried secretly and without due process of the law. The students who mocked Charles I were sentenced to be degraded from the monastery and university, to lose one ear in London and another ear at Oxford, and to pay a fine of two thousand pounds.[11] The Star Chamber was not to be trifled with.

In 1632, complaints about John Cotton were logged with the High Commission Court because he ignored the *Book of Common Prayer,* did not wear the surplice, did not use the sign of the cross in baptism, nor did he kneel for the sacrament. On January 21, 1634, John Cotton wrote a letter to John Williams, bishop of Lincoln, pleading with him for time to reflect on ceremonies that were troubling his conscience, including the practice of kneeling during Holy Communion when there was no room to do so because of the crowds. Cotton wrote:

> It is true indeede, y^t in Receyvinge the Communion, sundry of y^m doe not kneele: but (as I concyve it, & as they Expresse them-selves) It is not out of scruple of Conscience, but from ye store & multitude of Communicants, wch often doe so thronge one another in this great Congregation, that they can hardly stand, (much lesse kneele) one by another.[12]

Whether to stand or kneel was one of the same issues that concerned Hanserd Knollys four years later. Whereas Bishop Williams was inclined to be lenient with Cotton (as he also was with Knollys), the archbishop was not. Laud was essentially Arminian. Arminians rejected the Calvinistic view of predestination and emphasized free will, the intercessory role of the priest, and the importance of surplice and ritual. According to some, the Arminians were closer to Roman Catholicism than they were to the Puritans.[13]

The court judged Cotton guilty of nonconformity and Puritanism. In danger of death, he disguised himself and fled with his wife, Elizabeth Horrocks, to Boston, Massachusetts, on the ship *Griffin*. They arrived in Boston, September 4, 1633, after an eight-week voyage from the Downs.

When Cotton was made "teacher" in First Church, Boston, the pastor was John Wilson. As teacher, Cotton gave the sermons and instructed the congregation on what to believe. As pastor, Wilson led the worship and administered the sacraments. In many churches the tasks of pastor and teacher were combined.

Although Cotton wanted more church members, he insisted on having only those who would publicly attest to having had "a significant religious experience" and who would also conform to his ways. First Church of Boston grew in size, but it was difficult to assess the inner workings of the Holy Spirit in spite of the claims that were made. As for conformity, Cotton later joined Winthrop in banishing Roger Williams, Anne Hutchinson, John Wheelwright, and Hanserd Knollys.

Nonconforming Roger Williams

Roger Williams (1603–1683), a pioneer of religious freedom, was one of the first to be banished from Massachusetts because he criticized the church leaders for using civil government to enforce religious beliefs. He believed that liberty of conscience was a right that belonged to everyone. Although he accepted the basic principles of Christianity and was essentially a Calvinist, he did not believe that any religious group should try to control the beliefs of those who held different views. Roger Williams, like Hanserd Knollys, was a hero and a defender of religious freedom.

The son of a tailor, Roger Williams was so intelligent that, as a boy, he became a protégé of Sir Edward Coke (1552–1634), the great jurist and chief justice of the Court of Common Pleas. The two met when Roger Williams was a student at Charterhouse in

1621; Edward Coke was on the board of governors and affectionately referred to Williams as his son.

Coke was a brilliant prosecutor and writer who always argued in favor of the supremacy of common law over everything except Parliament. He owned sixty manors throughout England, but his career was a stormy one, and he created much of the storm.[14] In fact, Coke wrote a protestation to King James I, which was adopted by the House of Commons. This statement claimed the right to freedom of speech.

> That the liberties, franchises, privileges and jurisdictions of Parliament are the ancient and undoubted birthright and inheritance of the subjects of England: and that the arduous and urgent affairs concerning the king, state and defense of the realm and the Church of England and the making and maintenance of laws and redress of grievances which daily happen within this realm, are proper subjects and matter of counsel or debate in Parliament: and that in the handling and proceeding of those businesses, every member of the house hath, and of right ought to have, freedom of speech . . .[15]

To say that every member of the House had the right to freedom of speech was an inflammatory statement. It was a demand for tolerance. The king was so furious he tore up the protestation and imprisoned Coke in the Tower. The case against Coke was finally dismissed, and he returned to Parliament and to his criticism of the Crown.

As his student and protégé, Roger Williams was no doubt influenced by Coke's demand for freedom of speech. With a scholarship from Charterhouse, he continued his education at Pembroke College, Cambridge, where both religion and the classics were emphasized. Williams also learned shorthand so he could record the sermons he heard in church and the speeches he heard in the Star Chamber.

He then became the private chaplain to the household of Sir William Masham at Otes in Essex, where he met many famous people. Among those was Thomas Hooker, who had to appear before the Court of the High Commission for nonconformist views and who later founded Hartford, Connecticut. Oliver Cromwell and John Winthrop also visited William Masham from time to time. One can only imagine the intensity of their discussions around the dinner table.

John Winthrop and Roger Williams came from very different family backgrounds. Although both attended Cambridge, Winthrop came from a newly rich background and viewed himself as a great prophet and leader. Like most people in power, he thought he knew what was best for others and wanted to control their beliefs. In contrast, Roger Williams had more modest goals. He wanted freedom to live by his own beliefs and wanted others to have the same freedom.

In Boston, Roger Williams was staunchly against control by the established church. In his view, it was as domineering as the Church of England. He was also against the Massachusetts Bay Colony's seizure of the Indians' land without payment. As a result, it was not long before Roger Williams clashed with both John Winthrop and John Cotton.

Winthrop accused Williams of writing letters that were "full of anti-Christian pollution." In October 1635, Roger Williams was called to appear before the General Court to defend his point of view. When he would not admit to being in error, he was ordered to leave within six weeks and not to preach during that time. However, Williams continued to preach, so a warrant was issued for his arrest with the intent of shipping him back to England.

Captain John Underhill, who three years later was to become involved with Hanserd Knollys, was sent to arrest Roger Williams, but Williams escaped through the wilderness. He fled to Rhode Island and bought land from the Indians, then returned to England in 1643 to seek a charter for Rhode Island. While in England, Roger Williams wrote letters and controversial tracts on the liberty of conscience. He claimed that civil magistrates had no power, either civil or spiritual, on matters of the soul and that the church in New England should break its ties with Old England and develop its own order. In contrast, John Cotton insisted that the new order be his order, what he personally wanted, and not what the people wanted.

Eventually Roger Williams received his charter and returned to New England, and Rhode Island became firmly established. Here, he put his theory into action. Church and state were kept fully separate, and there was tolerance to worship according to one's own beliefs.

Roger Williams's *Bloody Tenent of Persecution* was published in 1644 and reprinted by the Hanserd Knollys Society in 1848 along with a series of very friendly letters between Winthrop, Cotton, and Williams discussing their disagreements regarding church and civil power. In his last letter to Cotton, Williams asked him to consider the question: "If the Lord Jesus were himself in person in Old or New England, what church, what ministry, what worship, what government, would he set up?"[16]

Anne Hutchinson's Search for Truth

Meanwhile, Gov. John Winthrop, like Elizabeth I, refused to separate civil government from ecclesiastical rule. People like Roger Williams were anathema to him, and Winthrop began to blame the unrest and dissatisfaction in Massachusetts on others who believed like Roger Williams in freedom of conscience.[17] Winthrop was strongly supported in this by John Cotton.

In England, Anne Hutchinson had been one of John Cotton's most enthusiastic followers and had his strong approval until, in New England, she disagreed with some of his sermons. Anne was to become a major threat to the religious and civil establishment in Massachusetts that demanded conformity. Like Hanserd Knollys, who was also from Lincolnshire, she was willing to sacrifice everything for freedom except her beliefs.

Baptized July 20, 1591, in Alford, Lincolnshire, Anne was born to Bridget Dryden and Francis Marbury, a pastor in the Church of England who was so outspoken as a young man that he was imprisoned twice. His clergy status was revoked in Alford, but in 1594 he went to London. When he was more careful about not criticizing Queen Elizabeth, he was allowed to resume his role. Anne lived in London from age fourteen to twenty-one and, no doubt, observed and was influenced by her father's increasing involvement in politics. When she was growing up, girls did not attend schools, but she was well-educated at home. She became aware of the Familists (Family of Love), a separatist movement of Dutch origin which died out during the Restoration when some members became Quakers. Outspoken herself, Anne was increasingly aware of how women were supposed to be silent. That was not her style.

In 1612, she married William Hutchinson, also of Alford. They had fifteen children, all but the last born in England. Anne was strongly influenced by John Cotton. She often went to hear him preach at St. Botolph Church in Boston, Lincolnshire, twenty-four miles from Alford, when she accompanied her husband there on his business trips. Cotton, like her own father, questioned some of the practices that he thought were too "popish" in the Church of England. Both he and her father served as models for her. They were not afraid to voice their disapproval, and later she did the same.

Anne was so intensely involved in a search for religious truth that, in 1634, she and her husband followed John Cotton to Massachusetts bringing with them some of their children and her widowed mother-in-law. They arrived on the *Griffin* in September 1634 and became members of First Church in Boston on June 12, 1636.

William Hutchinson was a successful merchant and invested in real estate. He was appointed selectman and also deputy to the legislative assembly. While he was involved in business and community affairs, Anne became more absorbed in theological discussions. She started to hold meetings in their home as she had done in England and soon attracted many laymen and clergy.

Originally, her meetings were to discuss the sermons of John Cotton, and she shared with others what she learned from him in England. She had especially liked hearing Cotton proclaiming that people were not born into sin but became sinners through their actions.[18] Anne was a well-trained and well-liked midwife who had given birth to so many babies herself and had helped so many others do the same that she could not believe they were born in sin.

Gradually, Anne Hutchinson began to expand on Cotton's sermons by sharing her own theological views. This included her criticism of legalistic Puritan dictates. Claiming to receive revelations directly from God through the Holy Spirit and through reading the Bible, she soon became a powerful and controversial figure in Boston. Like Luther, Anne maintained that the indwelling of the Holy Spirit was as important as "good works" and that God could be experienced through Bible study, not just through the observance of rituals.

Some clergy interpreted her criticism of the Puritan emphasis on "good works" as a personal attack on their preaching. Although Luther had stressed the importance of conscience over conformity, a concept that Cotton agreed with, it was unheard of for a woman to speak out on such matters. That was the real issue. An intelligent woman who argued for her beliefs, as did Anne Hutchinson, was a threat to the structure Cotton had designed.

Women were expected to be inferior intellectually and to accept the dictates of men without question.[19] They were not allowed to vote; their role was to bear children and care for the home. They could be publicly whipped if they disagreed with their husbands or the magistrates of the church or town. But Anne had come from an educated family and had observed her father questioning authority and tradition. She felt equally human and could do no less.

When Anne and William Hutchinson first followed John Cotton to Boston, Cotton supported her open-group discussions. In England, he had stressed the Holy Spirit as more important than the structure and rituals of the church. However, in New England, in his position of having more personal authority than when he was under a bishop and archbishop, he began to agree with Winthrop on the right of a few leaders, including himself, to govern the lives and beliefs of many. Anne's meetings became so popular that some sixty to eighty people attended them, but when she began to question parts of Cotton's sermons, he withdrew his approval of her.

The wrath of John Winthrop, who lived just across the street from the Hutchinsons, was even more vengeful. No doubt he observed the popularity of her meetings. Even prominent businessmen attended her biweekly meetings. Perhaps through his own windows he watched the many coming to her house and saw her as a threat to his power. Viciously, Winthrop called her an "instrument of Satan" and arranged for her to be tried by the General Court for heresy. Neither Anne nor a lawyer was allowed to speak on her behalf, and she was accused by Cotton of being a Familist and an Anabaptist. She denied both.

Placed in custody, she was then banished from the Massachusetts Bay Colony, primarily for "traducing the ministers." This was just two years after Roger Williams had been similarly banished. Others who agreed with Anne shared her fate of banishment. She was pregnant and forty-six years old when a group of them left for Aquidneck, now part of Rhode Island. Then, her husband died; she moved to Long Island Sound where she gave birth to a stillborn, deformed child. The final tragedy came when Anne and other members of her family were massacred. Only her eldest son, who had accompanied John Cotton to Massachusetts, survived.

After the massacre, Winthrop's antipathy for Anne and religious freedom was even more cruelly verbalized. He pronounced that her deformed child and the massacre of her family were proof of God's judgment against her.

Winthrop's concept that women's role in society was inferior to that of men stemmed from the long-held belief that women were the devil's gateway and the source of all evil. This belief had led to the witchcraft movement which began in Europe during the thirteenth century and lasted until the beginning of the eighteenth. In England alone, between 1563 and 1685, nearly one thousand women were executed and the condemnation of women continued in New England.

When Anne Hutchinson was put on trial and questioned by Winthrop, the proceedings reflected John Cotton's theory that the role of women in church was to be limited. A woman was only supposed to speak out when giving an account from some wrong-doing or when singing with the congregation. Women were not to ask questions, yet they often asked rhetorical questions with the intent of tricking their questioners. In Anne Hutchinson's trial in November 1637, she did exactly that.[20] And she was not the only woman in New England to suffer for speaking out in favor of religious freedom.

Hanserd Knollys, though a man, also disagreed with Winthrop and Cotton on the "proper" role of women. As to be seen later, both he and his wife, Anne Cheney, participated in church debates about baptism. Hanserd also publicly defended another controversial women who wrote a book and spoke out about her theological beliefs, not just at home but to whomever would listen.

The Banishment of John Wheelwright

John Wheelwright was another who felt the brunt of Winthrop's and Cotton's intolerance in Massachusetts. Wheelwright had been vicar of Bilsby in Lincolnshire and lived near the Hutchinsons and Marburys. Mary, sister of William Hutchinson, was John Wheelwright's second wife. Thus, three powerful nonconformist families from the same geographical area were dissenters from the Church of England and were related by marriage: the Hutchinsons, Marburys, and Wheelwrights.

John Wheelwright was the one who so greatly influenced Hanserd Knollys/Knowles in England by urging him not to worry so much about "good works" but to trust God's grace. One of the stories told about Wheelwright involves Oliver Cromwell, the Lord Protector of England who ruled after Charles I and who functioned much like a king although he refused that title.

It seems that Cromwell and Wheelwright had been at Cambridge together and argued endlessly about theology and government. Wheelwright usually won their debates. The two also competed in association football or soccer. According to tradition, football became popular in the twelfth century as a way to celebrate driving the Romans out of England with a flying wedge in the third century. It also celebrated driving out the Danes in the eighth century. Cromwell was said to have remarked years later that "he could remember when he was more afraid of meeting Wheelwright at football than meeting an army in the field, for he was infallibly sure of being tripped up by him."[21]

Wheelwright, like Cotton, had been silenced in England. When they arrived in New England on May 26, 1636, on the small ship *Griffin*, both were fleeing the authorities. On the voyage, they had alternated giving three sermons a day.[22] After landing in Boston, they started to attend First Church where the Rev. John Wilson was already established as pastor. John Cotton became teacher in the church. Some church members suggested that John Wheelwright also be added to the staff. However, Cotton did not want this. He resented Wheelwright's argumentative style. Perhaps the two had become competitive when they listened to each other's long sermons daily during the eight-week crossing.

Wheelwright was asked to leave First Church, so he formed a church in the part of Boston called Braintree and later Quincy, where he had a grant of two hundred acres. In Braintree, he was spied upon, his sermons carefully listened to by those who were looking for something that could be used against him. At last they heard it.

On January 20, 1637, a fast was being held in the Boston churches. In his sermon that day, Wheelwright spoke against those who "walked in a covenant of works." Winthrop got angry at this expression of dissent and called the court into session. Wheelwright was accused of sedition and contempt of court. Given a chance to retract his statement, he responded that if guilty of sedition he deserved death, but if they proceeded against him he would appeal to the king.

The trial continued and those on the side of religious freedom lost. Those on the side of authoritarianism and conformity won. This created so much controversy in the church that when John Wilson preached, half of the congregation would get up and leave.[23]

The animosity ran deep. Later the same year, fifty-eight Wheelwright partisans, including Captain John Underhill (who later became very involved with Hanserd Knollys), were required to turn in all their arms and ammunition. The town record of November 20, 1637, reads:

> Whereas the opinions and revelations of Mr. Wheelwright and Mrs. Hutchinson have seduced and led into dangerous errors, many of the people here in New England, inasmuch as there is

just cause of suspicion that they, as others in Germany in former times, may, upon some revelation, make some suddaine irruption upon those that differ from them in judgment; for prevention whereof it is ordered that all those whose names are underwritten shall (upon warning given or left at their dwelling-houses), before the 30th day of this month of November, deliver in at Mr. Cane's house, at Boston, all such guns, pistols, swords, powder, shot and match, as they shall be owners of or have in their custody.[24]

The reference to Germany in the above judgment was based on an event that had occurred some eighty years earlier. It was in 1529 when some of the freedoms given to the followers of Martin Luther were taken away by the Roman Catholic princes of Germany and Charles V. The Lutheran princes and inhabitants of fourteen cities had objected. They argued that withdrawing the right to worship as they pleased was not binding as it forced them to go against their conscience. This led to a bloody uprising.

Winthrop was worried that a similar kind of disagreement could occur in Massachusetts leading to a riot. So Wheelwright was sentenced to be banished, essentially because he agreed with Anne Hutchinson that "good works" were not enough to ensure salvation.

Then, three men of the Hutchinson family signed a remonstrance against Wheelwright's banishment. One was his brother-in-law, William Hutchinson, who had married Anne Marbury; the other two were Richard and Edward. William was especially influential in getting the sentence modified. He was a freeman and, therefore, could vote on such issues. He also owned considerable property, was a delegate for Boston to the General Court, and was on a committee in charge of allotting land around Boston to new settlers. Furthermore, he contributed to the establishment of a grammar school; needless to say, he was very influential.[25]

Although the Hutchinsons' intervention was effective, Wheelwright was disgusted. Along with some members of the Hutchinson family and others who were disaffected, he left the colony. Church records say they were dismissed. The word *dismissed* in such records is not a synonym for being expelled; dismissal is a letter of transfer from one church to another when members change their church affiliations.

Some of the Hutchinsons and their followers went to Rhode Island, others north to Maine. Still others, including Wheelwright, went to the province of New Hampshire where they bought land from the Indians and established Exeter in 1639. Wheelwright was well-liked in Exeter and, with thirty-four others, signed a combination in which they agreed to conform with English laws as subjects of King Charles. A combination was a document that declared the intention of a group of people to establish a local town government that would be acceptable to the Crown.

However, when Exeter became part of Massachusetts and, therefore, under Winthrop's control, Wheelwright had to leave. He went to Wells, Maine, where he purchased four to five hundred acres of land from Governor Gorges, who had received the land from his uncle Sir Ferdinando Gorges. When Wheelwright's sister-in-law Anne Hutchinson and her family were massacred in 1642, Wheelwright was no doubt overwhelmed by the family tragedy and concerned for his own wife, Anne's sister-in-law. She probably wanted to return to Exeter so she could be near other family members; so Wheelwright wrote to Governor Winthrop and apologized extravagantly (as was the style at the time) for being so argumentative.

> It repents me that I did so much adhere to persons of corrupt judgment . . . as a man dazzled with the buffetings of Satan . . . I confess that herein I have done very sinfully and do humbly crave pardon.[26]

Winthrop was not appeased by the apology and Wheelwright had to remain in Wells, Maine, for another four years. Finally, December 1, 1647, he was invited to Hampton, New Hampshire, to serve the church there as its third minister. In Hampton, he bought land that had once been owned by Rev. Stephen Batchelor, one of the founders of Hampton.[27] Ten years later, Wheelwright went to England and then returned. When he died in 1679, he left property in both England and New England.

This John Wheelwright was the same person who, in the previous chapter, was so important in helping Hanserd Knollys work through his agony of doubt so that he could confidently follow his own conscience in the service of God. Perhaps Wheelwright met up with the Hanserd Knollys's family again on his trip to England. After all, John Knowles/Knollys, probably Hanserd's son or nephew, bought land in Hampton where Wheelwright lived and was married there in 1660.

Meanwhile, Cotton and Winthrop had not tolerated Knollys's and Wheelwright's belief that it was necessary to experience the Holy Spirit as well as do "good works." Cotton and Winthrop wanted conformity, not to the Church of England, but to their own beliefs. They believed that they were the "elect," that they were the saints who were predestined to rule, and that their decisions were law. Even in New England, religious freedom was on trial.

Trial by the High Commission

Boston, Massachusetts, was named after Boston in Lincolnshire, England, and in both cities Hanserd Knollys was arrested. In 1638, just before he fled to New England, Hanserd was arrested for nonconformity in Boston, Lincolnshire, the same city from which John Cotton had been forced to flee for disagreeing with Laud.

With the permission of the Bishop John Williams, Hanserd had been lecturing and preaching close by in the villages of Woodenderby, Fulnetby on the Hill, and Wainfleet. Silenced in Wainfleet, he went on preaching until he was taken by order of the High Commission Court. This court was ruled by Archbishop Laud, who was then feuding with Bishop Williams. It was the bishop who had encouraged Knollys to continue preaching.

Williams was powerful, a keeper of the great seal and bishop of Lincoln from 1621 to 1641. Although Williams had assisted Archbishop Laud in Laud's rise to authority, there was no gratitude in return. Laud resented Williams for disagreeing with him, accused him of divulging the king's secrets, libeling against the Privy Council, and tampering with the king's witnesses. Laud had Williams put on trial in the Star Chamber and imprisoned.

The High Commission Court, in which Hanserd Knollys was tried, was founded in 1535 to deal with heresy, schism, nonconformity, and marital offenses. Those accused of violating the Act of Supremacy and the Act of Uniformity were tried with little or no evidence against them. If a minister did not read prayers on Wednesday, it was nonconformity; if two women quarreled in church, it was schism; witchcraft was heresy. A defendant before the High Commission Court had to take an oath before discovering the accusation and was also questioned severely before the trial.

This procedure was despised by the Puritans and by the common law judges who resented such powerful repression of nonconformity and insistence on Church of England rites and rituals. Noted for its arbitrary punishments, the High Commission found Knollys guilty of nonconformity to regulations that were imposed by the Crown and carried out by the Church.

This judgment against Hanserd occurred three years after his father was called to court because of Laud's rulings and two years after Hanserd resigned from his parish in Humberstone, renounced his ordination in the Church of England, and was lecturing in other parishes. While awaiting sentence, Hanserd was kept prisoner by the very man who had served the arrest warrant to him. He preached to his jailer and was so effective that, according to Hanserd's brief memoir, the man was "so greatly terrified in his conscience that he set open his doors and let me go away."[28] Although Hanserd escaped, he was not out of danger, so he hid out in London for six weeks until he could catch a sailing ship to New England. It was the summer of 1638, and although he talked his way out of jail this first time, this would not always be possible. He was to become one of those who, like Roger Williams, John Wheelwright, and Anne Hutchinson, were excluded from Massachusetts for defending religious freedom.

5

Escapes and Banishments

Stone walls do not a prison make, Nor iron bars a cage.

—Richard Lovelace, 1618–1658

Freedom From and Freedom To

When Hanserd Knollys escaped to America in 1638, England was in turmoil. Charles I, son of James, had dissolved Parliament back in 1629 because it would not comply with all of his demands, so there was no Parliament at all until 1640. There were few civil rights, food and jobs were scarce, and poverty was rampant. Emigration increased. Many early settlers sailed to the New World feeling so desperate about their homeland that even the wilderness offered more hope.

Some left England to escape persecution, to live out the political and religious hopes for freedom which the Reformation had inspired. Hanserd Knollys was one of these. Others were essentially businessmen wanting free enterprise and the opportunity to make money from trading, fishing, and lumber.

Dense forests covered much of the eastern coast, and old-growth lumber, especially tall straight timber for masts, was so valuable that in New Hampshire in 1643, four men were fined for felling trees wastefully. Traders and adventurers came looking for new challenges, and farmers came who wanted to own their land instead of renting it or worked for hire on land that belonged to others. In the colonies, labor was scarce and land was plentiful.

The difficulty was that impoverished people could not afford to buy passage to the opportunities in the New World. Many emigrants paid for their passage by signing contracts to be servants for three to seven years. After their "indentured servitude" they would be free to acquire their own land, which was almost impossible in England. Consequently, they signed up as servants even if they had technical or professional skills. Unfortunately, many worked so hard they did not live long.

Other emigrants came as young apprentices. In England, all children were generally expected to leave home by age fourteen and they did. Becoming an apprentice, domestic servant, or farm worker was most common. Only the poorest families did not employ children of other families. Many of the apprentices and servants came from the gentry class.[1]

London was the center for apprentices, and Hanserd Knollys paid over sixty pounds for the apprenticeship of one of his sons and also gave him an additional forty pounds, a large sum in those days. John Knollys/Knowles, a mariner who settled and was married in Hampton, New Hampshire, in 1660 at the time John Wheelwright was there, may have been this son. Early marriages were not customary except in cases of royalty when very early marriages were often arranged to ensure lines of inheritance and political alliances.

People labeled "criminals" were often sent to America although their only crime might be disagreement with the Crown or religious authorities. However, whether criminals, servants, or free, those who came to America in the early days were often as harshly controlled by civil and religious authorities there as they had been at home.

In 1619, a Dutch ship transported the first slaves to Jamestown for sale; by 1713, England claimed the exclusive right to bring slaves to America. For slaves, there was no freedom—at best, only permission to exist, if obedient. Their cries for personal, political, and religious freedom joined those of the other immigrants in the new country.

The importance of these early explorers, religious reformers, farmers and traders, and those brought involuntarily cannot be overemphasized in the history of America. The explorers opened the door to freedom; the others crowded through courageously. For some, however, the freedom was illusory.

Knollys's Rough Crossing

Hanserd Knollys was forty years old when he and his wife, Anne Cheney, and one or more of their children sailed on April 26, 1638, from Gravesend, England, on a ship commanded by Captain Goodland.

For Knollys's family, it was "a rough crossing of 14 weeks," and it was rough in several ways. A child of theirs died. Their water stank, and their bread and cheese turned green, yellow, and blue, rotten with mold, but they had to eat it anyway. When they arrived in Boston, Massachusetts, even the moldy food was almost gone, and Hanserd had only six farthings left. Fortunately, Anne had saved five pounds for emergencies, and a friend who had moved to Rhode Island loaned them his Boston house to live in. But, for several weeks, Hanserd was so poor he had to work "with a hoe."[2]

In his brief memoir, Hanserd did not mention the death of his child on board the ship. This was recorded by Governor Winthrop in his journal who wrote that a child of Hanserd Knollys died of convulsions during the voyage. It was a curious item for Winthrop to mention. He generally kept very brief notes which were often written long after the event and were not necessarily chronological. However, Winthrop was bitterly critical of Knollys. Was he implying, as he did with the death of Anne Hutchinson's child, that the death of Hanserd's child was evidence of God's judgment?

In spite of having a place to live, Hanserd was not allowed to stay in Boston. Some ministers reported to the magistrates that he was "antinomian." The word *antinomian* comes from the Greek *anti* (against) and *nomos* (law). It was widely used in a pejorative way for those who interpreted biblical, ecclesiastical, or civil law in ways that were contrary to what authoritarians claimed were right.

In essence, antinomianism, a doctrine that grew out of the Reformation, was the belief that legalistic obedience to Old Testament law was not necessary and that Christians were free of it because of God's grace. This was based on the belief that grace was experienced through the Holy Spirit. Those who disagreed worried that this freedom would lead to license. In England, a number of Separatists, including some Independents, were accused of sympathy with antinomianism doctrine. And, in New England, Anne Hutchinson had been accused of antinomianism as had John Wheelwright and, of course, Hanserd Knollys.

Clergy Conflict in Dover

When Hanserd Knollys arrived in Massachusetts in 1638, he was denied the right to preach or teach by Rev. John Cotton and Gov. John Winthrop. Like John Wheelwright, Hanserd was accused of being tainted with antinomian beliefs because he agreed with Anne Hutchinson about the importance of experiencing the Holy Spirit instead of the rigid Puritan focus on doing "good works." For this, he was banished from Massachusetts.

When he was getting ready to leave, two strangers heard of Hanserd by accident and invited him to settle along the Piscataqua River. The Piscataqua River is now the boundary between Maine and New Hampshire.[3] The word *piscataqua* is Algonquin for "dividing point of water." The river had a safe harbor with a rocky shore. As early as 1603, Martin Pring visited it. In 1614, Capt. John Smith was there. Land grants in the area were obtained in 1623 by Capt. John Mason and Sir Ferdinando Gorges.

After being forced out of Boston, Hanserd Knollys went to the area on the Piscataqua River called Strawbery Banke, which later became part of Portsmouth.[4]

The fishing was good, and Piscataqua became New Hampshire's first settlement. It was renamed in 1653 when the settlers asked the General Court of Massachusetts for a name change. They chose Portsmouth because it was, "a name most suitable for the place, it being the River's mouth, and a good harbor as any in the land."[5]

Dover, where Hanserd was later to preach, was seven miles north of Strawbery Banke. It was first settled by Capt. Thomas Wiggin in 1633. The trees there were suitable for great masts as well as building homes. Signatures of two Indians known as "Ould Robin Hood" and Wahowah or "Hope Hood" are on early land transfers made to settlers. Sometimes, there was relative harmony between the Native Americans and the settlers. At other times, there was great discontent and warfare.

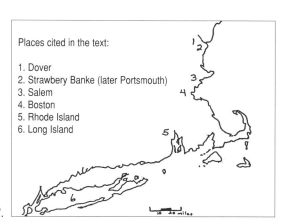

Places cited in the text:

1. Dover
2. Strawbery Banke (later Portsmouth)
3. Salem
4. Boston
5. Rhode Island
6. Long Island

New England.

Originally, Dover had an independent local government, and William Leveridge was the community's first minister. Although he was well-trained and well-liked, Leveridge left after two years because Dover was so small it could not afford to support him. George Burdett from Yarmouth, England, was Dover's second minister and a claimant to the role of governor. In those days, the title "governor" did not mean what it means now—the chief elected officer of a state. Then, it could mean an administrator of a town, a province, or a colony. In the early colonial period, a governor usually reported to a proprietor who held land granted to him by the Crown.

Hanserd purchased land in Strawbery Banke from Henry Jocelyn, who had received it as a grant from the Laconia Company five years earlier. When Hanserd started to form a church in Piscataqua, he was told to leave by a resentful George Burdett, who was the local governor at the time.

Then, Burdett got himself in trouble. He was accused of adultery with several women and also of writing a letter to Archbishop Laud claiming that the Massachusetts Colony was planning to become independent of England. Burdett's letter was intercepted and aroused the animosity of Massachusetts Governor Winthrop, who certainly did not want his loyalty to the Crown cast in doubt! Burdett fled to what later became York, Maine, and then returned to England where he was imprisoned.

After Burdett, Capt. John Underhill became governor of Dover. Underhill, a soldier, was first brought over by Governor

Winthrop to teach military practices to citizens. However, he was censured and disenfranchised from the church in Boston because he, too, was thought to be overly attracted to Anne Hutchinson's beliefs. Someone overheard him saying, "The government at Boston is as zealous as the scribes and Pharisees, and as Paul before his conversion." Although he denied saying it, his accuser stood firm and he was called into court.[6]

Forced to leave Boston, Underhill moved to Exeter and then to Dover where, as governor, he invited Hanserd Knollys to become the town's third minister. Everything went well in the beginning. The first church was built of logs, and Hanserd's name shows on tax records of 1638.[7] In referring to old records, it is important to note that by this time, *Knowles* and *Knolles* had become the more common ways to spell *Knollys*.

The year 1640 saw the arrival of another minister in Dover, Thomas Larkham. Born in Dorsetshire and educated at Cambridge, Larkham was a radical preacher who had been accused in England of heresy, witchcraft, and treason, so he fled. In Dover, Larkham's flamboyant preaching style made him popular. Like his predecessor George Burdett, he claimed both civil and church authority.

The town could not afford both Larkham and Knollys as preachers. The two disagreed strongly on many issues, including the baptism of children, burial rituals for the dead, and eligibility for church membership. Trouble erupted.

Historians writing two hundred years later disagreed on the details. One story is that Hanserd Knollys, at the request of his congregation, declared Thomas Larkham to be excommunicated. Angrily, Larkham grabbed Knollys's hat, accused him of not paying for it, and shook a halberd at him. (A halberd was a sixteenth-century weapon with a long shaft topped by an ax-like blade and steel spike.) To the halberd was tied a Bible.

As this story goes, Knollys flourished a pistol and Captain Underhill intervened by taking Hanserd into protective custody. Larkham sent for support from John Williams, the governor of adjacent Strawbery Banke. This version of the event concludes with Williams deciding it was Underhill who was guilty of provoking a riot.[8]

A different, and probably more accurate, version of the story says it was Knollys who went before the troops with a Bible on the long pole and Larkham who had the pistol and called the magistrates while Underhill armed some men to protect Knollys. This version was published by Thomas Leckford, an attorney, in 1642, along with a series of letters.[9] When the case went to court, nine men were sentenced to be whipped for participating in a riot but were spared. Captain Underhill and Hanserd Knollys were each fined one hundred pounds, which they could not afford to pay. Knollys wrote a letter to Winthrop on Underhill's behalf, and Underhill went to Boston to apologize. Although at first he was not allowed to speak, eventually his profuse apology was accepted.

Like Burdett, Underhill, and Knollys, Mr. Larkham also had his troubles after the halberd and Bible episode. In 1641, he was forced to leave Dover on suspicion of impregnating a "handsome widow." Returning to England, he preached at Travistock and served as army chaplain but was court-martialed for misconduct.

Again on Trial

Meanwhile, Hanserd Knollys complained in a letter to England that the government of Massachusetts was worse and more oppressive than the High Commission of England. Winthrop heard about the letter, accused him of slander, and took him into custody. The records of the Massachusetts Court of November 29, 1639, show Winthrop's accusations and his demand, which was sent to all public officers, that Hanserd leave Massachusetts in ten days:

> Whereas M[r] Hanserd Knolles of Dover vpon Pascay: hauinge by letters into England greatly Scandelized y[e] Church and Civill State of this Jurisdiction, and beinge vpon better consideration brught to see the greatnesse of his offence & therevpon hath oft & earnestly craued Libertye that he might come to giue Pubt satisfaction: I haue thought fit by the advise & consent of the rest of the Councell to graunt him these letters of Pubt Assurance: by w[ch] he shalbe in peace & saftye w[th]in this Jurisdiction duringe the time of his cominge stayinge, and returninge free from any

> arrest ore othere molestation by ore from any Awthy. heere he
> demeaninge himselfe well accordinge to the order of such Pubt
> Assu[ ] pvided that he shall not staye wth in this Jurisdiction
> aboue tenn dayes, after notice giuen him by the Governo^r or
> Dpty Govr this Assurance to be in force till the ende of the thirde
> month next and noe longer.

Having arrived in 1638 and being banned from Boston, within a
year Hanserd found himself forced to leave a second place in New
England. In addition, John Winthrop insisted he publicly apologize.
Hanserd wrote a letter to that effect and left it with Winthrop to be
sent to England. It was directed to Robert Simson in England.
Fragments of the apology remain and indicate he felt guilty for being
judgmental when one of his basic values was tolerance. He judged
himself harshly for his lack of love and intolerance of Winthrop.

First, Hanserd admitted that he had written something offensive to the Massachusetts magistrates and their method of
government and that he had criticized them unduly because they
did not allow him to settle in their jurisdiction. He wrote that he
should have blessed them and "even blessed their favors in the
[past] and so become in time [confirmed in] their love [and that of]
the brethren." Next, he profusely apologized for accusing Winthrop
and the court of being "more censorious about the faith as a witness
of Christianity than the High Commission of England."

> [My] being misinformed by such as favored those who, for their
> sinful miscarriage and dangerous errors, were censured, made
> me then think [so, as was thought] by many then. Experience
> since teacheth me now to profess there is no [oppression in the]
> Court there, [and] that I have sinned in speaking false of the
> Rulers and particularly about the chief Ruler Mr Winthrop who
> was then, and now is, Governor of the Massachusetts Bay.[10]

Hanserd's third apology in this long letter was for listening to
rumors about John Cotton having no firm creed: "Herein also I
[sinned in disregarding the] comeliness Mr. Cotton then had in the
eyes of Massachusetts."

His fourth apology was for having criticized those who used fans, wore hoops and costly apparel, and oppressed their brethren in bargaining. He had charged that there was "hardly so much as a face of Religion in New England unless upon Sabbath." He wrote that instead of saying that, he should have made allowances for those in poverty, "poor persons who have lost their faith living in the woods and famishing."

Perhaps he apologized to avoid going to prison when his wife was pregnant and he was without means of support. Perhaps he regretted ever sending his protest to someone who notified Governor Winthrop of its contents. Very likely, he sincerely regretted writing his original letter.

It may be difficult to believe that such a self-reproachful letter was genuine, but that was the writing style of the time. It was also consistent with Hanserd Knollys's self-image as a sinner for falling into the trap of hastily judging others.

The Magna Carta of Dover

In early colonial days, neither the people of Strawbery Banke on the Piscataqua River where Hanserd still owned property nor Dover, eight miles up the river, had any government delegated by the Crown. They were part of New Hampshire and were self-governing. Although records of Dover prior to 1647 no longer exist, it appears that Dover's civil government began when forty-one men, including Hanserd, signed the combination for self-government in 1640. Signed and sent to England, Dover's combination read:

> Whereas, sundry mischeifes and inconveniences have befain us, and more and greater may in regard of want of civill Government, his Gratious Ma'tie haveing hitherto setled no order for us to our knowledge. Wee whose names are under-written being Inhabitants upon the River Pascataquack have voluntarily agreed to combine ourselves into a body politique that we may the more comfortably enjoy the benefit of his Ma'ties Lawes together with all such Orders as shal bee

concluded by a major part of the Freemen of our Society in case they bee not repugnant to the Lawes of England and administered in the behalfe of his Majesty. And this wee have mutually promised and concluded to do and so to continue till his Excellent Ma'tie shall give other Order concerning us. In Witness whereof wee have hereto set our hands the two and twentieth day of October in the sixteenth yeare of the reign of our Sovereign Lord Charles by the grace of God King of Great Britain France and Ireland Defender of the Faith &c. Anno. Dom. 1640.[11]

Hanserd, whose surname was written in so many ways, signed the combination and spelled his name *Knollys* to show his preference in spelling. Later, the combination was found in the Public Records Office in London and still exists. It is known as the "Piscataqua Combination."[12]

Two hundred years later, Rev. Dr. Alonzo Quint began publishing in the *Dover Enquirer* some historical memoranda that he had been collecting for thirty-eight years. He probably also used Thomas Leckford's book, *Plain Dealing,* published in 1642 and republished in 1885, only five years before Quint began his newspaper column. He labeled the above combination *Dover's Magna Carta* and made the point that in this document there were no special privileges for clergy, nor for those with long pedigrees, nor for those in whose "veins ran the blood of the Plantagenets." Their names were written in the same columns with those of obscure laborers and with no marks of distinction.[13]

This is reminiscent of the original Magna Carta, sometimes called the Great Charter, that was granted by King John in 1215 to the barons and became the basis of both English and United States law. King John was forced to sign it or lose the support of his barons. The charter guaranteed many rights including feudal rights, freedom of commerce, procedures for trial, and standardized penalties for felonies. However, the rights were often withheld from the people.

When Hanserd Knollys signed the combination that Quint described as Dover's Magna Carta, it indicated Hanserd still wanted peace with England, not separation. The stated goal of the combination was to enable the settlers to "more comfortably enjoy the benefit of [the king's majestic laws] together with all such

[laws] as shal bee concluded by a major part of the Freemen of our Society."[14] In other words, the settlers wanted the same rights in New England that they had as freemen in their mother country.

The word *freemen* did not include all men. It referred to those who were entitled to vote because they were members in good standing of the Congregational Church. Although less ceremonial than the Church of England, the early Congregational Church in Massachusetts was just as controlling. If ministers and magistrates said "leave," there was no choice except to obey.

Dover, originally part of New Hampshire, was annexed by Massachusetts on October 9, 1641. Under the government of Massachusetts, whose seat was in Boston, Dover was allowed to retain much of its independence. It had its own court and taxes and was exempt from the Massachusetts ruling that only Congregational Church members could vote.

However, Hanserd Knollys and other dissenters who had previously incurred the ongoing wrath of John Winthrop and been banished were forced to sell their land along the Piscataqua River because it had been transferred to Massachusetts. A brief but confusing record reads, "Strawberry [*sic*] Creek [Banke] is granted Mr. Knollys his purchase, paying the thirty pounds to the courts satisfaction." Ten years later, this land was returned to the province of New Hampshire, and the property that was once owned by Hanserd Knollys was given to Capt. William Hawthorne for "beinge commissionor for this colonie, all that parcell of land bought of Mr Knollys, lyinge in Kettery, & abuttinge of Pascataque River, grannted to him & his heires for ever."[15]

Rejected in Long Island

After selling his land on Strawbery Banke, Hanserd Knollys, along with Edward and Timothy Tomlins and others, moved to Long Island. Part of Canada and much of the northern part of the United States including Long Island had been granted to William Alexander, Earl of Sterling, by James VI of Scotland and Charles I of England. These lands, like many early grants, stretched from the Atlantic to the Pacific. The land Sterling was granted was larger than all the king's other holdings. Poet, statesman, and scholar, the

Earl of Sterling never came to the colonies; he was busy being the secretary of state for Scotland for almost twenty-five years.

Shortly after Hanserd Knollys and several followers settled in Long Island, a protest was filed against them and John Winthrop and the Council of Massachusetts by James Forrett, a representative of Sterling. Probably this was related to the death of the impoverished Sterling in 1640 while his agent was in the process of selling the earl's vast estate. The protest read:

> Whereas Edward Tomlins and Timothy Tomlins togither wth one Hanserd Knollys Clercke and others have latly entered and taken possession of some parte of the longe Iland in New England, wch was formerly granted by the letters Pattents of o^r Sovereine Lord Kinge Charles to the Right Honora [ ] Witt Earle of Sterlinge and his heires: I James fforrett gentl [ ] by virtue of a Commission vnder the hand & Seale of the sayd Earle to me made for the dispossinge and ordiringe of the sayd long Iland, doe hereby protest.[16]

Once more uprooted, Hanserd was now forty-two years old and without money or means to support his family. His father, who was elderly, had written and asked him to return to England. Perhaps he was glad to do so.

> I returned with my wife and one Child about three years old and fhe was great with another Child and we came fafe to London on the 24th of December 1641 in which year the Maffacre in Ireland broke forth, and the next year Wars broke forth in England between King and Parliament.[17]

Hanserd Knollys had been away from the intolerance in England for three and one-half years, from July 1638 to December 1641. Hoping for freedom of worship, he had not found it. Nor did he find it after he returned home.

Futhermore, it was not until 1663 that the first permanent Baptist church was established in New England, in Swansea, Massachusetts, near Plymouth. The founder was John Myles, a Baptist minister from Wales who, like Knollys, was also persecuted for preaching on religious liberty.

Early marker in New England.

Destitute in London

It was 1641, the same year as the Ulster Rebellion, that Richard Knollys asked his son to return home. As the case had been filed against Hanserd for settling in Long Island, his decision to leave New England was probably easy to make. However, with a pregnant wife and three-year-old child, the trip back home was difficult. Anne was injured on the voyage, and when they arrived in England, Hanserd wrote that they had no place to go:

> I was ftill poor, and fojourned in a Lodging till I had but fixpence left, and knew not how to provide for my wife and Child, but having prayed to God and encouraged my wife to truft in God and to remember our former experiences.[18]

Having paid for their lodging out of the scant funds that he still had, Hanserd was at a loss to know how to support his child, his wife, and himself. Yet, Anne was always loyal in spite of poverty and illness; she trusted that something positive would happen. One day Hanserd went out to walk and meditate. He met a woman, a stranger, who said she and her husband wanted to provide lodging for him and his family about eight doors from where he was staying. Evidently, they heard of Hanserd's and Anne's plight.

The couple paid all of Hanserd's family expenses for fifteen weeks. If they had not, Anne Knollys might have died. Pregnant, she had fallen on the ship coming home and, badly bruised, had gone into early labor. Fortunately "two Doctors, an Apothecary and a Chyrurgeon, did daily attend her" without charge.

This same woman who provided housing also gave Hanserd twenty shillings that a Dr. Bastwick had given her for him. John Bastwick was a strong, outspoken Presbyterian who had evidently heard of Hanserd Knollys and could well understand his dilemma. Shortly before Hanserd returned to England, Bastwick had been fined and sentenced to the pillory, to have his ears cut off, and to be imprisoned for life. In 1640, the finally recalled new Parliament reversed Bastwick's sentence. However, Bastwick continued writing such inflammatory pieces that eventually he and Hanserd got into a publishing war of pamphlets.

Meanwhile, a group of friends gave Hanserd seven pounds. He asked them if they knew how he could get some students because he would rather work than depend on charity. One of these friends suggested that he go to the school on Great Tower Hill where the schoolmaster had just died to see if he could get some students who were now without a teacher. Hanserd did so and soon gained the reputation of being a fine teacher.

Shortly after this, he was chosen to be master of Mary-Axe Free School. Within a year, he had strengthened it greatly and eventually had 140 day students and 15 boarders.[19]

The Search for Knollys's Children

Many secondary references about Hanserd Knollys state that he had only one child. The original source of that error may have been John Winthrop's comment on the death of one of Hanserd's children. Yet, according to Knollys's own short autobiography, certainly the best source of information about this, Hanserd and his wife, Anne Cheney, had seven sons and three daughters:

> I married a wife, with whom I lived 40 years, by whom I had wiffue, 7 Sons, and 3 Daughters, who was a Holy, Difcreet woman, and a meet Help for me, in the ways of her Houfholdd,

and alfo in the ways of Holinefs; who was my companion in all my Sufferings, Travels, and Hardfhips that we endured for the Gofpel: She departed this Life the 30th of April 1671 in full Affurance of Eternal Life and Salvation.[20]

The names and dates of birth for all of Anne's and Hanserd's children have not been found. Civil records were not required. Parish records had been ordered during the rule of Henry VIII, but compliance to his order was not enforced until much later. Furthermore, Hanserd gradually stopped believing in infant baptism. Biblically oriented, his disagreement was based on the New Testament account of Jesus being baptized as an adult. Consequently, after he resigned as clergy from the Church of England, he probably did not have his children who were born after that date baptized as infants. With no civil birth records or baptismal records of a parish, determining names and dates of birth for his ten children has been impossible.

Furthermore, though most families in England lived in the same town or village for generations, Hanserd and Anne lived in several places in England, also in Wales, Massachusetts, New Hampshire, Holland, and Germany. He recorded some of these moves:

In the fpace of 40 years, that I and my faithful Wife lived together; we removed feveral times with our whole family, whereof once from Lincolnfhire to London, and from London into Wales; twice from London into Lincolnfhire, once from London to Holland, and from thense into Germany, and thense to Rotterdam and thense to London again.[21]

As many of his moves were made secretly to avoid persecution, it is not surprising that records of his ten children are so elusive. Intensive research has proven the names of only three sons: Cheney, Isaac, and John. Evidence of son John is a microfilm of a parish record. It shows a John Knollys was baptized March 11, 1633, at Goulceby, Lincolnshire, by his father Hanserd Knollys, minister in the Church of England.[22] This baptism was three years before Hanserd resigned from the Church of England in 1636. The record does not show John's age at the date of his baptism.

Record of another son comes from the *Alumni Cantabrigienses* which, using the modern spelling of *Knowles* instead of *Knollys*, says, "Cheney Knowles of Lincolnshire, Matric. pens. from Queens College, July 21, 1647, and received his B.A. in 1651–2; and his M.A. 1655." Cheney Knowles was a son of Anne Cheney and Hanserd Knollys and given his mother's maiden name as his first name. Cheney died in 1670. His will was probated the same year and provided more evidence of the family. He referred to his father as "Hanserd Knollis," to his mother, to his daughter Mary then living in London, to his "second brother John," and three other unnamed brothers. As we will see later, when Cheney wrote his will, Hanserd had been imprisoned and released several times, had been banished in New England, self-exiled in Rotterdam and Germany, and was desperately ill.

Like his father, Hanserd, and his grandfather, Richard, Cheney was ordained and served as clergy in Scartho. Records of the parish church of St. James in Great Grimsby show that twenty years later there were two more Cheney Knowles who lived in the same area; perhaps one was his son and the other his grandson.

Proof of a third son, Isaac, comes from Hanserd's brief autobiography in which he describes Isaac as "his last living sonne." This phrase for Isaac creates a problem for family historians. The problem is due to a claim in the International Genealogy Index (I.G.I.) that John Knowles of Hampton, New Hampshire, married Jamima Austin in 1660, and was the son of Hanserd Knollys. Hanserd, in 1672, wrote that Isaac was his last living son and died in 1671. This was twenty-seven years before the John Knowles of Hampton died. Hampton town records state "John Knowls being blind about 10 years Died the 5 Day December 1705." Obviously the records are not compatible. Of course, Hanserd might have assumed that John Knowles was dead if he did not respond to correspondence because of blindness or if authorities were interfering with mail. Father and son could also have lost touch with each other when Hanserd fled from imprisonment by going to Holland and Germany for several years when he was in his sixties. Perhaps Hanserd's phrase "last living sonne" meant the last one living in England. The puzzle remains.

Married in 1632, Hanserd and Anne could have had several children before escaping to New England in 1638. Although one child died on the ship going over, other children could have accompanied them, or been born after their arrival, or been left behind with relatives.

When they returned to England in December of 1641, Hanserd stated that they had a child with them who was "about three years old." Could this be Cheney? He also said that his wife Anne was pregnant. Could this be one of the Johns that Cheney mentioned in his will as a second brother. Either one could have grown up to be John the mariner who married Jamima Austin in Hampton in 1660. However, neither one was the John baptized in Goulceby in 1633. That child would have been eight years old, not three years old, when they returned to England, December 26, 1641. The one born in Goulceby could have been the one who died on the ship or could have been left at home with a family member. Probably, Hanserd and Anne had two sons who were named John. It was a frequently followed custom that if an older child died, a younger child was given the same name.

A Mystery in Charterhouse School

A different kind of evidence regarding John Knollys is found in the records of the famed Charterhouse School in London. Education always had high priority for Hanserd Knollys. Like his father, he wanted his children to be well-educated. In 1653, he persuaded one Bulstrode Whitelocke to sponsor the enrollment of his son John in Charterhouse School. At that time, there were forty-four students; each was chosen by a governor of the school.

Bulstrode Whitelocke (1605–1677) was one of the most powerful and controversial figures of the time. His second marriage in 1635 was to the sister of Lord Willoughby. Hanserd was Willoughby's family chaplain during the civil war, and it was probably through this relationship that Whitelocke sponsored one of Hanserd's sons.

Whitelocke was Keeper of the Great Seal and member of the Long Parliament. As an important political figure, he often negotiated with the king and Cromwell on behalf of the Parliament. Whitelocke believed that the army should not rule the country and that peace was needed among the factions. Whitelocke also opposed the belief that the Presbyterian form of church government was God's choice, but, like Hanserd, he was in favor of religious freedom and, like him, was rejected by some for believing this.[23]

With his political and social prestige, Whitelocke was on the Board of Governors of Charterhouse School. First established as a monastery in the Middle Ages by the Carthusian monks, it was taken over by Henry VIII in 1535. The school was founded there in 1609 and was very well-endowed by Thomas Sutton. It provided a classical education, and the students wore gowns. The famous Roger Williams, who was banished from Massachusetts and founded Rhode Island, had been a student at Charterhouse and a protégé of the great jurist, Edward Coke.

Charterhouse also had a chapel and a hospital which was given over to eighty elderly gentlemen who had been merchants or military officers. All of their expenses were paid, plus fourteen pounds a year. They lived in luxurious apartments and ate in a common hall.

Shortly after Hanserd's son John was accepted as a student in the school, it was discovered that he was going blind. Since Charterhouse had a hospital as well as a school, an allowance was given for treating his eyes. The Charterhouse archive record reads:

> On July 1, 1653 it was ordered that John Knollis, son of Hanserd Knollis, clerk [meaning clergy] presented by Bulstrode Whitelock, was too blind to be admitted. 3$ be allowed him weekly while being cured.[24]

Evidently the treatment was not effective enough for John to maintain the rigors of long academic studies. His place was given to someone else. Six months later, on December 20, 1653, the standing committee of Charterhouse approved "John Norris to take the place of John Knollis, who had been admitted for Lord Whitelock."

Surely this John in the Charterhouse records was not the John who was baptized by his father Hanserd in 1633 in Goulceby, Lincolnshire. If so, he would have been twenty years old in 1653. Charterhouse students were admitted between the ages of ten and fourteen.

Therefore, the John who was born in 1633 was probably the child who died on the ship en route to New England, and another child, born years later, was named John after his dead brother.

When Hanserd Knollys and his wife, Anne Cheney, returned to England in December 1641, they had a child whom Hanserd described as "about" three years old and Anne was pregnant. This three year old would have been fourteen if presented to Charterhouse in 1653 by Bulstrode Whitelocke. The child with whom his mother was pregnant would have been eleven years old if it were he who attended Charterhouse. The second John in Cheney Knollys's will could have been the eleven or the fourteen year old.

Although Anne and Hanserd's son Cheney went to Cambridge, this son John did not. As we will see in a later chapter, his apprenticeship was paid for by Hanserd. If his apprenticeship was for the purpose of becoming a mariner, then he was probably the progenitor of the Knowles family in Hampton, New Hampshire, where according to town records John Knowles and Jamima Austin "wer Joyned in marriage: 10: 5: mo 1660."

Another Charterhouse record reads briefly, "John Knollis for the Mr of the Hosp. apprentice 23 May, 1661." It is not known what happened to John directly after 1653 when he was rejected because of his poor sight. There must have been a special reason that he was listed there in 1661 in reference to the hospital. It implies that he returned for treatment but the details remain a mystery.[25]

Another mystery is about when John Knowles and his wife Jamima Austin married in 1660, they purchased considerable property in Hampton, New Hampshire. It was near where John Wheelwright once lived, the same Wheelwright who had been a pivotal advisor to Hanserd. Town records revealed that for at least his last ten years of life, this John Knowles was totally blind. Could this blindness be a crucial link identifying him as the John Knollys who was rejected from Charterhouse School because of his poor sight? This is still an unanswered question.

The Paper War between Bastwick and Knollys

Not all wars are fought with military weapons; some are fought with boycotts or censorship, and Hanserd Knollys was often caught up in pamphlet and paperwars over religion and politics. One such war was with the radical John Bastwick. Bastwick was the person who had sent twenty shillings to Hanserd by way of an anonymous woman when he returned penniless to London in December 1641. Later, the two men clashed because they held such different views about church government.

Bastwick, a physician and strong Presbyterian, was radically opposed to Roman Catholic rituals. Educated briefly at Cambridge, he went to Italy to study medicine and then to the Netherlands where he published two pamphlets in Latin against "popery" in the Church. Laud and other clergy were outraged, considering this a personal attack. Bastwick was excommunicated, barred from practicing medicine, imprisoned, and his books were burned, but he would not be silenced. He described the bishops as enemies of God and "the tail of the beast." This infuriated Archbishop Laud. On June 14, 1637, Bastwick was brought before the High Commission Court, and Laud accused him of sedition for libeling against the bishops, and thus against the king and state.[26]

Along with Bastwick, William Prynne, a lawyer, and Henry Burton, bachelor of divinity, were also accused. All were imprisoned, their trial was recorded, and they were convicted of "writing and publishing seditious, schismatical, and libellous books against the hierarchy of the church." Their pamphlets and books were burned, they were sentenced to lose their ears in the pillory, and they were fined five thousand pounds each. William Prynne also had his face branded with the letters "S. L.," which stood for seditious libeler.

When Bastwick's conviction was overturned by Parliament in 1640, he joined Parliament's army and started writing again. By this time, he had given up his bitter diatribe against the Church of England and instead began attacking the Independents (later called Congregationalists) and the Baptists.

After Hanserd Knollys fled to New England the following year, his library was searched and in it was found Bastwick's published defense. The cover read, *A brief relation of certain special and most material passages in the Star Chamber at the censure of three worthy gentlemen, Bastwick, Burton and Prynne.* Having this pamphlet was considered suspicious and held against Knollys because Bastwick's writings had supposedly all been burned.[27] Perhaps Bastwick heard about Knollys's interest in his defense against the Star Chamber and therefore sent the unnamed woman with the badly needed twenty shillings to Hanserd when he returned destitute to London.

John Bastwick's paper war with Hanserd Knollys began with a tract that Bastwick wrote, *Independence Not God's Ordinance*. In this, he claimed that the Presbyterian form of church government was what God wanted and that God was not in favor of independence in church structure.

Hanserd Knollys disagreed, and in 1645, he published his disagreement, *A Moderate Answer to Dr. Bastwick's Book Called Independence Not God's Ordinance*.[28] It was indeed a moderate answer, but Bastwick became enraged. The next year, in stronger retaliation, Bastwick attacked Knollys and others more directly. His attack on the cover of his new booklet read:

> The Utter Routing of the Whole Army of All the Independents & Sectaries . . . and All the Forces of the Three Generals and Commanders of the Sectaries, Hanserdo Knollys, J. S. & Henry Burton are all dissipated, with all their whibbling Reserves.[29]

The phrase "whibbling Reserves" was meant to be provocative, but Hanserd did not take the bait. His philosophy was "live and let live"; people should have the freedom to believe as they chose and the freedom to act according to their own consciences, as long as it did not interfere with the freedom of others.

Like most religious and political dissenters, Hanserd thought he was right. Unlike many, he voiced his opinions but did not try to impose them on others. Charles I and Archbishop Laud were quite the opposite; they insisted they had the right to dictate what everyone was to believe and do. Compliance to the law was the only safe measure. Taking any kind of heroic alternative usually led to exile or banishment, imprisonment, or execution.

6

War without Wisdom

There is nothing unhappier than a civil war for the conquered are destroyed by, and the conquerors destroy, their friends.
—*Dionysius of Halicarnossus, c. 20* B.C.

The Archbishop and His Wars

England was still in turmoil when Hanserd Knollys returned in December of 1641. Charles I had been in power since 1625 and had shown himself to be just as resistant to sharing power as his father had been. That resistance had promptly gotten him in trouble with Parliament. The first part of this chapter will focus on this complex political situation. Then, the focus moves to the similarities and differences between the Independents and Anabaptists, as well as the General Baptists and the Particular Baptists, and how disputes over baptism and who would be welcome in a church led Hanserd Knollys to establish his own Baptist church.

For eleven years, from 1629 to 1640, King Charles refused to call Parliament into session at all. Charles saw no need to consult with his subjects when he wanted to change a policy or impose a tax. After all, he was the king. Yet, his autocratic decisions and personally imposed taxes angered the people.

Under Charles, William Laud had become archbishop of Canterbury in 1633. Like the king, he was highly authoritarian. As the king raised taxes at will claiming it was his divine right to do so, Archbishop Laud demanded uniformity in worship, claiming divine right for the episcopacy. However, in 1639, when he tried to impose the *Book of Common Prayer* and the rituals of the Church of England upon both England and Scotland, the Scots revolted. This first Bishops' War took place the year after Hanserd Knollys had fled to New England.

The Scots firmly united against the English intrusion into their religious affairs. The Scottish army was strong and well-disciplined whereas the English army was poorly equipped and worse-disciplined. English men had been conscripted under pressure and resented being sent off to fight a bishops' war. The very name given the war was a reflection of the public's lack of commitment to the Archbishop Laud's demands. When it was clear that the English army had no stomach for the fight, a truce was signed without bloodshed.

Eventually, a treaty was made granting the Scots a free church and their own Parliament, but the treaty was vague and satisfied no one. Furthermore, Charles was unwilling to honor some verbal agreements the Scots thought they had won from him. Peace was short and political discontent grew.

Charles wanted to retaliate against the insubordinate Scots but could not afford to. He had difficulty raising troops and equipping them with horses. Men commonly evaded conscription by exemption if they could or bribery if necessary. Charles squeezed innumerable loans, contributions, and gifts from others, including the queen. However, these forced contributions were not enough to satisfy him.[1] On April 5, 1640, his financial greed drove him to call Parliament into session. But, it was so outraged at having been disbanded and ignored for the previous eleven years that it refused to cooperate with his requests for more money. After three weeks, Charles dissolved it, and it was dubbed the "Short Parliament."

During this period, one of Charles's and Laud's strongest allies was Thomas Wentworth, who had been made lord deputy of Ireland in 1632. In fiscal desperation and with Wentworth's cooperation, Charles obtained enough money from the Irish Parliament to start the second Bishops' War in 1640.

This war lasted less than a year. In the spring of 1640, the Scots invaded England. The king's soldiers were weak opposition. They

were out of control, violent against people and property, even
tearing down communion rails and altars in their drunken riots.
By September of that year, Londoners were anxious that the Scots
might blockade the city's coal-supply line. When the Scots
demanded that Charles pay them £850 per day for their upkeep,
Charles called Thomas Wentworth, who had become Earl of
Strafford, to lead the king's army against Scotland. Wentworth
lost, and the second Bishops' War ended in November of 1640.

Pressured by the Scots, Charles I then summoned Parliament
back into session. This became known as the "Long Parliament"
because it met off and on for twenty years (1640–1660). The Long
Parliament freed some political prisoners and passed a Bill of
Attainder. This bill permitted an arbitrary death sentence without
trial. It was used against Thomas Wentworth, Earl of Strafford, so
that he was executed in May 1641. Archbishop Laud was
impeached by the Long Parliament in 1640 but was held in prison
for four years before being tried in 1644. He was then judged guilt-
less by the House of Lords but guilty by the House of Commons
which, under the Bill of Attainder, was enough to have him
executed in 1645.

The Long Parliament also voted that the king could not impose
any taxes without its approval. It abolished the dreaded Star
Chamber, which had been so named because of the stars on the
ceiling in the room where it met, and disbanded the High
Commission, whose very name was so arrogant. Other acts specified that Parliament would meet at least every three years and
could not be dismissed without its own approval.

There was often great animosity among the members, against
the king, and sometimes against the army. Although many in
Parliament wanted to crush the Catholics and the rebellion in
Ireland, a strong block did not want the king to gain any control of
the army in the process because, in the Bishops' Wars, he had
shown himself to be incompetent in devising and carrying out any
form of military strategy.

In February 1641, new major disagreements arose in
Parliament. One was about the "Root and Branch Petition."[2] It
called for abolition of the episcopacy and all its "roots and

branches." This petition carried fifteen thousand signatures and was presented to the House of Commons for debate. It was not passed.

Animosity grew stronger that same year when John Milton, politician turned poet, published *Reformation Touching Church Discipline in England.* This was against the Church of England's claim that ordination was invalid unless it was performed by their bishops. Milton disagreed and also objected to what he thought was too much Catholic ritual in the Church. Furthermore, he claimed that people should be free to interpret Scriptures as they wished.

Protestation and the Great Remonstrance

Further protests arose when, in 1641, King Charles demanded money to finance his armies in Scotland and Ireland and reinstated the poll tax. This tax had first been established in 1222 and everyone over the age of fourteen was supposed to pay it. In 1381 there had been a so-called Peasants' Revolt against this tax. Landowners as well as peasants revolted. Rebels had marched on London, taken over the Tower, and executed the archbishop of Canterbury and the chancellor. The tax was dropped. When it was reinstated under Charles, it was as hated as ever.

Then, the Oath of Protestation was instituted. This oath required all men to swear loyalty to His Majesty, to the reformed protestant religion, and to the power and privileges of Parliament. A list was kept of all who, like the Quakers, did not believe in taking oaths and refused to do so. They were called "recussants."[3]

The *Protestation Returns 1641/2 Lincolnshire* shows that in Scartho, Hanserd's hometown, among those who signed the oath on March 16, 1641, were Hanserd's father and brother, Richard and Zachariah Knollys. Zachariah was the brother with whom Hanserd had argued and then prayed when they were adolescents. At the time of the signing, Hanserd was having trouble in New England. Later that same year, he received a letter from his father asking him to come home. The Bishops' Wars were over; Parliament had released Bastwick, Prynne, and Burton from prison; and Laud and Wentworth were now in prison for treason. It seemed safe for Hanserd to return.

Meanwhile, King Charles had become so high-handed that in November 1641, the House of Commons drew up the "Grand Remonstrance." It listed 201 political and religious grievances against the king. It also demanded that the army come under Parliament's control instead of under the king's control, that the king's ministers be approved by Parliament, and that the Church be reformed. The bill passed the House of Commons by only eleven votes. When John Pym, a Puritan and leading member of Parliament, presented the Grand Remonstrance to him, Charles I rejected it and brought an armed guard into the House of Commons to arrest five leaders including Pym, but they escaped. The king left London for the northern part of England, and the queen, who was Catholic, went to Holland to sell her jewels to raise money for him.

Charles I and the Civil Wars

Parliament was now polarized into two groups, Roundheads and Royalists. The Roundheads kept shouting, "Privileges of Parliament" while the Royalists cried out, "God bless the king."[4] The Roundheads were given that nickname because their hair was cut very short. Roundheads included members of Parliament, country gentry, lawyers, and merchants, especially from London and southeast England. Many, such as Oliver Cromwell, supported Puritan beliefs. These beliefs were fairly compatible with Presbyterianism, and the Roundheads became stronger when the Presbyterian Scots joined them.

In contrast, the Royalists (often called Cavaliers) supported Charles I. They were mostly peers and landowners and Catholics or staunch members of the Church of England. In the beginning of the war, their superior cavalry was an advantage. Yet, by the end of the war, when the Roundheads and the Presbyterians gained power, the estates of many Royalists were confiscated.

More religious controversy was raised by the Scottish Presbyterians who wanted Parliament to endorse a national covenant in exchange for the assistance of the Scottish army. Both Roundheads and Royalists enlisted troops and, in August 1642, the civil war broke out. In 1643, a "Solemn League and Covenant" was signed in which Parliament agreed to establish the Presbyterian Church in England in exchange for Scotland's troops joining Parliament's army against the king.

The conflict became even more explosive. To settle the disputes, an assembly was called to Westminster to reform the Church. This Westminster Assembly had representatives from various religious groups and met off and on for ten years (1643–1653). Although the representatives could not agree on many issues, the Presbyterians wrote their Westminster Confession of 1647, which is still their official statement. Presbyterians were particularly strong in Parliament and clashed with the Independents, who were the strongest in Cromwell's New Model Army. Two years later, it was required that all army officers sign the national covenant, but some refused. Then, Parliament's army and the Scots got together and defeated the Royalists in 1644 near York in the Battle of Marston Moor. Parliament gave Oliver Cromwell much of the credit for this.

With Sir Thomas Fairfax as the new commander, the Royalists were defeated once more, this time at Naseby in 1645. In disguise, Charles fled from Oxford where his court and army headquarters had been located. Laud was executed and the use of the prayer book was forbidden. In 1646, the civil war came to an end. Charles surrendered to the Scots; in contrast, his headquarters surrendered to Parliament. Then, the Scots made peace with Parliament and turned Charles over to parliamentary commissioners. The Presbyterian form of church government was required in England from 1647 to 1650, and the offices of bishop and archbishop were abolished.

Meanwhile, the war raged on in a different form in Parliament between various religious and military factions. In fact, conflict between the Presbyterians and the Independents became so bitter that on December 6, 1648, Col. Thomas Pride purged the Parliament of Presbyterians by the order of the army council. Thus, 140 members of Parliament were excluded from the House of Commons. What was left was called the "Rump Parliament," and it voted that the king be put on trial. Thomas Pride, as judge at the trial, signed the death warrant of Charles I. John Milton wrote a defense of the action.

Trial of Charles I.

Oliver Cromwell's Rise to Power

Oliver Cromwell (1599–1658) rose to political power during the reign of Charles I and this power was greatly enhanced by his military skills. Cromwell was born in Huntingdon, England, to nonconformist parents. Originally, his family was from Wales and their name was Williams. Thomas Cromwell, the powerful minister of Henry VIII, was a remote uncle of Oliver's, so the Williams family in those perilous times had adopted the Cromwell name. Thus, Oliver's father became Robert Cromwell. His mother was Elizabeth Steward. Both parents held nonconformist beliefs, which doubtless shaped their son, as did his early studies with Thomas Beard, an outspoken Puritan leader. A year at Sidney Sussex College at Cambridge University, which was primarily Puritan, reinforced the teaching he had received.

When Cromwell was eighteen years old, his father died and he dropped out of college, although he may have studied law briefly at Lincoln's Inn in London. In 1620, he married Elizabeth Bourchier and inherited land at Ely from his uncle. However, like Hanserd Knollys, Cromwell felt emotionally and spiritually at odds with himself. Finally, he had a conversion experience and wrote about it to a woman cousin: "Oh, I lived in and loved darkness and hated the light: I was a chief, the chief of sinners. This is true: I hated godliness, yet God had mercy on me."[5]

In 1628, Cromwell was elected to Parliament and sat in both the Short and Long Parliaments. Cromwell first gained his power as a parliamentarian, then as an army leader, and in 1654, as the lord protector. A very articulate politician, Cromwell, in one of his first speeches to the House of Commons, spoke out against the bishops. He also spoke on behalf of the multitude outraged by the king's taxes. He did not believe any king had the right to tax his subjects without their consent. Cromwell was also a Calvinist and an Independent who, like other Independents, believed congregations had the right to choose their own ministers, instead of having them assigned by the church hierarchy.

However, he was not as liberal in other ways. He was not willing to give up some of the political and financial advantages that went with his position and inherited property. According to the historian

Oliver Cromwell.

J. P. Kenyon, Cromwell "shared all the prejudices of the conservative small gentry class from which he sprang."[6] He was a power in the Parliament when the *Book of Common Prayer* was disallowed, bishops were rejected, and those who criticized Calvinistic creed or ritual were fined.[7] Two Anabaptist preachers who rejected Calvinism denounced Cromwell as the "Beast of the Apocalypse,"[8] a term Hanserd Knollys later applied to Charles II.

As an outspoken member of Parliament, Cromwell was a natural military leader of the Roundheads (a term which he considered demeaning and which he forbid his troops to use). His strategy was well-planned. He organized, trained, and insisted on strictly disciplined troops who were to be well paid and treated fairly. They were not allowed to swear or get drunk.

Chaplaincy and Civil War

When the civil war broke out in 1642, Cromwell went to Cambridge University to intervene so the colleges would not send their plate to the king to be melted down and used to fund the Royalists. He successfully raised a troop of cavalry from his childhood home of Huntingdon and was able to get permission from the House of Commons to raise a regiment of cavalry to protect Cambridge.

As further protection, in 1644, Edward Montague was directed by Parliament to "regulate" Cambridge University and get rid of "scandalous ministers" and to destroy what were termed "superstitious pictures and ornaments." The destruction in churches by the soldiers was excessive and led to great bitterness. A Royalist news sheet attacking the Roundheads was published at Oxford, and a Roundhead news sheet that attacked the Royalists was published in London. Naturally, they had very different tales to tell about the course of events.

In 1643, when Cromwell asked for volunteers for Parliament's army, Hanserd Knollys signed up as chaplain. The duties of an army chaplain were diverse. Chaplains preached and encouraged soldiers before battle and ministered to them afterward. Between battles, chaplains were expected to be politicians, lecturing and preaching in the towns against the error of being loyal to the king. They also served as emissaries to the House of Commons to keep the members up-to-date on details of battles and the overall state of the war.[9]

Within the chaplaincy of Parliament's army, there was wide diversity, from the free-love libertines of the Familists sect (often called the Family of Love) to those who denied church rituals and attributed all things to the Holy Spirit.[10] This became a basic belief of the "Children of Light," later known as the Society of Friends (or Quakers). George Fox (1624–1691) recorded the beginning of this movement in his *Journal*. He was not only against ecclesiastical customs but also was against oaths, titles, and military service.[11] Within the army, there were also chaplains who held more traditional Protestant views, namely that a covenant with God which included "good works" was the path to salvation.

At this time, the gentry of Lincolnshire were more concerned with local issues than with the conflict between the king and Parliament. Their complaints were against enclosure laws, loss of common rights, and enforced change.[12] However, in 1643, when the cities of Lincoln and Gainsborough were plundered by the king's troops, Lincolnshire residents became very involved indeed. Gainsborough, where Hanserd had taught school before going to New England, was occupied by the king's forces led by the Earl of Kingston, although the earl claimed he was not certain of whose side he was on.[13]

With such uncertainty, it is not surprising that Kingston was easily overpowered at Gainsborough on July 16, 1643, by Parliament's army, which was under the leadership of Francis

Willoughby. He, like Cromwell and Hanserd Knollys, was under Montague's orders which led to trouble. [14]

Willoughby was the fifth Baron of Parham and had been appointed by Parliament to be lord-lieutenant in the Lindsey district in Lincolnshire.[15] Willoughby's home was in Knaith, three miles from Gainsborough. During his first term of service as a chaplain in 1643, Knollys was personal chaplain to Willoughby's family, went to his home daily, and tutored Willoughby's son for the university. Later, he dedicated a book to the Willoughbys, an interpretation of the biblical Song of Solomon.

Power Politics in the Army

Three political and military powers, Francis Willoughby, Edward Montague, and Oliver Cromwell, had off-and-on conflicting relationships that eventually led to Hanserd's decision to resign from the chaplaincy.

Montague, usually referred to as "Manchester" because of his earldom, was a member of both the Short and Long Parliaments. While Charles I still ruled, Manchester seemed to favor the Puritans so much that on January 3, 1642, the king accused him of treason. At the outbreak of the war two months later, Manchester was cleared by both Houses of Parliament. His conflict with Cromwell and Willoughby arose because, from Cromwell's perspective, Manchester was not aggressive enough and therefore lost important battles.[16] He defended his caution with, "If we beat the king ninety-nine times, he is king still, and so will his posterity be after him; but if the king beats us once, we shall all be hanged and our posterity be made slaves."[17]

Looking for someone to blame, Manchester then accused Willoughby of being weak because, when attacked by a Royalist army from Newcastle, Willoughby's troops had retreated and many deserted. In despair, Willoughby had written to Cromwell, "Since the business of Gainsborough, the hearts of our men have been so deaded that we have lost most of them by running away."[18] In response to the letter, Oliver Cromwell's troops marched in and won the major battle of Gainsborough on July 28, 1643, and he was made lieutenant-general under Manchester six months later.

According to historian Anne Laurence, who cites many primary sources, Knollys first served in Manchester's army which, in 1643, was called the Eastern Association. Other armies of Parliament were led by the Earl of Essex and Sir William Waller. Chaplains in all three armies were predominantly Presbyterian, but in Waller's army there were also "rebellious Brownists."[19] Chaplains were appointed by colonels and paid by warrant. The rate of pay was similar to that of a benefice but sometimes in arrears. Consequently, some chaplains continued to serve a church or lecture or tutor. Knollys did all three.

Meanwhile, Parliament asked the embattled Charles I to make Willoughby an earl and assign him to be one of the commissioners to the Scottish army. However, Cromwell complained to the House of Commons that Willoughby had been too tolerant with his troops. Although Cromwell was tolerant about religion, he insisted on very strict discipline in the army.

He was also in favor of the Self-Denying Ordinance of 1645, which was to prohibit any member of Parliament or peer from holding an army commission. That would remove incompetent officers from command but allow the successful Cromwell to be reappointed on his merits. Cromwell's troops were so successful that the House of Commons approved a new army that would attack the king's troops, not just defend against them. Largely due to Cromwell's influence, the successful new army was put under the major-general, Edward Montague, second Earl of Manchester, and Cromwell became Manchester's second in command. In 1645, Parliament's New Model Army defeated the king's army at the battle of Naseby. The county was in chaos as nine hundred Royalists were killed. The king's position was hopeless, and he surrendered in 1646, thus ending the first civil war.

Willoughby was impeached in 1647, imprisoned for four months, and then offered his freedom if he would post bail. He refused to do so but escaped to Holland where he joined the Royalists who were living there in exile. The next year, Willoughby's estates were sequestered by Parliament because he had sided with the king. On the day Charles II was restored to the throne in 1660, Willoughby was declared governor of Barbados for his loyalty to the king, and two years later his confiscated property in England was returned to him.[20] Meanwhile, Manchester had changed his loyalty from the Parliament's army, which was essentially Puritan, to that of the Royalists.

Hanserd Knollys had resigned from the army, disillusioned with the commanders' failures to keep their commitment to Puritan principles. He wrote in his brief memoir, "I did perceive the Commanders sought their own things more than the Cause of God and his People."[21] The date of his resignation is not clear, but he rejoined the New Model Army sometime after it was formed in 1645.

The Downfall of Charles I

The reign of Charles I was fragmented and intolerant. In 1645, Cromwell, comparing this disunity in government with the temporary unity that existed at that time between Protestant groups, wrote, "Presbyterians, Independents, all had here the same spirit of faith and prayer; the same pretense and answer; they agree here, know no names of difference: pity it is it should be otherwise anywhere."[22]

By comparing the unity of spirit between Presbyterians and Independents, Cromwell was lamenting the fact that unity did not exist between the Parliament, the Crown, and the army. In spite of his years of effort, Cromwell was unable to reconcile them to each other. War without wisdom continued.

The army no longer trusted Charles. In 1647, he was put under surveillance at Hampton Court Palace. He escaped but was captured and taken to the Isle of Wright for two and one-half years. There, he secretly negotiated with the Scots to invade England. He was a Scot, having been raised in Scotland. In disguised handwriting and coded letters sent out in a glove or in the laundry, Charles offered his support of the Presbyterian Church in England in exchange for the support of the Scottish army.

In 1648, the second civil war broke out, first in Wales when some officers and soldiers revolted and Cromwell was sent to

A Continuation of the

NARRATIVE

BEING

The laſt and final dayes Proceedings

OF THE

High Court of Iuſtice

Sitting in Weſtminſter Hall on Saturday, *Jan.* 27.

Concerning the Tryal of the King;

With the ſeverall Speeches of the King, Lord Preſident, & Solicitor General.

Together with a Copy of the

Sentence of Death

upon CHARLS STUART King of England.

Publiſhed by Authority to prevent falſe and impertinent Relations.

TO thoſe Proceedings of the Tryall of the King, I ſay, Imprimatur, GILBERT MABBOT.

London, Printed for *John Playford,* and are to be ſold at his ſhop in the *Inner Temple, Jan.* 29. 1648.

A writing that covered the trial and execution of Charles I.

control them.[23] Then, the Scottish Engagers' Army was defeated at Preston. The Presbyterians in Parliament preferred Charles as king but the Independents in Parliament wanted more freedom. Charles played them against each other.

Army records list Hanserd Knollys as chaplain of E. Whally's Regiment of Horse. Whally, a colonel, appointed him to the position in 1649. Part of the regiment mutinied. A declaration against Leveler principles was published.[24] Led by John Lilburne, the Levelers planned to overthrow the government by revolt. The Baptists, some of them had been Levelers, renounced their connection to Lilburne and his movement. Knollys was one who signed the renouncement.

The army demanded that Charles be tried for treason. Labeled tyrant, traitor, murderer, and public enemy, Charles was led to the scaffold on January 30, 1649. The army had to hold back the crowd. Charles, claiming that he had not been at war with Parliament but that Parliament had started the trouble, offered forgiveness to those who had initiated his trial and its outcome, including Cromwell. Then Charles carefully tucked his hair under his cap so it would not interfere with the executioner's ax. He apologized for taking so long and maintained his innocence until the ax fell. According to bystanders who recorded the event in shorthand, the crowd let out a mighty groan.[25]

Anabaptists Versus Baptists

Principles and beliefs were not only debated in the army and in Parliament; acrimonious debates also permeated the churches.[26] Three groups that had some similarity and some major dissimilarities were often confused—the Anabaptists, the General Baptists, and the Particular Baptists. The Anabaptists were a sect that originated during the Reformation in Germany, the Netherlands, and Switzerland. Like the Lutherans and Calvinists, they preferred personal faith to traditional rituals. Like the Baptists, they read the New Testament story of John baptizing Jesus as an adult and interpreted this to mean baptism should be the free choice of persons old enough to understand what it meant. Yet, they also believed unbaptized children were saved, that the Lord's Supper was to be an expression of love rather than ritual, and that church and state should be separate. Some favored communal living in which possessions would be shared equally and polygamy permitted.

Persecution of Anabaptists was severe. Under Henry VIII, some were burned at the stake. Some were buried without any of the rites of the established Church. One parish record says that George Piper, an Anabaptist, was "tumbled in ye ground." Another one records that Bernard Stoniford, a bricklayer, was "hurled" into a grave.[27] However, the Anabaptists were different from other Separatists because they opposed civil government and war. They thought all magistracy was unchristian and could not be saved.

A key issue the Anabaptists and Baptists agreed upon was that baptism should be for believers, not for infants. This led to ongoing confusion and trouble. It was fueled by a Dr. Featley, who wrote a book dedicated to the Parliament in 1645 with the long title, *The Dippers Dipt, or, the Anabaptists Duck'd and Plung'd over Head and Eares, at a Disputation in Southwick.* Featley recommended that all Anabaptists be severely punished if not utterly exterminated and banished from both church and kingdom because:

> They flock in great multitudes to their Jordan, and both sexes enter into the river, and are dipt after their manner with a kind of spell. . . . They defile our rivers with their impure washings, and our pulpits with their false prophecies and fanatical enthusiasms, so the presses sweat and groan under the load of their blasphemies.[28]

During Elizabeth's reign, while the number of Anabaptists had gradually decreased, the prejudice against them did not. Although Baptists shared the Anabaptists' belief in adult baptism, they did not endorse polygamy or shared possessions, and when they were confused with Anabaptists, they resented it.

Within the Baptists themselves, there were two main groups in England. One was called the General Baptists. They were descendants from the English Separatists in Amsterdam, who, according to historian Murray Tolmie, were strongly influenced by the Anabaptists.[29] The General Baptists were founded by Thomas Helwys, who was strongly against John Smyth and the Mennonites in Holland as well as being against the Calvinists and the Church of England back home. In fact, Helwys's book, *A Short Declaration of the Mistery of Iniquity*, was an attack on the whole Christian world, according to E. B. Whitley. Additionally, Whitley continues that with apocalyptic fervor, Helwys claimed it was his task to set the world right. However, Helwys's concept of a "right"

Inscription by Thomas Helwys.

world would not have pleased everyone. In 1611, he had an advertisement posted in London that advised readers using Scripture as his basis. The advice from Prov. 9:8 was, "Rebuke the wyfe, and they will love thee." And for Prov. 29:1 it was, "They that harden their neck, vvhen they are rebuked fhall fuddenly be deftroyed, and cannot be cured."[30]

The General Baptists as a whole believed salvation was "generally" for anyone. They were also very strict about the Lord's Supper. In the New Testament story, the disciples sat; they did not kneel. Therefore, the General Baptists were against kneeling. They were also against cutting the communion bread with a knife because the same story speaks of "the breaking of the bread."

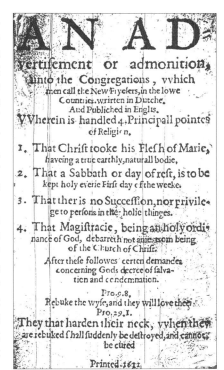

Helwys's advertisement posted in London.

The other Baptist group was known as the Particular Baptists and, later, as the Calvinist Baptists. They were not an offshoot of the Anabaptists or the General Baptists. They developed from what was known as the Jacob/Jessey Independent Church in England. Like Presbyterians, they were Calvinists who believed salvation was a more selective process, only for the "elect." This was the belief of most of the early Puritans in New England, including Hanserd Knollys.

General and Particular Baptists agreed on the administration of the Lord's Supper and on baptism by immersion. The most divisive element between them was their disagreement over singing in church and the role of women, but there will be more on that later.

From Independents to Baptists

Slowly and painfully, Hanserd Knollys came to realize he could not change the Church of England. In 1644, he began attending Henry Jessey's Independent church, whose members were later known as Congregationalists. This church had been founded almost thirty years earlier in 1616 by Henry Jacob. It was the first Independent church in London.[31]

Jacob wanted recognition for churches that chose to be self-governing instead of being governed by the Church of England or by the throne. He did not ask that these Independent churches replace the established parish churches but that they be accepted as valid and voluntary at a time when attendance in the Church of England was required, not voluntary. Although his church was allowed to exist, it was not truly accepted, and some of its members left for New England.

In 1637, Henry Jessey, who had been ejected from his church in Yorkshire for nonconformity, was called to serve Jacob's church. As early as 1638, the same year Hanserd Knollys fled to New England, members of the congregation were struggling to clarify their concepts about baptism and whether it should be by sprinkling or immersion, and for children or adults.[32] Henry Jessey believed in tolerance, so weekly discussions were held on the pros and cons of infant baptism. Like the splitting in the early English churches in the Netherlands, Jessey's church also split.

Henry Jessey.

One group followed Praise-God Barebone (sometimes spelled *Barbone*), a member of Parliament who broke away from Jessey's church to form his own Independent church. Another group followed John Spilsbury and became the first Particular Baptist church. This group did not believe infant baptism was valid, only the baptism of those old enough to be believers.

William Kiffin (1616–1701), of whom we will hear more later, was a successful businessman and friend of Hanserd Knollys for fifty years. Both their signatures can be found on several important documents including the Proceedings of the General Assembly of Baptists held in 1689. Kiffin was one of those who left the Jacob/Jessey church and joined the Spilsbury congregation.

When Hanserd Knollys was attending the Jacob/Jessey Independent Church in 1644, the church was still arguing about infant baptism. Jessey wanted one of Hanserd's children to be baptized. Hanserd disagreed; church records show his wife, Anne, was also against infant baptism.[33] Meetings in the church and public meeting were held to discuss the issue. Members of the congregation disagreed, but their disagreements were without rancor. Although intoleration was the rule of the land, the tolerance of this early church was remarkable. Membership was open to any who had been baptized, either as infants or as believers. Talented laypersons were allowed to share in the ministry, and the church voted that it would remain in harmony with other new churches that were forming.

One of the most notable writers of the time was Henry D'Evers, a Baptist who was imprisoned in the Tower but released on bail and died in 1686. D'Evers was especially known for his comprehensive treatise on baptism of believers and of infants. It was strongly criticized by many but even more strongly defended by William Kiffin and Hanserd Knollys.

Ranters, Levelers, and Other Sects

In addition to the Church of England, and the Presbyterian, Independent, and Baptist Churches, smaller and more radical groups developed. Some were religious sects known as the Seekers, Familists, and Ranters; some were political sects known as Diggers and Levelers. Baptists and Independents were often accused of belonging to either or both groups.

The Seekers were not an organized group as much as they were independent thinkers seeking answers. John Milton, the poet who

was also the Latin secretary to Cromwell's Council of State during
the interregnum, was a Seeker. Another one was Sir Henry Vane the
Younger, a Puritan who had been governor of Massachusetts before
Winthrop but who returned to England. A member of the Long
Parliament, Vane later opposed the restoration of Charles II to the
throne and, for this, was executed. Another well-known dissenter
was Roger Williams, who defined himself as a Seeker in his later life.

The Familists believed all should live as a loving family. This
sect originated in Holland. It was an offshoot of Anabaptism and
was a pantheistic sect with a passive attitude toward the world.
Anne Marbury Hutchinson had been accused of being a Familist
when she was banished from Boston.

The Ranters were more radical. According to Ranter doctrine, a
man could not be free from sin until he had committed each sin
while believing that it was not sinful. Therefore, their reasoning
went, in order to be perfect, one had to have committed every sin.
Using this argument they justified their behavior, including being
naked when taking communion.[34] They believed a church should
be full of enthusiastic sinners not feeling guilty as they ranted and
raved. Drunkenness and adultery in public was almost expected.
An authority on the Ranters, G. F. L. Ellens, noted that Parliament
acted against them with only partial success.[35]

Hanserd Knollys, normally very tolerant, opposed the Ranters'
licentious behavior. Debates were held on whether or not church
membership should be only for believers or should also be open to
sinners who did not believe. This led to a debate on whether
nonbelievers should pray or not. Hanserd said "no." If nonbelievers prayed, it would be only outward conformity. He claimed
it was their duty not to pray if they did not believe, that only
believers should pray.

On the political front there were two main sects, the Diggers
and the Levelers. The Diggers were a small group of extremists led
by Gerrard Winstanley. They wanted a form of agrarian communism that would eliminate all manors and landlords, and they
tried to establish such a commune on a hilltop in Surrey. They dug
up St. George's Hill and planted beans to demonstrate that all the
land belonged to all the people. The Diggers were not a serious

threat to Cromwell. They believed in passive resistance and were easily put down by Gen. Thomas Fairfax.

The Levelers were more powerful, especially in the army. They were led by Lt. Col. John Lilburne, who believed that all Englishmen were born equal and had equal rights. Greatly influenced by Sir Edward Coke, the great jurist who had sponsored Roger Williams in Charterhouse School, Lilburne wanted a society that was more level than the current one. Thus, his adherents were called "Levelers." They thought the monarchy and House of Lords should be abolished and the common law revised. Essentially a political group, the Levelers also wanted complete religious toleration. They were not successful in achieving their goals.[36]

Oliver Cromwell was the object of hero-worship by John Lilburne, but Cromwell did not want the "leveling" of society. Instead, Cromwell wanted unity of spirit. Like the Diggers and Levelers, he too failed to get what he wanted.[37] Lilburne came to resent Cromwell's typical small gentry position and, like Bastwick, published many inflammatory pamphlets on the subject, including one titled *An Impeachment of High Treason Against Oliver Cromwell*.[38]

Between 1647 and 1650, John Lilburne was imprisoned several times for his radical beliefs. Hanserd Knollys was sympathetic to him and, to the horror of some, prayed publicly for Lilburne's release from imprisonment in the Tower. Lilburne was finally acquitted in a very dramatic trial, but his party died out. Their demands for democracy and separation of church and state were too extreme for the times.[39]

Gathering a Church and Healing the Blind

In 1645, Hanserd left Jessey's church and "gathered" his own in London. This was one of the very first Particular Baptist churches. Many old records speak of a "gathered" church to indicate the element of choice at a time when, theoretically, there was no choice. Since everyone was supposed to attend services and pay tithes to the Church of England in the parish where they lived, nonconformist worship was usually held in homes. Nonconformist clergy did not receive income from tithes, nor were they paid salaries. They received free-will offerings and took jobs outside the church to sustain themselves. Hanserd did this by teaching school and working for the government for several years while he ministered to the same church for almost fifty years.

After Hanserd Knollys gathered his church, Henry Jessey, minister of the Independent church that Hanserd had attended, changed his mind and decided that baptism should be only for those who were old enough to believe, not for infants. So, in 1645, Henry Jessey was baptized by immersion by Hanserd Knollys.[40] Jessey was then accused of being an Anabaptist and imprisoned several times, but he continued to serve his church until his death in 1663. The major difference between the two men was that Knollys believed faith should precede baptism and Jessey did not think that was necessary.

A revised edition of the 1644 London Baptist Confession of Faith was written in 1646. Hanserd helped write it to reflect a more Calvinistic orientation. He also signed it along with representatives from the seven other Baptist churches in London, including his long-term friend William Kiffin, of Devonshire Square Church, and a French congregation in London that had similar views.[41]

During his long ministry, Hanserd Knollys's church moved a number of times. Its first year, 1645, the church met next door to Great St. Helen's Church in London. Knollys was a powerful preacher, and so many people came to hear him that he was asked to move. He next located to Finsburg Fields, where he had both his home and school and, it is said, sometimes preached there to very large groups of people.

In 1652, the Knollys's church started meeting in Swan Alley, Coleman Street. Following this, it moved to George Yard in Whitechapel. At the time of his death in 1691, it was meeting at Broken Wharf, Thames Street in London.[42] When he was out of town, or in prison, or self-exiled to Holland and Germany, his assistant served the congregation. In fact, Hanserd's last letter to the church, written just before he died, was a plea that they take care of his assistant.

Hanserd Knollys's heroic yet modest stance in an atmosphere of never-ending animosity must have touched his listeners at the heart. In 1646, Thomas Edwards, who wrote *Gangraena* and seemingly did not like Hanserd, nevertheless recorded the healing of a blind woman by Hanserd. Edwards claimed he got the story from a minister who was present at the healing and who saw and heard the entire process.

The story goes that the event occurred near Aldgate in London during a large meeting of many dissenting churches and clergy. Even Henry Jessey, the minister of the early Independent church was there. The blind woman was placed in the middle of the room to pray aloud, and others joined her. Then Hanserd prayed for her fervently and asked for a blessing. Next, she was anointed with oil and healed.[43]

And Then Another Church

Although Hanserd and his family lived in many places, it was while Charles I was in prison awaiting his execution that Hanserd returned home to Scartho. The House of Commons had voted to disband most of the army in 1647. But, the army had not been paid and did not want to go home until it was. There was not enough money to go around so the political scene in London was very stormy. Yet, in country villages such as Scartho, it was relatively peaceful. Scartho had been the home of Hanserd's youth. His father and several other relatives had served as vicar in St. Giles Church before the installation of Hanserd and, later, one of his sons.

Early memories of his family must have touched him deeply when, on October 12, 1648, Hanserd Knollys was installed in St. Giles. His father had been installed there in 1613 and when Hanserd was first ordained in 1629, he had sometimes preached for his father. In fact, he had sometimes preached as often as four times a day—twice at the church in Humberstone where he was assigned, once in the nearby village of Holton-le-Clay, and once in Scartho, for his father. In 1641, when Hanserd was rejected in New England, Richard Knollys had written to ask him to return home, but Richard evidently died shortly thereafter. Unfortunately, during the years of the civil war, records were so poorly kept that the date and place of his father's death is uncertain.

When Hanserd returned to St. Giles, it was twelve years after he had resigned from the Church of England and three years after he had become a Baptist and gathered his own church in London. Charles I was in prison. The Presbyterians were in control and recommending toleration of other religions. The congregation in Scartho had been served by the Knollys family for so long that it probably did not object in the slightest to Hanserd Knollys's affiliation as a Baptist. In a small Lincolnshire town such as Scartho, church government did not seem as important as it did in London where the Presbyterian form of church government was popular because it was similar to the city's constitution.[44]

While serving the church in Scartho as well as his church in London, Hanserd probably traveled between the two churches from time to time. He had an assistant in London, as did most Protestant clergy who served more than one church. He remained active and loyal to both. In fact, in 1656, Hanserd drew up a petition for the Scartho parish. It was addressed to Oliver Cromwell as Lord Protector and to the council and was signed by nine inhabitants, including four who signed with a mark. This petition was entered into the *State Papers* on May 15, and in parenthesis on the petition Hanserd was identified as "patron of the church." His request, made on behalf of the town, was:

> Our parish church is much decayed, and the spire ready to fall. We beg your order to Thos. Clayton and 5 other inhabitants to take down the spire, and in 3 years' time to repair the south aisle and other parts of the church.[45]

Repairs were allowed and, later, Hanserd's son Cheney Knollys served as vicar in the same church. Cheney died twenty years before his father and in his will made Hanserd one of his beneficiaries.

With the Wisdom of Solomon

Throughout his life that lasted almost a century, Hanserd Knollys was always a passionate teacher and student. While living in London and serving the church he had gathered, he expanded his already fine education by studying with one of the best-known scholars of the time, Christian Ravis (1613–1677), whose surname was sometimes spelled *Ravius* or *Rave*. Born in Berlin, Ravis was a deacon at the Church of St. Nicholas. He had studied theology and languages at Wittenberg, became a professor of oriental languages including Samaritan, Syriac, Arabic, and Ethiopian, and lectured in many of the great cities on the continent.

In 1638, Christian Ravis went to Oxford, England, and was given an allowance by the archbishop to travel in search of manuscripts in eastern languages. Each place he went he was warmly welcomed by the British embassy. After great success, Ravis returned to Oxford University in 1645, took the covenant, and was elected fellow of Magdalen College, which had been founded in 1458. But, in 1648, when he did not receive the chair in Arabic at Oxford, he returned to the continent.[46]

During the years that Ravis was in London, 1645–1648, Knollys studied Hebrew with him and become familiar with his extensive writings in Latin and oriental philology. This led to the publication of Knollys's own book, *The Rudiments of the Hebrew Grammar* in 1648. Hanserd so valued languages for the study of Scripture that he wanted others to have the same opportunity. Throughout his entire life, Hanserd Knollys never stopped studying, translating, and writing.

Another one of his small books was *An Exposition of the First Chapter of the Song of Solomon*. This was the book that Hanserd dedicated to Lord Willoughby, Baron of Parham, and to his wife and children, "As I fulfilled the daily courfe of my miniftery in your Lordfhips Houfe." Such a dedication verifies Hanserd's role as family chaplain and tutor to Willoughby's children when the civil war was being fought in Lincolnshire.

Hanserd's book was printed in London in 1653 during the interregnum, and in the margins of his book, Hanserd included some editorial notes in Greek. He evidently expected it would be read by others who were well-educated, able to read Greek, and who would appreciate a verse-by-verse allegorical interpretation. He also explained his purpose of the book.

Wherein the Text is analyzed, the Allegories are explained and the hidden mysteries unveiled according to the Proportion of faith. With Spiritual Meditations upon every Verse By Hanserd Knollys.[47]

Clearly, Hanserd did not always take the Bible literally. He saw the allegorical meaning and reminded Baron Willoughby that the Song of Solomon was like a marriage song and each person had a part to play. The Spiritual Husband was to be interpreted as the Church Beloved, the gracious wife as the Spouse of Christ, and the children as the Daughters of Zion. Knollys directed them all to learn their parts. He probably composed it when Willoughby was in prison or exiled. No doubt referring to the king, Hanserd, in just one sentence, captured his lifelong belief in religious freedom:

[It] is a great sin, and of dangerous consequence, for the people of God to submit unto any impulsive or coercive power of the supreme magistrate imposing or prescribing a false worship.[48]

War without wisdom made no sense to Hanserd, nor did obedience to any authority who did not allow religious liberty.

7

Trials and More Trials

New opinions are always suspected, and usually opposed, without any other reason, but because they are not already common.

—*John Locke, 1632–1704*

Censorship and Freedom of the Press

Holland and Germany were the centers for book publishing during the seventeenth century; Dutch literacy was the highest in the world with Leiden as its most important center of learning. In fact, the Dutch press was the first free press, and the *Leiden Weekly* and *Amsterdam Gazette* were widely read throughout Europe because of their freedom from censorship.[1] René Descartes (1596–1650), philosopher and scientist, praised Holland with the comment, "There is no country in which freedom is more complete, security greater, crime rarer, the simplicity of ancient manners more perfect than here."[2]

With the invention of the printing press, with the use of the vernacular instead of only classical languages, and with the publishing of books, pamphlets, and newspapers, knowledge continued to grow at a rapid rate. New attitudes were formed on the basis of new knowledge. However, in most countries, including England, the press was not free. Censorship for the purpose of controlling public opinion existed as long as writing itself.

The first *Index of Prohibited Books* by Pope Paul IV was issued in 1559. In England that same year, Elizabeth I chartered the

Stationers' Company and arranged for a system of licensing. This company became a monopoly that published, printed, and sold books and pamphlets. It could seize and burn all unlicensed books and put their authors in prison. Then, toward the end of Elizabeth's reign, the punitive Star Chamber also got involved in controlling the publishing field. Only Oxford and Cambridge Universities were allowed to have presses; all other printing was restricted to London.

Yet, the use of secret presses proliferated. In 1643, just two years after Hanserd returned from New England, Parliament reinforced Elizabeth's early law which required that all books and pamphlets be licensed. This again required that a book be approved by the Stationers' Company before being published.[3] By the time Charles I was beheaded in 1649, there were six licensed newspapers in London, all weeklies published on different days. There were also three Royalist papers that were highly critical of the army and Parliament. However, the press was not to be suppressed and there were many unlicensed secret presses.

John Milton (1608–1674), one of the world's greatest poets, fought prepublication censorship. He was hired by the council to be secretary for foreign languages during the protectorate because he

could write Latin, Italian, and French fluently, was loyal to the Parliament, and was opposed to bishops and kings. In fact, in his *Tenure of Kings* he justified the execution of Charles I as a tyrant. Not only interested in politics, Milton argued, in his *Doctrine and Discipline of Divorce*, that marriage required intellectual as well as physical compatibility. Although he was imprisoned briefly during the reign of Charles II for supporting the Parliament, he continued to write and encourage those who had Puritan leanings. In his

John Milton.

Areopagitica, he conceded that some writers could rightly be punished after publication for what they wrote. Yet, he defended the freedom of the press to print without censorship.

Stoned for Preaching Tolerance

Hanserd Knollys was a staunch Calvinist who believed in freedom of the press, that people should make their own choices about what to believe, and that all should be tolerant of others who might believe differently. This message was widely unpopular; many thought tolerance meant indifference or the absence of values when actually it meant freedom to believe and speak out according to one's conscience. Hanserd did not expect to receive toleration for himself for he was so outspoken; yet he wanted it for others. Because he wrote and preached in favor of toleration, he was stoned.

Stoning was a form of capital punishment and part of the Old Testament law that continued into New Testament times. Blasphemy, idolatry, and adultery were punishable by stoning. People such as Zachariah (c. 800 B.C.), the son of a priest, was stoned "in the court of the house of the Lord."[4] Stephen, the first Christian martyr, was stoned to death for prophesying, and Paul was also stoned and left for dead.

It was in the sequestered parish of Dallinghoo, near Wood-bridge in Suffolk County, England, that the people turned against Knollys, leading to his stoning in 1646 when he was preaching on Col. 3:11: "Christ is all and in all." Suffolk was an ecclesiastical province divided into fourteen presbyteries. The people were so angered by something he said that they stoned him out of the pulpit. Their wrath may have been activated by either Hanserd's sermon (to preach on political issues was common at that time) or by a letter he had written to John Dutton of Norwich in January 1645. In the letter Knollys had complained, "The city Presbyterians have sent a letter to the synod [Westminster] dated from Sion College, against any toleration."[5] Hanserd's letter was intercepted and published and angered the Presbyterians who were rising in power.

This event transpired shortly before the Presbyterian form of church government was required of all churches, including the

Church of England. The Presbyterians were not in favor of religious toleration at that time. In fact, the clergy of London sent out a manifesto against it and a petition was presented to Parliament asking that Anabaptists, Brownists, and all other sectaries who did not conform to Presbyterian government be banned from public service. Clergy who did not conform were ejected from their churches, especially the Baptists and Congregationalists. They were called "sectaries" or "Independents." The requirement that all churches conform to Presbyterian government lasted from 1647 to 1650.

Hanserd was not only stoned, which must have been very painful, but the doors of the meetinghouse were also shut against him. He was then attacked by "a malignant High Constable" and imprisoned in Ipswich.[6] Perhaps there was another reason for the violence against Hanserd. Suffolk County had been the ancestral home of the powerful Governor Winthrop of Boston, Massachusetts. Since Knollys had criticized Winthrop when writing to England in 1638, perhaps Winthrop had complained about Knollys to his friends back home. On the other hand, perhaps the congregations in Suffolk were even less open-minded than the several committees that put him on trial.

The Committee for Plundered Ministers

During the three years that Presbyterian church organization was required of all English churches, the Presbyterians often used committees that acted as judge and jury to avoid legal processes. These committees had more latitude than the courts and sometimes assessed penalties that were more severe or more lenient than those imposed through the courts. Hanserd Knollys was called to appear before three such committees.

The first was the Presbyterian Committee for Plundered Ministers, which had ordered his arrest and held him without bail in Ely House. This committee was appointed by Parliament in December 1642. It was to "consider of the fittest way for the reliefe of such Godly and well affected ministers as have been plundered."[7] London was strongly Presbyterian, and in Bow Church in London a complaint was filed against Hanserd questioning his right to preach. Hanserd described the incident:

They at last carried me before the committee, and asked me several questions, to which I gave sober and discreet answers. Among others, the chairman, Mr. White, asked me who gave me authority to preach. I told him, the Lord Jesus Christ. He then asked me whether I was a minister. I answered that I was made a priest by the prelate of Peterboro, but I had renounced that ordination, and did here again renounce the same.[8]

Hanserd was then asked to preach for the committee and used Isa. 58 as his text: "Cry aloud, spare not, lift up thy voice like a trumpet, and shew my people their transgression, and the house of Jacob their sins" (KJV). The Presbyterians were Calvinists, as was Hanserd Knollys, and all Calvinists centered their worship on the Bible. His sermon was so biblically grounded and so powerful that the committee let him go.

Several other times when ordered to stop preaching, Hanserd immediately said that he would certainly continue to preach, both publicly and from house to house because he would obey Christ who commanded him, rather than those who forbade him.

More Committees, More Judgments

The Committee of Examinations was another body to judge Hanserd Knollys. In 1645, he was accused of creating great disturbance for the ministers and people of Suffolk. In his defense, which cost him sixty pounds, Hanserd preached three biblically based sermons for the committee. He also had witnesses of good repute who testified in his favor. On the basis of this, the committee recommended to the House of Commons that Hanserd be released. Thus, he was acquitted and granted the liberty to preach anywhere in Suffolk when there was a need due to the absence of a minister.

The third committee before which Hanserd appeared was the Committee of the Chamber, also called the Queen's Court. Once more he was accused of preaching without Holy Orders because he had renounced his ordination. The committee told him to stop preaching; he said he would not stop because he had to obey Christ. Evidently, the issue was settled to the committee's satisfaction. The proceedings of the committee from 1643 to 1647 are now housed in the British Museum. Included is a notation from June 21, 1645, that the church should pay Hanserd "Knowles" for his work at Dallinghoo "for the services of the cure during the time of his service." It must have been the depth of his personal faith and the way he encouraged others to have faith that moved his hearers, judicial or not.

In contrast to the stoning he received and the interrogation by committees, he was, in time, deeply appreciated in Ipswich where he had been imprisoned. In 1649, the year that Charles I was beheaded, a group of citizens of Ipswich wrote to Oliver Cromwell and thanked him for allowing Hanserd and his friend William Kiffin to work in their town. The original letter, among the Tenison MSS in the Lambeth Palace Library, states:

> We cannot sufficiently express our thankfulness to the honourable house, and your honour for that great favour wch out of yr sense of our present condition you were pleased to shew unto us, that there is liberty granted to Mr. Knollys and Mr. Kiffin according to our desire to come among us, whose labours (through God's blessing) are like to bee not only very comfortable to us in particular but very profitable to the state in generall; yet as there is noe good Action but finds opposition, soe we have heard that this is much opposed by some, who (as wee are informed) doe labour to hinder it. Now if any such should be, who are thus contrary minded, our humble and earnest desire is, that your honour; would be pleased to continue your former favour unto us, that we may not be deprived of this great good that is coming unto us.[9]

This complimentary letter to Cromwell from Ipswich came thirteen years after Hanserd had resigned as clergy in the Church of England because he did not think his preaching and the rites of the Church were making any difference in the lives of his congregation. It was ten years after he had been banished from Massachusetts and three years after being stoned out of a church in Suffolk. The letter was sent in 1649 when the interregnum was just beginning.

The word *interregnum* refers to a period between two kings. It lasted for eleven years from the beheading of Charles I in 1649 to the restoration of Charles II to the throne in 1660 when he returned from exile. During the interregnum there were two different forms of government, the commonwealth and the protectorate.

New Rule in the Commonwealth

The first five years of new rule were called the "commonwealth." It was declared by the Rump Parliament, which took its orders from the army. The commonwealth, with most of the power in a one-house Parliament, has been called an experiment in republican government. The experiment was not effective.

Supposedly assisting, yet often directing the Rump Parliament, was a Council of State made up of forty-one members. Oliver Cromwell was the first chairman of the council and, under his influence, it tended day-to-day affairs. However, when the council wanted to disband the army to save money, crisis ensued. The army's pay was so long overdue that the army had lost its trust in Parliament. Cromwell tried to mediate between the army and Parliament but was unsuccessful. So, he sided with his troops and marched them out of London to consolidate their remaining power.

The Rump Parliament assumed its power in January 1649 and granted freedom of worship to all except Catholics, Unitarians, and members of the Church of England. It voted to abolish the Church of England, the House of Lords, and the monarchy. It also declared church attendance was no longer mandatory.

Meanwhile, Cromwell invaded Ireland, confiscated much property, and ordered massacres at Drogheda and Wexford. He then invaded Scotland and defeated the Scots, but the young Charles II was crowned king of the Scots in January 1651. The war continued between the forces of Charles and Cromwell and Charles finally fled to France. The Rump Parliament was then accused of corruption and dissolved by Cromwell. He replaced it with the "Parliament of Saints."

Sometimes this was called the "Nominated Parliament" because so many members were Protestant clergy, handpicked by Cromwell and the council. These "saints" were representatives

The great seal of the commonwealth.

from Independent churches. One of them was the fiery Anabaptist minister nicknamed "Praise-God Barebone," who had left the Jacobs/Jessey Independent Church to form his own. He was also called "Barebones," and this Parliament became known as the "Barebones Parliament."

The experienced, more conservative members of Parliament thought the new clergy of the Barebones Parliament were entirely too naive, incompetent, and radical. After eight months, Cromwell dissolved it. As historian E. I. Woodward commented, "The sinners seemed more numerous than the saints."[10]

Cromwell as Protector

The commonwealth came to an end in April of 1653 and was followed by a very different kind of rule, the protectorate. It lasted from December 16, 1653, to May 25, 1659. Cromwell was made lord protector at the instigation of the army and a new constitution of government was drawn up, which included a union of Scotland and England.

On September 12, 1654, when Cromwell made a speech to the new protectorate Parliament, he proclaimed four fundamentals that were needed in government. The first fundamental was that government should be by a single person and Parliament. The "Single Person" of Cromwell's speech was Cromwell himself as lord protector. His second point was that parliaments should not make themselves perpetual. Third, liberty of conscience was a natural right. And fourth, the militia should be "well and equally placed" under Parliament.[11]

In the years that followed, the roles and control of Parliament and the militia often changed as did the interpretation of his third point, the "right to liberty of conscience." People felt safe to speak up for what they believed. When a movement developed to offer the Crown to Cromwell, many were opposed to having another king and said so. Hanserd Knollys and eighteen other Baptists, including John Clarke, who had been with Hanserd in New England, sent Cromwell a fervent request that he not accept the title. The military also objected, and Cromwell refused the throne in May of 1657 with, "I am persuaded to return this answer to you, that I cannot undertake this government with the title of king. And that is my answer to this great and weighty business."[12]

Under Cromwell, many changes were attempted and some succeeded. He attempted to create a stronger Protestant Church using what were called "Triers and Ejectors." The Triers were lay army officers and clergy. They were supposed to determine the fitness of clergy who might be too outspoken in politics or religion. The Ejectors were laymen who, under the direction of the Triers, ejected the clergy who were considered to be too radical.

Other important changes during Cromwell's protectorate were that Jews were allowed to return to England after being exiled for 350 years, and toleration was extended to Quakers. Civil marriages were legalized, feudal tenure became obsolete, and industry could establish its own prices without government interference. Although scholars have disagreed in their assessment of Cromwell's rule, they do agree that he was a zealous patriot who restored political stability after turbulent civil wars.[13]

When Cromwell died in 1658, his inefficient son Richard tried to rule the protectorate. His brief reign was so chaotic he resigned after eight months and the army took over. Then, the three generals of the armies in England, Ireland, and Scotland disagreed among themselves on who should rule the country and how.

George Monck.

Gen. George Monck rose to power. Monck, a competent soldier, had supported Oliver Cromwell, been in command of Parliament's army in Ireland, and was commander-in-chief in Scotland. He had also supported Richard, Cromwell's son, and marched against the Royalists when they tried to take over after Richard's resignation. However, Monck quickly changed his mind. His fear of monarchy during Cromwell's protectorate was now outweighed by his fear of anarchy.

To avoid anarchy, Monck had the Long Parliament recalled. It included the Rump, plus the ninety-six Presbyterians who had been purged in 1648. Immediately, the Long Parliament voted to dissolve itself in favor of the Convention Parliament which, in 1660, invited Charles II to return from exile. After eleven years without a king, monarchy seemed preferable to being ruled by a powerful protector, or by a parliament of "saints."

Dissent in Excise and Customs

Although clergy in the Church of England received tithes and rental fees from their parishes, the nonconformist clergy did not.

As a nonconformist clergyman, Hanserd Knollys received none of the financial support from tithes that supported clergy in the Church of England, and his church was too poor to help support him. It was necessary for him earn a living in other ways.

First, he was the post examiner at the customs and excise offices. The Custom House was where all the king's duties were collected on imports and exports in London. The excise office was where the town business of excise taxation was transacted by nine commissioners and numerous clerks.

Taxes were high. During the civil war, an excise tax had been put on alcoholic drinks—ale, beer, cider, and perry, which was a wine made from pears. This tax was supposed to finance Parliament's army. But when Charles II was restored to the throne in 1660, the income from these excise taxes was transferred from supporting the army to supporting Charles's lavish lifestyle.

According to the *State Papers: Domestic Series* (March 29, 1653), Hanserd received a salary of £120 but resigned from his work at customs and excise "for more beneficial employment." This may not have been a voluntary resignation. It seems that the Regulators of the Excise Office found someone who was willing to take the job at a 40 percent reduction in salary. By letting Hanserd go, the Regulators were then able to divide the wages that were saved among themselves.[14] That was probably their original not-so-hidden agenda.

Later during the commonwealth, Hanserd held another civil position. It was as clerk of the check. He checked on expenditures and even questioned the financial honesty of a ship's surgeon. The "Letters and Papers Related to the Navy," which are in the *State Papers* of May 22, 1655, have a somewhat confusing statement. It seems that a certain Capt. John Parker, of Truelou King's Road, Bristol, reported to the navy commander that when he came into port to convoy guns for a new frigate, Hanserd questioned the ship's surgeon about the use of funds that had been given for the sick and wounded. The details were not included in the *State Papers,* but evidently Hanserd either resigned from his position in disgust, as he had from his chaplaincy in the army, or was fired for questioning authority. The record states:

Another clerk of the check has been appointed in place of Mr.
Knowles [Knollys], who is troubled by them about the money he
received for sick and wounded men; he handed it to the surgeon
before the ship came out, and it as been laid out in necessaries for
the men.[15]

Other records do not show whether Hanserd continued in
another form of civil service after this unpleasant situation or
returned to teaching and serving the church he had gathered in
London.

An Impartial Outsider

Hanserd Knollys well understood the penalties for independent thinking and action when he pleaded with churches to be
more tolerant. After all, he had been tried by the High
Commission, imprisoned and banished, and fled for his life on
many occasions. In spite of that, the importance of religious liberty
was one of Hanserd's deepest convictions. His name was attached
to two pleas for toleration that were sent to the deeply polarized
Parliament. One plea was in 1651 and the other in 1654 when he
was working as clerk of the exchequer. On April 3, 1657, he sent a
similar plea to Cromwell because his belief in the need for civil and
religious toleration was an ongoing theme in his life.

Within Parliament, battles over religious beliefs ran rampant
among the Roman Catholics, Presbyterians, Independents,
members of the Church of England, and Separatists. The
Separatists, including the Pilgrims and Quakers, wanted complete
separation from the Church of England and what they called all
"popish rituals." Although the Presbyterians and Independents
had different beliefs about church structure, their theology was
similar enough that they were often allies. But not always.

There is an interesting old record directed to the king and court
by an unknown writer. Obviously an ardent supporter of the
Church of England, he nevertheless described himself as "An
Impartial Outsider" when, in 1672, he compared nonconformist
sects. The Presbyterians, he wrote, are the least to be feared:

They are partly devided [*sic*] among themselves, some being for three-quarters conformity, some for half, some for a Quarter, & a few of them for none at all; and those few, it is doubted, are something akin to the Jesuits. . . . The Independents are the next considerable party, and in some respects more considerable than the former, if not for number, yet for their unity among themselves, & from the danger that may arrise [*sic*] from their evil Principles. . . . Among their Evil principles, this is the worst. They hate Monarchy. . . . The Independants & Anabaptists, with some few of the fiercer Presbyterians, are proud & censorious;—quakerlike they will denounce judgments both upon Kings—and Kingdom, upon any pretended miscarriage they do but hear of. These are great frequenters of Coffee-houses. . . . The Quakers most truly deserve the character of rude, saucie, unmannerly, with all the ugly names that belong to an illbred person; it is not wrong to them to say they are mad, & fitter for Bedlam than sober companie.[16]

After this blast against those who criticized the monarchy including Quakers, Independents, and Anabaptists, as well as "fiercer Presbyterians" and those who were "something akin to the Jesuits," the same author compared Presbyterians and Independents. The Presbyterians, he wrote, were "more in number by much, generally for Government by Bishops, weak in their Politicks & open in their councils, and by their rebellion gott all power into their hands." In contrast, the Independants were "more united, for no government, cunning, subtile persons, secret & close in their designs, cheated them out of it, & made fools of them ever after." This unknown, self-described "impartial" author continued:

Both parties are rich & have great interest in trade, and have made it their great designe to cast all the reproach of Ignorance, Lazyness, and immorality upon the conformed clergy, that they might take off the esteem of the people from them, which hath in a great measure succeeded.[17]

This kind of criticism probably reflected the thinking of many people including Charles II, although he said it differently. With more restraint, he claimed Presbyterianism was "not a religion for gentlemen."[18]

Fifth Monarchy and Newgate Prison

Meanwhile in 1660, Hanserd Knollys was back in prison because of a movement known as the Fifth Monarchy. It was an extreme and short-lived Puritan political-religious sect based on a puzzling interpretation of the biblical book of Daniel, written about 164 B.C. and replete with symbols, visions, and predictions of apocalyptic events. At that time, Assyria, Persia, Greece, and Rome were seen as the first four world monarchies; the Monarchists claimed that they would be the fifth world power.

Some Fifth Monarchists were Presbyterians; many more were from the Independent or Baptist Churches or one of the sects. Led by Thomas Venner, the Fifth Monarchists staunchly believed that they were saints, and as saints, they would rule with Christ on earth for the next one thousand years.[19]

When the movement first developed, the Fifth Monarchists supported Cromwell and the Barebones Parliament of 1653 because they thought they themselves would take over next. However, when the protectorate was established and they knew they had no chance of ruling, they turned against Cromwell. Anna Trapnel was one who wrote strongly against him. In 1654, she claimed to have visions that God would "batter" Cromwell. When she visited the Fifth Monarchist members of the Barebones Parliament, some local clergy accused her of subversion. She was arrested and imprisoned for two months.

Finally, the Fifth Monarchists drew up a petition for Parliament in which they accused Cromwell of worse tyranny than that of Charles I. Cromwell responded to this by imprisoning some, warning others, and barring those who would not take a loyalty oath from entering the House of Commons. Thomas Venner led the Fifth Monarchists in two armed uprisings in 1657, during the protectorate and again, in 1661, after the restoration of Charles II to the throne. Although the uprisings were easily suppressed, when Venner and a small group of followers continued to claim that a Fifth Monarchy was coming and that it would be ruled by Christ and his saints, he and twelve others were executed.[20]

Cromwell's army attempted to quash all elements considered to be subversive. Although there is no evidence that Hanserd Knollys was a Fifth Monarchist, he was judged guilty by association because some of the participants who joined the sect were from his church. Hanserd had also visited Anna Trapnel.[21] This was held against him, and along with four hundred others who refused to take Oaths of Allegiance and Supremacy, Hanserd Knollys was put in prison for four and one-half months. During his imprisonment, he was allowed to preach daily to other prisoners and summarized the experience matter-of-factly:

> In the year 1660—Venners Rifing and others made an Infurrection in the City of London, my felf and many others were taken out their own dwelling houfes and brought to Woodftreet Counter, and many to Newgate, and other Prifons, though we were innocent, and knew not of their Defign; at which time I suffered Imprifonment 18 weeks, till we were delivered by an Act of Pardon at the King's Coronation, unto all offenders, except Murderers.[22]

It could not have been a pleasant stay. Newgate Prison was foul, ugly, and full of lice. Built in the twelfth century, it was notorious for its deplorable conditions and dungeons where men and women, debtors and murderers, were herded together with or without hope for a trial. Misery due to tyranny was constant. Only those with money or influence had any safety or comfort; they bribed their jailers, but if they ran out of money, their lives also ran out.

When an execution was scheduled, crowds often surged around the gallows. Being pilloried, branded on the forehead, and having one's nose slit or ears cut off were common punishments. Those who bravely faced the flames, the rope, or the ax were highly esteemed. When Dr. Bastwick lost his ears to the executioner, his daughter carried them away in a clean handkerchief.[23] Many of the condemned carefully planned their dying speeches, which were recorded at the event in shorthand. Historian William

Haller tells a story of Archbishop Laud, who, when led to the block, ordered that the cracks between the boards be filled up so that his blood would not fall on those underneath and in his final speech declared, "Lord, I'm coming as fast as I can."[24]

Restoration and Another Flight to Freedom

Charles II (1630—1685), son of Charles I and Henrietta Maria of France, grew up during the civil wars against his father. When his father was executed in 1649, Charles II was proclaimed king in Scotland by those Scots who were Catholic and by the Church of England. However, when Cromwell defeated the Scottish army, Charles fled to France in 1651 and lived there with little money or power. The restoration of Charles in 1660 was greatly due to General Monck and to the new Convention Parliament.

Monck, who supported Cromwell after the execution of Charles I, worried about the people's restlessness after the Lord Protector's death in 1658. Cromwell's son tried to rule, but was so unsuccessful he was forced to resign. Then, Monck changed his loyalties and assisted the transition so that Charles II was called to England and restored to the throne. At that time, the Church of England was also restored to full power as the Church of state.

However, the anger of Charles II and other Royalists against Cromwell had not been assuaged by Cromwell's death. About three years later, his embalmed body was dug out of its Westminster tomb and hung up on the gallows at Tyburn where criminals were executed. When his body was taken down, it was buried under the gallows and his head was impaled on a pole on top of Westminster Hall where it remained throughout the reign of Charles II.

During the Restoration, most prisoners who had been accused of being Fifth Monarchists were pardoned and released, including Hanserd Knollys. Although Hanserd returned to preaching at All Hallows Church, he was still suspect.[25] Fifth Monarchists were accused of "visiting with the Presbyterians," and the Presbyterians were accused of encouraging people to reject the Church of England's *Book of Common Prayer*. Some previously accused Fifth

Monarchists began to leave England. Only a few weeks after his release from prison, Hanserd, still a suspect, fled with his wife, one son, and one daughter to Holland. The *State Papers* (1661–1962) read:

> [The Fifth Monarchists] have bought a small ship to convey each other abroad. Mr. Knowles [Knollys] and others, who were in Newgate, are sent into Holland, where they are in good condition, but act their business more secretly than here; they only wait an opportunity.[26]

It would be interesting to know what secret business and opportunity the writer of the above *State Papers* was referring to. More than likely, the Fifth Monarchists were suspected of continuing political agitation. Hanserd then went to Germany where he built a house and remained for three years. During this time, Hanserd was writing his language grammar books and endorsing even more controversial writers. One of them was Benjamin Keach.

The Banning of *Instructions for Children*

Benjamin Keach (1640–1704) was a General Baptist who was self-taught. When he began preaching in 1659, he was imprisoned for doing so without official sanction. Later, he became a Particular Baptist and wrote between forty and fifty pamphlets that were often inflammatory. He knew that deliberately publishing something that might be controversial often invited punishment. Therefore, he knew what the outcome might be when he published his book, *Instructions for Children*, in 1664.

Unlike his other books and pamphlets, Keach's *Instructions for Children* was not written for political purposes. It was a book for teaching children how to write capital letters, easy syllables, and lists of words that had one, two, or three syllables. However, it also included a Baptist catechism for children, which led to his imprisonment. Preapproval of anything to be published had been reinstated during the Restoration. Keach did not seek this approval nor did he put his name on the book as author. Yet, because he was

Benjamin Keach in a pillory.

so outspoken publicly, it was soon known to be his. Hanserd Knollys's passionate introduction to the book irritated non-Baptists.

> This little book, Instructions for Children, I have read and taught to scholars about 40 years [*sic*] in London . . . so I do commend it to all Religious Parents who are willing to catechize their children. . . . I could wish that all English schoolmasters in and about that city (nay throughout the nation) would make use of it for the Instruction of their Scholars.[27]

If Keach thought he had preserved his own safety by not having his name on the book, he was wrong. Keach's trial in 1664 was recorded in Ivimey's *History of the Baptists, Vol. I.* It clearly illustrates how trials were conducted so that the accused had no defense. The judge at Keach's trial was Lord Clarendon, the man behind the rigid Clarendon Code. Clarendon insisted that Keach be pilloried and his books burned in front of him so that he would suffer physically and also be publicly disgraced.

However, Keach's physical punishment and the burning of his books did not destroy what he believed to be important in the education of children. Hanserd Knollys continued to point to its usefulness, and John Cotton used the book as the foundation for *The New England Primer*, which became required study in Massachusetts. In 1667, Clarendon, who had judged Keach so harshly at his trial, was himself impeached and banished for treason and tyranny.[28]

Return from Germany

Hanserd Knollys's faith was again challenged when he decided to leave Germany and return to England. He had built a house in Germany but was unable to sell it before leaving so he had very little money. In the port of Cullen on the way home, he was tricked by the unscrupulous skipper of a hired boat that was to take him and his family to Rotterdam. Hanserd had paid him in advance and the skipper had agreed, in writing, to pay all tolls and licenses en route. However, after the skipper paid only two tolls, he refused to go further without more money. Hanserd and his family were suddenly stranded in a strange port, and his wife, Anne, became very sick.

Suddenly, a gentleman who was in charge of the toll collectors and skippers of the boats appeared and asked what was going on. Although he and Hanserd did not speak the same native language, they were able to communicate in Latin. When the gentleman heard what had happened, he commanded the skipper to return all of Hanserd's money and to arrange for a free and safe passage for the entire family. Apparently he also told others about the dishonest skipper because, after Hanserd arrived in Rotterdam, something occurred which he claimed was due to divine intervention on his behalf:

> God made two Catholicks in Cullen inftrumental to prevail with Prince Dewit, to fend me by a Bill of Exchange 160 Rix Dollers for a Houfe that I had Built in his country and could not sell, which I received at Rotterdam.[29]

What a relief this must have been to receive the money for the sale of his house in Germany when he was almost destitute in

Rotterdam. Hanserd's wife and children were then able to return to England, and he was to follow. However, while they were living in Germany, their home in England had been illegally confiscated. His wife and children had no place to live; and, when Hanserd arrived back in England, he found them staying at a friend's house in London. Later, this led to an agonizingly long legal case.

In 1664, almost twenty years after the publication of his first book on Hebrew grammar, four new language books by Hanserd were printed. Two were on Hebrew, *Linguae Hebraicae delineatio* and *Radices Hebraicae Omnes.* One was a Latin grammar book, *Grammaticae Latinae Compendium,* and another was Greek, *Grammaticae Graecae Compendium.* The following year, another book of his about languages in the academic field that was so dear to him was published. In this book he dealt with all three languages and titled it, *Grammaticae Latinae, Graecae, and Hebraicae.*

Evidently he had been working on these books while self-exiled in Holland and Germany when Charles II was ruling so irrationally. To Hanserd, war and intoleration, without the wisdom that can come through studying the Scriptures, preferably in their earliest languages, was ultimate foolishness.

Grammar books did not generate much income, so on his return home Hanserd once more began to teach school. He had given his school and its students to one of his sons and to one of his daughters and her husband, but the date he gifted them is not known. It could have been when he was put in Newgate Prison with the Fifth Monarchists or when he fled to Germany. It appears to have been before 1664 when he discovered his house had been confiscated illegally.

In Defense of Women and Song

Always a defender of religious freedom, Hanserd Knollys was never afraid to do what he believed was right, whether writing, teaching, preaching, working with his children in running a school, or encouraging his friends. Four years after he wrote the introduction to Benjamin Keach's book for children, Knollys supported him again when Keach introduced congregational singing in his church in 1668 at the end of the Lord's Supper.

Keach, author of many radical pamphlets and the controversial children's book endorsed by Hanserd, was one of the first nonconformists to have a congregational hymn sung in his church. It seemed so appalling to some members that they left his church permanently. The argument about music during worship had deep roots from the past. In the Roman Catholic Church, music was the responsibility of the priests as the Gregorian chants required trained choirs. The chants, which were developed from the 600s to the 1400s, were always sung in perfect unison.

Congregational singing did not begin until the Reformation when Martin Luther published the first Protestant hymnbook in 1524. It had eight hymns and five tunes. Gradually, more French and German tunes were added.[30] Luther liked music and wrote:

> I would not give up my humble musical gift for anything . . . next
> to theology, there is no art that can be compared with music; for
> it alone, after theology, gives us rest and joy of heart.[31]

John Calvin allowed only words from the Bible to be used in hymns. Generally, they were psalms set to well-known melodies of the time. Because the English nonconformists were primarily Calvinists, their first hymnbooks consisted of psalms set to music.

However, when a woman by the name of Katherine Sutton wrote hymns, the controversy became more intense than when Luther and Calvin introduced singing in their churches. In the dispute over this, Hanserd Knollys rose to her defense by claiming that her hymns were as good as prayers.

Katherine Sutton also wrote a book titled *A Christian Woman's Experience of the Glorious Workings of God's Free Grace,* published in Rotterdam in 1663. This was another radical departure from tradition. Women were not supposed to speak in public about religious matters, much less write about them. So, religious liberty was once more on trial. Hanserd probably knew Katherine Sutton in Rotterdam; he preached there on the need for toleration of women and did not agree with the tradition that women were supposed

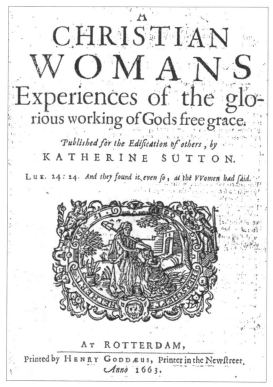

The cover of Katherine Sutton's book.

to be silent. In fact, he wrote a preface to her book saying she was "an effectual means of the conversion of many."[32]

Her book began with confessions of what she was ashamed of:

> I had once hard thoughts of the people of God, yet being on a time perfwaded to go to hear them, I went though not out of love to them, but to vvatch vvhat I could obferve; and being then over perfwaded againft them, and the Minifters Text (that then preacht) was Rom. 2:4, 5, 6 . . . Verily at this opporunity the dread of God did much fmite upon my heart, that I fo long finned againft his patience and goodnefz. . . . The very firft night after he began to work on my heart, I fell under his temptation, that I should not eat any more, but rather die, and then I should ceafe from finning againft the Lords goodnefs.[33]

Katherine Sutton's conversion led to her awareness that she was avoided because she was so vain. Hanserd Knollys's introduction to her book was addressed to Courteous Readers. He pleaded that they be especially courteous with her sudden and unexpected transitions from one thing to another. He added that many who heard her in her family and other families turned to the Lord. "She opened her mouth with wifdom, and in her tongue was the Law of kindness as Solomon fpake of the virtuous woman."

Issues of women speaking out and congregations singing out continued to be seen as major problems in Baptist churches. Both subjects were debated at the first combined National Assembly of the General and the Particular Baptists. This was held in 1689 and was intended to be a forum for discussion, not legislation. However, although both Baptist groups emphasized the autonomy of local congregations, they disagreed on other matters including the role of women and the singing of hymns during worship.[34] Their disagreements on singing became so bitter that joint Baptist assemblies were discontinued after a few years. They believed there could be no benefit from further discussions.

On Being a Beneficiary

Benefits come in different ways and from different sources. During his lifetime, Hanserd Knollys received different kinds of benefits from many kinds of people. He benefited from his first bishop John Williams, who encouraged him in the ministry. He benefited from John Wheelwright who helped him sort out his theological beliefs concerning his role in the Church. He benefited from strangers who provided housing for him and his family when he arrived in London destitute, from friends who showed him how to get students, and from more friends and family who simply loved him.

Hanserd was also a beneficiary in several wills. Thomas Taylor, a shipwright in Wapping, Middlesex, whose will was proven January 10, 1658, made Hanserd one of his beneficiaries. This occurred before Hanserd fled to Germany. A wealthy man, Thomas Taylor owned freehold lands, copyhold lands, and tenements in

Essex. Traditionally, freehold land was land held in perpetuity because of loyalty to the king or service as a knight. Copyhold land was land that belonged to a lord and was leased. Thomas Taylor also received fees from farm rentals of a manor in Norfolk and from lands and tenements in Middlesex County. Although wealthy, he died fairly young when one of his sons, Caleb, was still underage.

In his will, Thomas Taylor instructed his wife to bring up their son Caleb until he was twenty-one, and he made "Master Hanserd Knowles" a beneficiary because he was so grateful to him for having been Caleb's schoolmaster.[35] Probably Caleb was one of Hanserd's day students or a boarder in his school. The same year that Thomas Taylor's will was proven, Hanserd bought land and a house in London and remodeled it for a home and school. Perhaps he was able to do this because of the money he had just inherited.

Almost twenty years later, another known benefactor of Hanserd was Ann Grave, a widow of St. Botolph-without-Aldgate, London. In her will, dated February 10, 1675, and proven March 20, 1676, she left many large bequests including "provision for the maintenance of eight, poor, aged, decayed ministers." Hanserd's name was first on her list.[36] At this time he was seventy-eight years old. The amount of the "provision" she left for Hanserd was not specified. William Kiffin, Knollys's longtime friend, was one of the executors of Ann Grave's will, so she evidently knew and trusted Kiffin and was committed to the ongoing work of the Baptist churches.

Hanserd Knollys lived for another fifteen years after Ann Grave's will was proven. How might this man, still so passionately preaching what he believed to be true, have felt when he was described as one of eight "poor, aged, and decayed" ministers? And, how might he have felt had he known that after his death, the Hanserd Knollys Society would be established in his honor in England?

8

To Owe Nothing but Love

I desire to owe no man anything but love . . . and if Death seize my body, that I may leave enough of my own behind me to pay all my debts, and a little for the relief of God's poor, and some of my poorest natural relations.
—Hanserd Knollys, 1598–1691

Foreign Affairs and More Wars

International conflict had been escalating for years after Hanserd Knollys's return to England from America. The wars with the Dutch were the ones that affected him most directly; three were fought within thirty years. The first one was during the interregnum and lasted from 1652 to 1654. It started when Parliament forbade any foreign ships from bringing cargo into port that had not been produced in England.

The Dutch not only brought in products from their various colonies, but they refused to lower their flags in recognition of England's dominance when they entered the waters between England, France, and the Netherlands. The powerful navies of England and the Netherlands fought nine battles in two years. Then, England blockaded the Dutch coast, and the Dutch faced starvation; a treaty was signed April 22, 1654.

The second war with the Dutch was ignited when England took New Netherlands in 1664 and renamed it New York, after the Duke of York. The duke was Charles II's brother, later to become James II and reign only three years, from 1685 to 1688.

Meanwhile in April 1660, Charles II, with the help of his advisor Edward Hyde, prepared a declaration stating Charles's

desire for amnesty, for freedom of conscience, for fair settlement of
land disputes, and for the army to receive its back pay. Similar to a
campaign speech, it was successful and won him back his throne.

However, problems developed over which he had no control.
By 1665, the plague and Great Fire of London had so devastated
England that Dutch ships were able to enter the Thames and burn
the British war ships at Chatham. When the Treaty of Brenda was
signed July 11, 1667, the Second Dutch War was over. By this treaty,
the Dutch got Surinam in South America and the Spice Islands in
the West Indies; the English got New York, Delaware, and New
Jersey. But the treaty did not lead to lasting peace.

Two years later, when Louis XIV of France wanted to expand
his country, he sent French troops into the Spanish Netherlands
(now Belgium). In retaliation, Sweden, Holland, and England
signed a Triple Alliance against France in 1668. This was such a
threat to Louis that he made a financial settlement with Sweden
and secretly signed the Treaty of Dover with Charles II in 1670. In
this treaty, Charles agreed to support France against the Dutch,
and Louis XIV agreed to support Charles with hidden payments so
that Charles need not ask for so much money from Parliament.

A great admirer of the pomp, ceremony, and lavishness of the
French court, Charles converted to Catholicism. Since Charles's
wife and brother were also Catholic, his conversion increased the
fear of many that England might be forced to return to
Catholicism. As protection against that, Parliament insisted
Charles make peace with Holland in 1674 and de-emphasize the
alliance with Catholic France.

The Controlling Clarendon Code

Neither the king nor the Parliament thought of themselves as
being intolerant; each was certain of being right. Sir Edward Hyde
believed the same of himself.[1] A longtime member of Parliament,
Hyde had tried to reconcile Parliament and Charles I after the
Grand Remonstrance of 1641 but failed. When a petition against
episcopacy was presented in 1641, the same year Hanserd
returned from New England, Edward Hyde had opposed it. He

Sir Edward Hyde.

also was opposed to excluding clergy from government positions.

Charles I had been executed in 1649 and the army had taken over. During the commonwealth period, Charles II was a poverty-stricken fugitive until he was restored to the throne in 1660. Hyde had joined him in exile and had become his close advisor. They were so close that Hyde encouraged his daughter to become pregnant by Charles's younger brother, James, Duke of York and future king. She persuaded James to marry her in September 1660, shortly before their child was born.[2]

Because the duke was a well-known womanizer who did not want marriage to interfere with his many mistresses, he married her secretly. When Charles II discovered the subterfuge, Hyde protested fervently that he knew nothing about his daughter's sexual liaison with the duke before their marriage and that she certainly should be decapitated. The king had no desire to execute her, so he accepted the clearly fanciful explanation and, in 1661, made Hyde the Earl of Clarendon.

As such, Hyde had great power. The very restrictive Clarendon Code, a series of laws made between 1661 and 1665, was named after him. Essentially, the code reestablished the Church of England and penalized dissenters and Roman Catholics through four separate acts.

First was the Municipal Corporations Act of 1661, which required all persons who worked for city governments to renounce the Presbyterian Covenant, which had been established years earlier, and take communion in the Church of England. Second came the Act of Uniformity of 1662, which required all clergy to use the Church of England's revised *Book of Common Prayer* in public worship. Third was the Conventicle Act of 1664 that prohibited groups of more than five nonconforming persons from meeting for worship unless they were family. Last was the Five-Mile Act of 1665. This act barred nonconforming clergy from living in or visiting any city or town where they had taught or preached before the act was passed. It also prohibited them from teaching anywhere. Through this act, some two thousand clergy lost their living. Some of these acts affected only the clergy but not the Conventicle Act. It affected both lay and clergy because it prohibited the worship meetings of many nonconformers. The penalty for this offense was three months in prison and a fine. For the second offense it was six months, and for the third it was banishment to America for seven years.[3] Hanserd Knollys was later imprisoned for disobeying the Conventicle Act of the Clarendon Code when he met with more than five people after his return from Germany.

Another connection between Knollys and the Earl of Clarendon is found in a remarkable collection of unpublished manuscripts from this period which is in the famous Dr. Williams's Library in London. The collection includes manuscripts of Roger Morrice (c. 1626–1702), an ejected minister. His *Entring Book* is an important political diary that Morrice kept from March 1677 to April 1691. In his diary, he mentions how Edward Hyde, Earl of Clarendon, unsuccessfully attempted to get Hanserd Knollys to support the king's proposed changes to the penal codes. Obviously, although Knollys was out of favor, he had great influence with many people and was well worth courting.

The Plague and the Great Fire

Although the penalties for not conforming to the Clarendon Code were severe, of even greater severity was the Great Plague that hit London in late 1664, shortly after Hanserd Knollys returned from Germany. Of course this was not the first time a plague had hit England. In 1630, Cambridge University had been completely closed because of a serious outbreak, and the vice-chancellor wrote, "Myself am alone, a destitute and forsaken man, not a Scholler with me in the college, not a Scholler seen by me without."[4]

When the plague hit London in 1664, it terrorized all who lived there. It was an infectious fever transmitted by rats and fleas, especially in overly crowded situations where the poor often lived. Starting first in London, in the neighborhood of Drury Lane, the plague lasted almost two years. Most people who were able to leave London, including the king, court, and clergy, fled to the country, and the city became so deserted that grass grew in the streets. Trade was almost nonexistent. Many people were quarantined and had a red cross painted above their doors with the words, "Lord have mercy upon me." There were no sewers. Refuse was supposed to be taken by cart and dumped outside city limits, but it was more often secretly dumped into the Thames. Instead of leaving town, Hanserd chose to stay with his church in London, which was made up mostly of people who were too poor to escape.

Samuel Pepys (1633–1703) was secretary of the Admiralty, a member of Parliament, confidant of Charles II and James II, and a brilliant diarist. According to Pepys's famous *Diary*, which he had started writing July 1, 1665, there were 7,496 deaths in London during the week of August 31, 1665. Of that number, 6,102 were from the plague. It became worse. Mortality records show that in two years over sixty-eight thousand persons died of the plague in London alone.[5] Another who wrote about the plague was Daniel Defoe (1660–1731), a nonconformist merchant as well as an author. He was a secret agent for the Tories and later for the Whigs. Perhaps best known for his *Robinson Crusoe*, he also wrote

A Journal of the Plague Year about how the plague affected ordinary people. In it are many details that shed light on what happened during that tragic time.

Two years after this plague, the Great Fire raged through London for seven long days, February 2—9, 1666. Beginning in the home of the king's baker on Pudding Lane near London bridge, the fire spread rapidly. The wind was high, the streets were narrow, the houses were built of wood and crowded together. In some places, great hooks were used to pull them down.[6] People tried desperately to get their possessions out of their homes, but the pitch and tar used in building and construction only made the situation worse. In five days, over thirteen thousand houses were destroyed, as well as eighty-nine churches. Again, Hanserd remained in the city during the Great Fire as he had during the plague, so he could continue to minister to his congregation.

The Friendship of William Kiffin

Through these difficult times, Hanserd Knollys had a long-term friend in William Kiffin (1616—1701). Although they served different churches in London, they were friends and colleagues for fifty years. After Hanserd's death, it was Kiffin who added to and published the very brief memoirs Hanserd had written twenty years earlier after his wife, Anne, and son Isaac died the same year.

William Kiffin was born in London in 1616. He was nine years old when he contracted the plague and recovered, although his parents both died from it, and he was taken care of by friends. Like Hanserd, he too had a conversion experience. It happened when Kiffin was running away from a glover (a maker of gloves) to whom he was apprenticed. He ran into a church where a sermon was being preached on the duty of servants to their masters, and as he listened he imagined the preacher knew all about him. He was so moved by what he heard that he returned to his master, determined to seek out more Puritan ministers. This he did.[7]

Shortly before Hanserd Knollys started attending the Jacob/Jessey Independent Church, Kiffin was a member of it. Then, he came to believe that baptism should not be for infants but

William Kiffin.

should be based on personal choice so he left to form a Baptist church with John Spilsbury, one of the first in London.

Kiffin became a very wealthy man making a large fortune in wool and international trade especially with Holland. From 1656 to 1658 he represented Middlesex in Parliament and was also pastor of Devonshire Square Baptist Church in London for sixty-one years. Hannah, one of his daughters, married Henry, a grandson of Oliver Cromwell.

Like Hanserd, Kiffin was arrested many times, once by General Monck, the general under Cromwell who was largely responsible for the restoration of Charles II. However, Kiffin's great wealth and political connections offered him considerable protection.

Hanserd did not have the protection that continuing wealth often provides. Sometimes he was seriously impoverished; other times he had substantial funds. W. T. Whitley, in his *History of the English Baptists*, does not give his references but claims that Knollys, like Kiffin, was sometimes involved in trade with the

Dutch, although for a much shorter period of time.[8]

Kiffin certainly did not need financial support from his congregation. Thomas Crosby (1683–1752), one of the earliest Baptist historians, wrote of an interesting encounter between William Kiffin and Charles II.[9] At one time, the king tried to borrow forty thousand pounds from Kiffin in return for favors he had granted him. Kiffin refused, but offered the king a gift of ten thousand pounds, probably assuming that the larger amount would never be repaid. The king accepted, and Kiffin reportedly said he had thus saved thirty thousand pounds. Contemporary historian B. R. White said that the forty thousand pounds the king asked to borrow would have been the equivalent of one million dollars in the 1960s.[10]

Some years later, Charles II's brother James II, who only ruled from 1685 to 1688, had a different kind of encounter with both Kiffin and Knollys. James tried to bribe Kiffin with an offer to make him an alderman of London if he would enlist Baptists' support in the suspension of all penal laws against dissenters and Catholics. Fearing the Catholics would regain control of the country, Kiffin refused. When James made the same request of Hanserd, he was again turned down. The king relieved his anger by throwing Hanserd into jail! Hanserd was then eighty-four years old.

Prison, Death, and the Need for Faith

During an earlier period, from 1666 to 1670, following the plague and Great Fire, life was relatively peaceful for Hanserd Knollys. Then, on May 10, 1670, he was once again imprisoned by order of the Lord Mayor of London while meeting with his congregation in George Yard, White Chapel. His arrest was due to the Second Conventicle Act of the Clarendon Code.

Hanserd refused to comply with the act and continued meeting with larger groups, so he was jailed in the Bishopsgate Compter. However, he was allowed to preach to other prisoners twice a week in the Common Hall. Since most of the prisoners went to hear him, he certainly had more than the five listeners there. Later, Hanserd was discharged at a session of Old Bailey, the central criminal court.[11]

After being released, Hanserd became very ill. He described it as a "painful gripping of the guts" that brought him "near to the grave." "Satan," he said, "was very busy tempting me in the night season, sometimes suggesting to me that I was but a hypocrite and at other times that my evidences for heaven were not good."[12] This sickness, coming so soon after the release from prison was another trial of faith. Two "Doctors of Physick" visited Hanserd daily but were unable to help him although they had cured sixteen others of the same illness.

Hanserd decided to take no more medicine but instead to rely on prayer. He was anointed by his longtime friend William Kiffin and the fiery Welsh preacher Vavasor Powell. The two of them and many other ministers and laymen prayed continuously for Hanserd. He recovered, although he was very weak for a long time.

That same year, two of his sons and one of his grandchildren died. Another grandchild had smallpox and was expected to die. Then one of his daughters-in-law had a stillborn child, and she also faced death. The deaths of so many family members in such a short time was another trial of faith.

Then a greater blow fell. On April 30, 1671, Anne Cheney, his beloved wife of forty years, died after six months of "great weakness and pain in her face." She and Hanserd had been so close throughout their marriage that at the very moment she breathed her last breath, Hanserd knew it. He was in his church preaching at the time, but his intuition was so strong that he interrupted his sermon to give thanks to God for having given her to him.

Anne was buried in Bunhill Fields, as was Hanserd Knollys twenty years later. Her tombstone inscription, preserved in Herald's College, London, was:

> Here lyeth the body of Mrs. Anne Knollys daughter of John Cheney Esq. and wife of Hanserd Knollys (Minister of the Gospel) by whom he had issue 7 sons and 3 daughters. Who dyed April 30th 1671 and in the 63rd year of her age.[13]

On the vertical stone over her grave were some lines of poetry that were not written in Hanserd's style. However, if sung to the tune of a hymn, such as "A Mighty Fortress Is Our God," the words could take on a certain majesty.

> My only wife, that in her life,
> Lived forty years with me,
> Lies now at Rest, for ever blest,
> With Immortality.
> My dear is gone—left me alone
> For Christ to do and dye,
> Who dyed for me, and dyed to be
> My Saviour-God Most High.[14]

Six months after his wife died, his son Isaac, whom Hanserd described as his "beloved son" and his "only son then living," sank into severe depression. Grieving for his mother, he died on November 15, 1671. Hanserd was disconsolate. According to his own account, he was still weak from his own illness and wept often. The death of Isaac, who had helped care for him when he was sick the year before, was almost more than Hanserd could bear.

Perhaps it was to help him recover from his great sadness that his friend William Kiffin encouraged him to write about his life. And so he began, "I, Hanserd Knollys, was born at Cawkwell. . . ." The bits and pieces of his life that he recorded were poignant but brief and incomplete. His sentence about the death of his favorite son Isaac as his "only living son" is tender but puzzling. Perhaps Hanserd's use of the phrase "only living son" meant that Isaac was the only one who was living near him in London. Hanserd originally had three daughters and seven sons; two of his sons died while he was so sick in 1670.

When Hanserd's son Cheney wrote his will in 1670, he mentioned his "second brother John" and three other brothers whom he did not name. That would indicate that five of Hanserd's sons were alive in 1670. But, in Hanserd's memoir, two of them, including Cheney, died that year and Isaac in 1671. But what about the other two? Were these sons so financially secure that Hanserd saw no reason to mention any financial support of them in his autobiographical notes?

The puzzle is not yet solved. Could Cheney's two other brothers have been living elsewhere? Perhaps they were Cheney's brothers-in-law, not biological brothers. Perhaps when Hanserd was in Holland and Germany for several years he lost touch with his other children.

Possibly the John Knowles of Hampton, New Hampshire, was indeed Hanserd's son but was believed to be dead. If he was the same John who, according to parish records, was baptized by his father Hanserd Knollys in Goulceby, then contact between them could have been lost due to distance or due to John's blindness the last ten years of his life. It is to be remembered that Hanserd had a son John who, after being admitted to the famous Charterhouse School, was excluded due to his eyes. John of Hampton supposedly wrote his will in 1693 (two years after Hanserd died). It was proven December 31, 1705, but that date could have been recorded wrong. It was given as the same date as the death of his wife, so the issue is still unresolved.[15]

Finances and Aging

With the deaths of so many in his immediate family within a year, Hanserd Knollys recognized he was getting older and was reasonably sure that he would be persecuted and imprisoned again (which of course happened). He did not want others to have to pay his debts. When he died he wanted "to owe no man anything but love" and have enough money so he could leave something for the poor and for his own poorest "natural" relatives.

Throughout Hanserd Knollys's life, his livelihood came from several sources. He taught, worked for the government, and preached where and when he could for voluntary offerings. It appears that he was sometimes involved in Dutch trade, perhaps with William Kiffin, his friend of fifty-four years.

Hanserd's involvement in Dutch trade is a reasonable assumption because the people of Hanserd's church, whom he served for so many years, were very poor. Yet, Hanserd had had enough money to flee to Wales, Holland, and Germany when he was released from Newgate Prison. At the time Charles II was restored to the throne, Hanserd also had sufficient deposits with Weavers' Hall that he was also able to build a home in Germany, so he must have had money from somewhere. However, this does not mean he was always financially secure. Quite the contrary, evidence shows that several times he was poverty-stricken and worried about it.

In his memoir, he reviewed his financial support of three sons, as well as one daughter and her husband. He did not mention his other four sons and two other daughters. One child had died as an infant aboard ship on the way to New England. Perhaps the others were no longer alive or had not needed financial assistance. His memoir says:

> To my Eldeft Son, I had given £60. per Annum during his Life which he enjoyed above 21 years ere he died. To my next Son, that lived to be Married, I gave the full value of £250. in money, Houfe, School, and Houfhold Goods, and left him 50 Scholars in his School-Houfe. To my only Daughter then living, I gave her marriage above £300. in money, annuity, Plate, Linen, and Houfhold-ftuff and left her husband 50 Scholars in the said SchoolHoufe in Partnership with my faid Son. To my youngeft son, that lived to be married I gave more than £300. Sterling, befides it coft me above 60 pounds in his apprenticefhip and £40. afterwards. . . .[16]

The phrase "above 21 years" in the second line in the above quote did not mean his eldest son was in his twenties. It was used for anyone who was over twenty-one, regardless of how old that person was. The ongoing support of one son was a substantial sum, and his gifts to his children were also significant, so estimating his income and expenses is difficult. They obviously fluctuated greatly. In fact, Hanserd was forced to borrow two hundred pounds to pay Isaac's debts when Isaac died and Isaac's wife remarried. Is it possible that the sixty pounds he paid for a son's apprenticeship was for the John Knowles of Hampton, New Hampshire, who was a mariner? Or, for a different son, also named John, who had such poor sight he was limited in what he could do?

His granddaughter, he wrote, had been with him for three years and was then nineteen years old when she took over the responsibility of caring for the student boarders and running Knollys's household. The husband of his only surviving daughter left "with her consent" and moved to the country. Perhaps he was the son-in-law who had helped to run the school in the past.

Whatever the reason, Hanserd stopped writing his memoirs, although he continued publishing other books. His last bit of writing was at the age of ninety-three when he wrote a letter to his church just before he died. William Kiffin added the letter to Hanserd's earlier memoir and it became part of the booklet published in 1693 and referenced in this book as *Life and Death*. It still rests in the archives of the British Museum.

Hanserd Knollys Sues the Army

Throughout the time of his illness, the death of his wife, sons, and grandchildren, and the writing of his brief memories, Hanserd Knollys was involved in a legal battle to regain his home and school, which were illegally taken from him.

The case had a long history. In 1658, before he was imprisoned during the Fifth Monarchists uprising, Hanserd Knollys had bought "an old armory house" from the Artillery Company of London for three hundred pounds. He then spent an additional four hundred pounds to remodel it and used it for his home and schoolhouse for about three years. When he fled to Holland and Germany in early 1661, he allowed some people to live there during his absence. That was when Colonel Legge took it by force.

Colonel Legge was "a Bed-Chamber man, and Lieutenant of Ordnance," who wanted the house himself. In order to acquire it, he charged Hanserd Knollys in the Court of Exchequer for keeping his house and grounds away from the king. The Court of Exchequer was the common law court which heard cases regarding the king's revenue. (The other two courts were the King's Bench, which dealt with criminal cases, and Common Pleas court, which was for civil cases between individuals.)[17]

When Legge lost the case in the Court of Exchequer and could not seize Hanserd's house legally, he brought in Red-Coat Soldiers. They took possession of the house, gardens, and goods by force. Legge also took two hundred pounds that Hanserd had on deposit in the Weavers' Hall and gave it to the king, along with even larger sums of money he had taken from other accounts.[18]

This happened just after Charles II was restored to the throne and wanted more money. To solve the problem, he had levied a new tax which was euphemistically named "The Free and Voluntary Present." Understandably, the king did not question the "present" that Legge had appropriated from Knollys, and, understandably, Hanserd was deeply concerned when he discovered that his house and savings had been taken as an enforced "tax." Hanserd Knollys had his attorney file a suit against the king to recover what was his, but it took years before the case was finally resolved.

His first petition was in 1670, just after his release from imprisonment for disobedience to the Conventicle Act. This was also the same year that he was so sick and so many of his family members died. Having been in Germany, Holland, and prison, he had not been able to live in his own house for nine years. His case, as recorded in *The Calendar of State Papers* reads:

> Petition of Hanserd Knollys to the King for confirmation of his purchase under the late usurped authority of the old artillery ground, Spitalfields, and the armoury room which was obstructed on a former petition by a caveat put in by Col. Legg, late Master of the Ordnance.[19]

Evidently there was no response to Hanserd's suit. Three years later he filed a second petition. In this, he explained that in 1658 he had bought the old armory house on the artillery ground near Spitalfields from the Artillery Company for £300 and spent £460 more in repairs and remodeling. The case had become more complicated.

Colonel Legge had died; his lieutenant, David Walter, had taken over the house. The *State Papers* revealed Hanserd asked that someone be appointed to examine the petition and have Legge's executors and David Walter repay the £760 cost to him. If the decision was not to pay him, Hanserd asked to be granted a low-cost lease for ninety-nine years because he had been denied the use of his property for over ten years and thereby been impoverished. An investigation showed that Colonel Legge had indeed ejected Hanserd from his home illegally and that David Walter was not claiming title to it. Therefore, the investigators recommended to the king that Hanserd be reimbursed or be given a long lease with a low rental fee.

Suddenly, a new difficulty arose. Another investigation revealed that Hanserd had not had a clear title to the property in the first place because the house had originally been built on land belonging to the Crown. He had bought the house without knowing the history of the land beneath it.

To resolve this, the officers of the ordinance held another hearing and decided against giving Hanserd a long-term lease at a low rental fee. By this time, the property, which had been under dispute for years, was now being used in a strange way. According to the papers, it was "necessary for airing the stuff in the Tower."[20] That seems to mean that the land was needed by the army or prison staff as a place to hang out the laundry.

Finally on June 22, 1674, it was recommended that Hanserd be reimbursed the money he spent "as it may best suit his Majesty's occasions." Whether the payment was ever made or not is not known. Although Hanserd won the case, actually paying him may not have "suited" His Majesty. Certainly, he never got back his savings of two hundred pounds that Colonel Legge had illegally taken from his account in Weavers' Hall.

Imagine what it was like for Hanserd Knollys during the years 1670–1674. He had been imprisoned and became desperately ill after he was released. He also lost at least three sons, two grandchildren, and his dearly beloved wife. Furthermore, he had a major struggle trying to regain his property from Charles II's army. Perhaps it seemed like the end of the world.

In 1672, the king issued the Declaration of Indulgence, which removed restrictions on nonconformists and Catholics. The Parliament did not approve, forced the king to withdraw it, and passed what was known as the "Test Act of 1673." This required those in office to take communion and pledge loyalty to the Church of England. Some were unwilling to do it.

Then, a factitious plot was developed in 1678 by a Titus Oates called "The Popish Plot." Oates claimed there was a plan to murder the king, massacre the Protestants, and set up a Catholic government under James, the Duke of York, with the help of the French. The lies of Oates were uncovered as well as the secret financial arrangement that Charles had with Louis IV. Parliament met again and tried to arrange matters so that the Catholic James II could not succeed to the throne, but the House of Lords rejected the plan.

The Last Days of the Apocalypse

The word *apocalypse* refers to a prophetic revelation, usually leading up to a final disaster like the end of the world. One of Hanserd Knollys's last books, printed in 1679 when he was eighty-one years old, was a parable titled *An Exposition of the Book of Revelations.*

The biblical Revelations was sometimes called "the Apocalypse" because that was the first word in the text originally written in Greek. Its theme was the struggle between good and evil and the final triumph of Christ and the Church. The writer of the biblical book conceived it when he was a prisoner on the island of Patmos and had visions of the future. Political enemies of Rome, especially those who refused to worship the emperor, were sent to work in stone quarries on Patmos.

Hanserd intended his own book to be a parable of this ancient writing and on the title page quoted Luke 8:10: "To you it is given to know the Myfteries of the Kingdom of God, but to others in Parables." In the margins, he gave references and summaries in both English and Greek of his most important points. This was to help readers understand the signs of the "last days" and what was to come. He then implored those who might read his book to seek "to communicate the same publicly for the Glory of God, and the Benefit of his Church, and people."

He also made comparisons. In the New Testament book of Revelations, some likened the "Beast" to Nero, who was the cruel Roman ruler at the time it was written. In Hanserd Knollys's parable, Charles II was the "Beast" because of his ongoing oppression and cruelty. London was compared with Jerusalem and England with Egypt. Hanserd knew, from personal experience, what it was like to have civil rights revoked, to have home and money confiscated, and to be imprisoned by the "Beast." With the passion of a prophet he wrote:

> Some of them [i.e., ministers and members of churches] shall be deprived of all their Civil Rights, Priviledges and Liberties: their Estates will be Confiscated, Proscribed, or Decimated &c. Their Person confined, imprisoned or banished &c and in fine all their Livings and livelihood taken from them by the Beast, and his Instruments of Cruelty.[21]

In the same book, while pointing to the signs of the times, he pleaded for toleration of those who held different religious perspectives. Time and again he used the phrase "in my opinion," meaning he did not believe his opinion to be the only one, nor necessarily the right one. Time and time again he pleaded for the clergy to focus on their assigned task of declaring grace. He was also against clergy demanding corporal punishment. In the margin of one page, he used a Bible reference to restate his point:

> Although the Ministers of the Gospel may declare the righteous Judgments of God against ungodly men, according to his written word, yet They ought not to sit in Judgment and pass Sentence of Corporal punishment upon any man. (Luke 12:14; Acts 6:4)[22]

Hanserd sometimes spoke and wrote like a prophet, but he did not view himself that way. Instead, like the writer of Revelations, he most often called himself "servant," and at the end of this parable, as with most of his other books, he signed himself, "The moft unworthy of all Servants of Chrift. Han. Knollys."

Two years later he wrote another short book, *The World That Now Is and the World That Is To Come.* This was also in the prophetic, apocalyptic vein, and again he pleaded for toleration. His plea took the form of frequently asking the reader to "consider" what he was saying. By using the word *consider,* he avoided taking an authoritarian position which so often elicits rejection of an idea. "Consider," he suggested, "that God offered Jesus Christ to poor, lost, miserable sinners."[23] He then went on to say that if people are willing to *consider* and receive this idea, then they can work out their own salvation because of grace working within.

Hanserd Knollys never forgot what John Wheelwright had taught him some sixty years earlier when he was so racked with doubt: if persons are willing to consider and trust, then they will experience spiritual grace.

Religious Freedom and the Bill of Rights

Love had certainly not been Charles II's goal. When Charles died in February 1685, England's political situation became even more explosive. His brother James II ruled for only three years 1685–1688. His reign ended in chaos. Determined to restore Roman Catholic power, James dissolved Parliament and issued two Declarations of Indulgences, one in 1687 and another in 1688. These supposedly gave freedom to all religious denominations.

All previous laws against Catholics and nonconformers were canceled. They were allowed to worship publicly instead of in homes hidden on back streets. James wanted to be thanked for this. Kiffin advised the Baptists that although they could hold their meetings in the open, it was not necessary to thank the king for that.

Furthermore, Protestants interpreted the declarations as favoring Roman Catholics because James promptly appointed numerous Catholics to high office. He also staffed his army with many Catholic officers, in spite of the Test Act forbidding it.

Louis XIV of France was known as a cruel tyrant and a firm Catholic with a strong army that could support James.

Furthermore, James was married to a Catholic and presumably would be succeeded by a Catholic. Anxiety over this was intensified in 1688 when James's son was born. Since the reign of Bloody Mary, all of Protestant England feared the return of a Catholic government.

As a result of this dread, two political parties had developed in Parliament. One party was made up of the "Tories." They were strongly for the monarchy. Most of them were landowners and members of the Church of England. The other party was made up of "Whigs," who favored the power of Parliament over the king. Many Whigs were nonconformists and businessmen. In spite of their strong differences, James's follies drove the Tories and the Whigs into a political alliance that was strong enough to drive him out.

One of the king's serious mistakes affected William Kiffin, Hanserd Knollys's good friend. Two of Kiffin's grandsons, Benjamin and William Hewling, were hung for nonconformity. This took place in spite of the fact that nonconforming families were licensed, for fifty shillings, to protect them from legal proceedings, and the Hewlings had been so licensed. In truth, charging for a license was a way for the king to raise more money. It did not save the people he wanted to get rid of. When James tried to get Kiffin's support for his policies, the bereaved grandfather grimly reminded the king of the death of his grandsons and said "no."

Because of persecutions such as these, in 1688 the Parliament offered the Crown to William III of Orange. He was a Dutch Protestant and the husband of Mary, daughter of James II who was raised Protestant although her parents converted to Catholicism.[24] William was invited to come to England, overthrow James, and save England from Catholicism. When he landed with his troops, Kiffin was one of those who welcomed him. James II escaped to France and the throne was declared empty. On April 11, 1689, the Crown was awarded jointly to William and Mary in Westminster Abbey.

Parliament promptly passed the Toleration Act of May 24, 1689. This act granted the judiciary independence from royal dictate, which was an important step. It also granted freedom of worship to nonconformers if they would take certain oaths of allegiance to the civil government. It allowed Baptist churches to be licensed, although they had to pay tithes to the Church of England. However, licenses were not offered to Catholics and Unitarians, and all dissenters were excluded from public office. Thus, it was a limited toleration.

Parliament next issued the Bill of Rights on December 1, 1689. This granted freedom of speech to Parliament members and protected them from retaliation for what they said in parliamentary debate. The king was restricted and could no longer interfere with Parliament or the courts, nor could he levy taxes without approval.

By the time this Bill of Rights was passed, Hanserd Knollys had only two years to live. He had been exiled, stoned, and imprisoned many times for his beliefs. Yet, he was still writing, preaching, and moderating Baptist association meetings. His voice was weak, but his mind was alert and his faith was powerful. So much so that Benjamin Keach, who was ill and expected to die, was brought to him for final prayers.

When Keach was brought for final prayers, Hanserd added, "Brother Keach, I shall be in heaven before you." And so it was. Hanserd died two years later at the age of ninety-three. Keach, much younger, lived another fifteen years.

During his final two years, Hanserd Knollys sometimes had to be carried to church and other meetings, such as when the Calvinist Baptists held their first national meeting in London in 1689. Two purposes of this national meeting were to seek ways to raise money for impoverished ministers and to help ministerial students better understand Latin, Greek, and Hebrew.[25] These stated purposes were surely a tribute to Hanserd Knollys who, though often impoverished financially, was still rich intellectually, competent in four languages, and deeply respected for his toleration and faith.

His influence continued in many ways, even in America. In 1696, a John Farmer and his wife, who had been part of Hanserd's church, arrived from England and became members of the first Baptist church in Philadelphia.[26]

The Final Imprisonment

Ever a defender of religious liberty, Hanserd Knollys was imprisoned for the last time for six months when he refused to use his great influence to sway Baptists to support the king when he wanted to suspend parts of the penal laws. According to historian Joseph Ivimey, a lord came from the court and asked Hanserd and "his friends of his persuasion" to accept a new act of toleration. It was to allow English nonconformists to worship where they pleased and to have their own ministers. At the same time, they were to be excluded from public office. Hanserd replied to the request, "I am old, and know but few men's minds . . . I am of the opinion that no liberty but what came by Act of Parliament would be very acceptable, because that would be stable, firm, and certain."[27] Hanserd chose prison as a dissenter rather than be a traitor to his own beliefs.

The reasons given for Knollys's final imprisonment were the two previous Acts of Uniformity in 1552 and 1559 during Elizabeth's reign. These acts imposed fines on Protestants and Catholics who did not attend worship in the Church of England. The Clarendon Code, requiring the use of a revised prayer book, was also used against him, as well as the Test Act of 1673, which was passed by Parliament as part of a larger penal code. Based on earlier acts, it excluded nonconformists and Roman Catholics from military and public office by requiring all officers to pledge allegiance to the Church of England and take communion in it. This was the test. Protestants who refused the pledge could not take a government position. Catholics were not allowed to vote, hold public office, own land, publish their own material, or import religious items from Rome. Five years later, another act excluded all Catholics from Parliament; in Scotland, government officials were required to be Protestant.

When Hanserd Knollys's refused to cooperate with the king's wishes, he may have shared the general Protestant apprehension that repealing the acts would have allowed the Catholics to seize control of the country and surpass even the Church of England's intoleration of dissent. He did not want this to happen. He had spent his life preaching and teaching tolerance from a biblical perspective.

Hanserd Knollys continued to defy the Conventicle Acts of 1664 and 1670, which disallowed groups of more than five people to meet in unauthorized worship. He would not conform to an act he considered to be intolerable. Some of his adherents took similar action. The *State Papers* of July–September of 1683 include a letter sent from a James Warner to Mrs. Jane Harvey that speaks of meetings being suppressed generally, "though when I am with Mr. Knowles, we keep our public meetings, which I determine to do to the end."[28] By this time, Hanserd had been released from prison and was doing what he believed was right for him to do—to go on preaching and trying to manage financially so he would owe nothing but love when he died.

The Great Dissenter's Cemetery

Hanserd Knollys died September 19, 1691, after a very brief illness. He was sick for only five weeks and bedridden only ten days before his death. It was during this time that he wrote his last letter to the church where he was pastor. In this letter, he commended them for their faith in times of liberty and persecution, especially when he was in Newgate Prison. He asked them to encourage the "younger brethren," to support his assistant, and thanked them for taking care of the meetinghouse. He also reminded them not to be lukewarm in their faith but to be zealous and to continue to study the Scriptures.

When he died, Hanserd Knollys was buried in Bunhill Fields near his beloved and faithful wife, Anne Cheney. Some of the world's greatest nonconformers were buried at Bunhill Fields, and he ranks as one of the most courageous.

Bunhill Fields, known by several names, was first used as a burial ground by the Saxons. Gradually, it became a cemetery for dissenters because other cemeteries would not accept their bodies. So, bodies were taken there for burial from various parts of England. In the time of Edward VI, the old charnel house of St. Paul's was emptied and many cartloads of bones brought out. Thus, it was called "Bonehill" for a time. Corrupted like many words, *Bonehill* became the present *Bunhill*.[29]

The Society of Friends had its own section in the cemetery and the bones of George Fox (1624–1691), founder of the Quakers, and George Whitehead (1636–1723), another Quaker who was imprisoned on several occasions, lie there. So do the remains of Daniel Defoe (1661–1731), writer of *Robinson Crusoe*, and John Bunyan (1628–1688), author of *Pilgrim's Progress*, whose words are quoted in the preface of this book and who, like Hanserd Knollys, became a Baptist and joined Parliament's army.[30]

Perhaps people such as these, whose faith gave them courage, may not "rest" in peace because tolerance is still on trial and courage is so often required in the cause of freedom. Hanserd Knollys had this kind of faith and courage. Determined to owe nothing but love, he also wrote that when he died he hoped to be greeted by his Lord: "Well done, thou good and faithful Servant. Enter thou also into the Joys of thy Master."

Deeply committed to his personal religious values, he was also committed to social values of independent thinking and toleration. Not a rebel by nature, he was willing to conform to civil and ecclesiastical authorities when conforming did not go against his conscience. When it did, he wrote and spoke against it, in spite of the consequences.

Physically imprisoned many times, Hanserd was always free spiritually because of the strength of his faith and his toleration of others. His enthusiasm for work and his willingness to suffer for what he believed had no end. His last letter to his church closed with words that seem appropriate to use here to end this book:

> And now my dearly beloved Brethren and Sisters, I commit you all to the Word of his Grace, which is able to build you up, and to give you an Inheritance among them which are Sanctified. So I remain, while in this Tabernacle. Hanserd Knollys.[31]

Endnotes

Preface

1. Daniel Boorstin, *Hidden History* (New York: Harper & Row, 1987), 58. Everything he writes is well worth reading.

2. Christopher Hill, *Collected Essays Vol. III: People and Ideas in 17th Century England* (Brighton, Sussex: The Harvester Press, 1986), 3.

3. Barbara Tuchman, *Practicing History: Selected Essays* (New York: Ballantine Books, 1982), 208. A "must" for anyone who enjoys reading history or feels compelled to write about it.

1. Rulers, Reformers, and Discontent

1. See Will Durant, *The Reformation* (New York: MJF Books, 1957), 283. A useful resource for this period.

2. H. G. Wells, *The Outline of History,* Vol. 2 (New York: Garden City Books, 1949), 752—53.

3. George Trevelyan, *England in the Age of Wycliffe* (London: Longman's Green & Co., 1906), 82. For a definitive biography see H. B. Workman, *John Wyclif: A Study of the English Medieval Church,* 2 vols. (1926).

4. Wycliffe, "On the Pope," in *English Works,* F. D. Matthew, ed. (London, 1880), 477.

5. Letter from Erasmus, to John Batt, 12 December 1500, quoted by Preserved Smith, *Erasmus* (New York, 1923).

6. E. E. Reynolds, *The Field Is Won: The Life and Death of St. Thomas More* (Milwaukee: Bruce Publishing, 1968).

7. Quoted in Will Durant, *The Reformation,* 418.

8. *Cambridge Modern History,* 12 vols. (New York, 1907), Vol. II, 713.

9. Johannes Janssen, *History of the German People at the Close of the Middle Ages,* Vol. XIV (St. Louis, Mo.: n.d.), 503. For current research, see *Calvinus Sacrae Scripturae Professor: Calvin as Confessor of Holy Scripture,* Wilhelm H. Neuser, ed. (Grand Rapids, Mich.: Wm. B. Eerdmans Publishing Co., 1994).

10. Roland Bainton, *Hunted Heretic: The Life of Michael Servetus* (Boston: Beacon Press, 1953), 209—11.

11. Joyce Youings, *The Dissolution of the Monasteries* (London: Allen & Unwin; New York: Barnes & Noble, 1971).

12. W. K. Jordan, *Edward VI: The Young King* (Cambridge, Mass.: Harvard Univ. Press, 1968).

13. Hester W. Chapman, *Lady Jane Grey: October 1537—February 1554* (Boston: Little, Brown, 1963). See also, Karen Lindsey, *Divorced, Beheaded, Survived* (Reading, Mass.: Addison-Wesley Publishing, 1995).

14. Edward B. Underhill, "Historical Introduction," *The Records of the Church of Christ Meeting at Broadmead Bristol: 1640—1687* (London: J. Haddon, 1848).

15. David H. Wilson, *King James VI and I* (London: Johnathan Cape, 1956). See also Antonia Fraser, *King James VI of Scotland, I of England* (N.Y. Knopf, 1975).

16. David Matthew, *James I* (London: Eyre & Spottiswoode, 1967). Well-organized and with extensive references.

17. Alden Vaughan, *The Puritan Tradition in America 1620—1730* (New York: Harper & Row, 1972), 11. Contains a wealth of information on sources.

18. J. P. Kenyon, *Dictionary of British History* (Hertfordshire: Wordworth, 1994). An indispensable brief guide.

19. Catherine Drinker Bowen, *The Lion and the Throne: The Life and Times of Sir Edward Coke* (Boston: Little, Brown, & Co., 1956), 35.

20. M. W. Beresford, *The Lay Subsidies and the Poll Taxes* (Canterbury: Phillimore & Co., 1963).

2. Rebellion and Family History

1. *Letters and Papers Foreign and Domestic of the Reign of Henry VIII*, Vols. 11 and 12, James Gardener, ed., and summarized by R. W. Goulding, Loath Old Corporation Record (Lowth, 1891), 186–95.

2. The Hanserd Knollys Society, *Publication of the Works of Early English Writers* (London, n.d.).

3. Thomas Armitage, *A History of the Baptists* (New York: Bryan and Taylor, 1887), 426–27.

4. J. M. Ross, "The Theology of Baptism in Baptist History" *The Baptist Quarterly*, Vol XV #3 (July 1953).

5. Armitage, *A History of the Baptists*, 427.

6. Walter Wilson, *The History and Antiquities of Dissenting Churches*, Vol. I. (London, 1808). Includes information about the ministers in these churches.

7. David Hey, *The Oxford Guide to Family History* (Oxford, England: Oxford University Press, 1993), 15–61.

8. Alan Rogers, *A History of Lincolnshire* (Chichester, Sussex: Phillimore & Co., 1985).

9. Quoted in *Lincoln Wills*, Vol. II, C. W. Foster, ed. (Horncastle: W. K. Norton & Sons, 1918), xxii.

10. For her opening speech to Parliament, see J. A. Froude, *Reign of Elizabeth*, Vol. I (Everyman's Library), 11.

11. Lincoln Record Society Publications 23, xxi.

12. *Gentleman's Magazine* (London, April 1764), 156.

13. Will and Ariel Durant, *The Age of Reason Begins* (New York: MJF Books, 1961), 3–45.

14. A. L. Rowse, *Sir Walter Raleigh: His Family and Private Life* (New York: Harpers & Bros., 1962).

15. Sir Walter Raleigh, *Selection* (Oxford, 1917), and Willard Wallace, *Sir Walter Raleigh* (Princeton: University Press, 1906), 241–42, Raleigh's *Works VIII*, 591.

16. James Culross, *Hanserd Knollys: A Minister and Witness of Jesus Christ, 1598–1691* (London: Alexander and Shepheard, 1895), 28.

17. A. R. Maddison, *Lincolnshire Wills, First Series, 1500–1600* (Lincoln: James Williamson, 1888), xv.

18. Peter Heath, *The English Parish Clergy on the Eve of the Reformation* (London: Routledge and Kegan Paul, 1969), 113.

19. See also Edward Gillett, *A History of Grimsby* (London: Oxford University Press, 1970), 94.

20. Maddison's information is from Harlequin MS 1052. Landowne MSS.207, 275.

21. George Matthews, ed., *Abstracts of Probate Acts of the Prerogative Court of Canterbury* (Surry, Sylvanhurst, Godalming, 1926), 164.

22. A. R. Maddison, ed., *Lincolnshire Wills, Second Series, 1600–1617* (Lincoln: James Williamson, 1891), 58–59.

23. David Hey, *The Oxford Guide to Family History*, 38–39.

24. A. R. Maddison, *Lincoln Pedigrees, I*, 451.

25. Parish records of St. Lawrence Church, Snarford, Lincolnshire.

26. Maddison, *Lincolnshire Wills I, 1500–1600*, #155.

27. *Calendar of Lincoln Wills, Vol. II: 1506–1600* (London: British Record Society, 1902), 171.

28. Christine Garrett, *The Marian Exiles* (Cambridge University Press, 1938. Reprinted 1966). An important book with detailed research.

29. B. R. White, *The English Baptists of the 17th Century* (London: Baptist Historical Society, 1983). A valuable brief introduction to the General and Particular Baptists and the differences between separatism and Puritanism. Also by B. R. White, *The English Separatist Tradition* (London: Oxford University Press, 1971).

30. John Smyth, *The Works of John Smyth Fellow of Christ's College 1594–1598*, Vol. I, W. T. Whitley, ed. (Cambridge: For the Baptist Historical Society, 1915), liv. See also James R. Coggins, *John Smyth's Congregation* (Ontario: Hearald Press, 1991).

31. Stephen Brachlow, *The Communion of the Saints: Radical Puritan and Separatist Ecclesiology 1570–1625* (New York: Oxford University Press, 1988). An academic study of Elizabethan ecclesiastical ideals used by Henry Jacob and John Robinson.

32. John Robinson, *On the Lawfulness of Hearing Ministers in the Church of England* (1634). See also F. Powicke, *J. Robinson* (1620).

33. William Bradford, *History of the Plymouth Plantation: 1620–47* (New York: Alfred Knopf, 1959).

34. J. E. Neale, *Elizabeth and Her Parliaments 1584–1601* (New York: W. W. Norton, 1966).

35. C. W. Foster, ed., *State of the Church in the Reigns of Elizabeth and James I*, Vol. 1 (Lincoln Record Society, 1926).

36. W. D. J. Cargill Thompson, "Sir Francis Knollys's Campaign Against the *Jure Divino* Theory of the Episcopy" in *The Dissenting Tradition*, C. Robert Cole and Michael Moody, eds. (Athens: Ohio University Press, 1975), 39–77.

3. Cambridge and Conversion

1. Terrick V. H. Fitz Hugh, *The Dictionary of Genealogy* (New Jersey: Barnes & Noble, 1985), 136.

2. Arthur Young, *A General View of the Agriculture of the County of Lincoln*, 8 vols. (London, 1799).

3. Harlein MS. 618. (Printed in *Tudor Lincolnshire* by Gerald Hodgett for the History of Lincolnshire Committee, 1975), 193.

4. Hanserd Knollys, *Life and Death*, 8.

5. G. Lipscomb, *History and Antiquities of the County of Buckingham* (London, 1847).

6. *The State of the Church Volume I*, Vol. 23 (Lincoln Record Society, 1926), 200.

7. Bob Lincoln, *The Rise of Grimsby*, Vol. I (London: Farnol, Eades, Irvine, and Co., 1913), 105–07.

8. Thomas Allen, *History of the County of Lincoln* (London: John Saunders, 1834), 227–28.

9. A. R. Maddison, *Lincolnshire Wills, Second Series, 1600–1617* (Lincoln: James Williamson, 1891), #157.

10. Thomas Allen, *History of the County of Lincoln*, Vol. IV (London: John Saunders, 1834), 240–41.

11. Hanserd Knollys, *Life and Death*.

12. Bob Lincoln, *The Rise of Grimsby*, Vol. I (London: Farnol, Eades, Irvine & Co., 1913), 104.

13. Gerald Hodgett, *Tudor Lincolnshire* (Lincoln: History of Lincolnshire Commission, 1975), 139–49. A detailed history of the fifteenth and sixteenth centuries.

14. *Life and Death*, 2–3.

15. V. H. H. Green, *Religion at Oxford and Cambridge* (London: SCM Press, 1964). A fine history with extensive academic endnotes.

16. Quoted in H. C. Porter, *Reformation and Reaction in Tudor Cambridge* (Cambridge: Cambridge University Press, 1958), 211.

17. Henry Martyn Dexter and Morton Dexter, *The England and Holland of the Pilgrims* (Baltimore Publishing Company, 1978), 257.

18. John Venn and J. A. Venn, eds., *Alumni Cantabrigienses,* Part I, Vol. III (Cambridge University Press, 1924), 31.

19. F. A. Reeve, *Cambridge* (New York: Hastings House, 1964), 28.

20. Arthur Gray, *Cambridge History* (Boston: Houghton Mifflin Company, 1927), 106–08.

21. V. H. H. Green, *Religion at Oxford and Cambridge* (London: SCM Press, 1964), 85–87.

22. Carlisle, *Endowed Grammar Schools in England and Wales,* Vol. I, 797.

23. Champlin Burrage, *The English Dissenters Vol. I: 1550–1641* (New York: Russell and Russell, 1912. Reissued 1967), 94–117.

24. *Life and Death,* 5–7.

25. A. R. Maddison, ed., *Lincolnshire Pedigrees,* Vol. 50 (London: Harleian Society, 1902), 242–44.

26. *Publications of the Lincoln Record Society*, Vol. II (Lincoln, 1914), 24.

27. Maddison, *Lincolnshire Wills, II, 1660–1617,* #32.

28. *Dictionary of National Biography.* Useful but needs checking.

29. Thomas Cooper, *Lincoln Episcopal Records 1571–1584.* C. W. Foster, ed. (Printed for the Lincoln Record Society, 1912), 177–78. These records from the Bishop's *Act Book and Register,* and the *Liber Cleri* of 1576 are invaluable.

30. Ernest E. Crake, *Parish Registers of St. Giles Church, Scarthoe* (Lincoln: J. W. Ruddock, 1926), 15.

31. Conrad Russell, *The Crisis of Parliaments: 1509–1660* (Oxford University Press, 1971), 314–15.

32. *Life and Death,* 11.

33. *Life and Death,* 15.

4. The Elect and Elected in Colonial New England

1. Quoted in George Frances Marlowe, *Churches of Old New England* (New York: MacMillan Co., 1947), 7.

2. Alden Vaughan, ed., *The Puritan Tradition in America 1620–1730* (New York: Harper & Row, 1972), 63–70.

3. Capt. John Smith, *Travels and Works,* 3 vols. (Reprint, Univ. of North Carolina, 1986.), Vol. II, 722.

4. Henry Dexter and Morton Dexter, *The England and Holland of the Pilgrims* (Baltimore: Genealogical Publishing Co., 1978).

5. Samuel G. Drake, *The History and Antiquities of Boston: 1630–1770* (Boston: L. Stevens, 1856), 218.

6. See William G. McLoughlin, *Soul Liberty: The Baptist Struggle in New England, 1630–1833* (University Press of New England, 1991).

7. Drake, *The History and Antiquities of Boston,* 131.

8. Edmund S. Morgan, *The Puritan Dilemma* (Boston: Little, Brown, & Co., 1958). Well-researched on Winthrop and others.

9. Quoted in Reginald C. Dudding, *History of the Parish and Manors of Alford with Rigsby and Ailby with Some Account of Well in the County of Lincoln* (Alford, Lincolnshire, 1931), 146.

10. Dudding, *History of the Parish and Manors of Alford with Rigsby and Ailby*, 145–47.

11. Emily Easton, *Roger Williams: Prophet and Pioneer* (Boston: Houghton Mifflin Co., 1930), 107.

12. Champlin Burrage, *The Early English Dissenters*, Vol. II (New York: Russell & Russell), 262–63.

13. Clive Holmes, *Seventeenth Century Lincolnshire* (Lincoln: Society of Lincolnshire History and Archeology, 1908), 112–13.

14. Catherine Drinker Bowen, *The Lion and the Throne: The Life and Times of Sir Edward Coke* (Boston: Little, Brown & Co., 1956).

15. Quoted by Emily Easton, *Roger Williams*, 91.

16. Roger Williams, "Mr. Cotton's Letter, Examined and Answered" (London 1644), printed in *Bloody Tenent of Persecution*, Edward Brian Underhill, ed. (London: J. Haddon, 1848), 439.

17. John Winthrop, *The History of New England* (Boston: Little Brown, 1853). This contains Winthrop's journal. The Massachusetts Historical Society also published Winthrop's papers and correspondence in five volumes, *The Winthrop Papers*.

18. Selma Williams, *Divine Rebel: The Life of Anne Marbury Hutchinson* (New York: Holt, Rinehard, & Winston, 1981).

19. Ben Barker-Benfield, "Anne Hutchinson and the Puritan Attitude Toward Women" in *Anne Hutchinson: Troubler of the Puritan Zion*, Frances Bremer, ed. (Huntington, N.Y.: Robert Krieger Publishing Co., 1981), 99–112.

20. Rosemary Keller, "New England Women: Ideology and Experience in First Generation Puritanism," Rosemary Radford Ruether and Rosemary Skinner Keller, ed., *Women and Religion in America Vol. II: The Colonial and Revolutionary Periods* (San Francisco: Harper & Row, 1982), 132–92.

21. Charles H. Bell, *History of the Town of Exeter, New Hampshire* (Boston: Farwell & Co., 1888), 4–8, 431–33, 454–55.

22. George Bancroft, *History of the United States of America: Vol. I* (Routledge, 1891), 272.

23. Drake, *The History and Antiquities of Boston*, 219.

24. Nathaniel Bouton, *Provincial Papers of New Hampshire, Vol. I, 1623–1686* (Concord: George Jenks, 1867), 130–31.

25. "Memoir of Governor Hutchinson," *New England Historical and Genealogical Record*, Vol. I, 4, (October 1847), 298.

26. Quoted by Warren Brown, *History of Hampton Falls* (Manchester: John Clark Co., 1900), 166.

27. Joseph Dow, *History of Hampton, NH, Vol. II* (Salem, Maine: Salem Press, 1893), 1039–40. Dow's genealogy of Hampton needs careful comparison with George F. Sanborn and Melinda L. Sanborn, *Vital Records of Hampton, New Hampshire, Vol. I* (Boston: New England Historic Genealogical Society, 1992).

28. *Life and Death*, 3.

5. Escapes and Banishments

1. David Hey, *The Oxford Guide to Family History* (Oxford: Oxford University Press, 1993), 113.

2. *Life and Death*, 17.

3. James Savage, *Winthrop's History*, I (Boston: Little & Brown, 1853), 392.

4. *New Hampshire Provincial Papers*, 1:68, 208.

5. Jeremy Belknap, *The History of New Hampshire*, Vol. I, 1784 (Dover: Stevens, Ela, and Wadleigh, 1831. Reprinted by Heritage, 1992).

6. Belknap, *The History of New Hampshire*, 23–24.

7. Nathaniel Boulton, *Documents and Records of the Province of New Hampshire: 1623–1686*, Vol. I (Concord: George Jenks, State Printer, 1867), 129–33. See page 118 for Boulton's statement of sources used.

8. Boulton, *Documents and Records of New Hampshire: 1623–1686*, 119–24.

9. Thomas Leckford, *Plain Dealing or News from New England*, J. Hammond Trumbull, ed. (Reprinted New York: Garrett Press, 1970), 102–04. Leckford mentions that Dover was briefly called "Northam," alias "Pafcattaaqua."

10. *Suffolk Deeds, Liber I* (Boston: Rockwell & Churchill, 1880), #19. The pages are not numbered in this book; the numbers given are case numbers.

11. Nathaniel Boulton, "The Dover Combination," *New Hampshire Papers*, Vol. 27 (Concord, N.H.: Edward Jenks Printer, 1877), 700–01.

12. See also C. E. Potter, *History of Manchester* (Manchester, N.H.: C. E. Potter Publishing, 1856), 101–16. Written with more fire than most histories.

13. Alonzo Hall Quint, *Historical Memoranda of Ancient Dover Vol. I*, John Scales, ed. (Dover, N.H.: 1900), 21.

14. Boulton, *Documents and Records of New Hampshire*, Vol. I, 126. See also Vol. X, 701–02.

15. Boulton, 197.

16. *Suffolk Deeds, Liber I* (Boston: Rockwell and Churchill, 1880), 21.

17. *Life and Death*, 18.

18. *Life and Death*, 18.

19. *The Founders: Portraits of Persons Born Abroad Who Came to the Colonies in North America Before the Year 1701* (Boston, Mass.: Vol. III, 1926. Reprinted: Baltimore Pub., 1976).

20. *Life and Death*, 8.

21. *Life and Death*, 28.

22. Microfilm of *Parish Records, Goulceby*, FHL 432506.

23. Bulstrode Whitelocke, *Memorials of the English Affairs*, Vol. II (London: P. Ponder, 1682), 476 f.

24. Bower Marsh and Frederic A. Crisp, *Alumni Carthusiani: A Record of the Foundation Scholars of Charterhouse, 1614–1872* (Privately printed, 1913). Original records were used for this and, according to the master of Charterhouse, were copied accurately.

25. By personal correspondence with Charterhouse.

26. William Laud, *A Speech Delivered in the Star Chamber, June 14, 1637* (Printed by Richard Badger, 1637), 9.

27. James Culross, *Hanserd Knollys* (London: Alexander and Shepheard, 1895), 28.

28. Hanserd Knollys, *A Moderate Answer to Dr. Bastwick's Book Called Independence Not God's Ordinance* (London: Printed by Jane Coe, 1645).

29. Champlin Burrage, *The Early English Dissenters*, Vol. I (New York: Russell & Russell, 1912. Reissued 1967), 367–68.

6. War without Wisdom

1. Mark Charles Fissel, *The Bishops' Wars: Charles I Campaigns Against Scotland, 1638–1640* (Cambridge: University Press, 1994), 111–52.

2. William Haller, *The Rise of Puritanism* (Morningside Heights, New York: Columbia University Press, 1938), 325–63.

3. W. F. Webster (transcriber), *Protestation Returns 1641/2 Lincolnshire* (Mapperley, Nottingham, n.d.).

4. Helen Douglas-Irvine, *History of London* (New York: James Pott & Co., 1912), 227. A very readable source.

5. Maurice Ashley, ed., *Cromwell* (New Jersey: Prentice Hall, 1969), 13. A well-balanced compilation of some of Cromwell's letters with editorial remarks.

6. J. P. Kenyon, *Stuart England* (London: Penguin Books, 1978), 171.

7. Thomas D. Macaulay, *History of England,* Vol. I (Reprinted N.Y.: Harper & Bros., 1879), 128.

8. Will Durant, *The Age of Louis XIV* (New York: MJF Books, 1963), 194.

9. Ivan Roots, *The Great Rebellion: 1642–1666* (London: Batsford, 1966). See also Geoffrey Aylmer, *The Struggle for the Constitution: 1603–1689,* 2nd ed. (New York: Humanities Press, 1968).

10. Leo F. Solt, *Saints in Arms* (Stanford, Calif.: Stanford University Press, 1959), 32.

11. Hugh Barbour, *The Quakers in Puritan England* (Yale University Press, 1964). Compare wth Barry Reay, *The Quakers and the English Revolution* (New York: St. Martin's Press, 1985), also note the foreword by Christopher Hill.

12. Alan Rogers, *The History of Lincolnshire* (Phillimore: Chichester, Sussex, 1985).

13. See Philip Taylor, ed., *The Origins of the English Civil War: Conspiracy, Crusade, or Class Conflict?* (Boston: D. C. Heath & Co., 1960). A series of essays with opposing views on the cause of the war.

14. Thomas Edwards, *Gangraena,* Vol. III (1646), 97f. Facsimile ed. by M. M. Goldsmith & Ivan Roots (Exeter: Rota Press, 1977).

15. Sidney Lee, ed., *Dictionary of National Biography,* Vol. XXI (London: Smith, Eldert & Co., 1909), 502–05.

16. *Calendar of State Papers: 1644–5,* 5.

17. Quoted in *Dictionary of National Biography,* Vol. XIII, 676.

18. Edward Totham, "Lincolnshire and the Great Civil War" in *Memorials of Old Lincolnshire,* E. Manuel Sympson, ed. (London: George Allen & Sons, 1911), 267. See also *Transactions of the Royal Historical Society* (1899), 53.

19. Anne Laurence, *Parliamentary Army Chaplains 1642–1651* (A Royal Historical Society Publication, Suffolk: Boydell Press, 1990).

20. *Calendar of State Papers 1661–8,* 167, 179, 234, 264.

21. *Life and Death,* 20.

22. Quoted by Solt, *Saints in Arms,* 51–52.

23. Charles H. Firth, *Oliver Cromwell and the Rule of the Puritans in England* (London: Putnam, 1901. Reprinted 1935.).

24. Laurence, *Parliamentary Army Chaplains,* 58, 143.

25. C. V. Wedgewood, *The Trial of Charles I* (London: Collins, 1964), 188–93. The book is well-documented with numerous early references and the discrepancies between them are noted.

26. Murray Tolmie, *The Triumph of the Saints: The Separate Churches of London 1616–1649* (London: Cambridge University Press, 1977), 8.

27. J. Gurhill, ed., *Gainsborough Parish Registers* (London: Elliot Stock, 1890), 38–39.

28. Edward B. Underhill, *Confessions of Faith and Other Public Documents* (London: Handon, Brothers, & Co. for the Hanserd Knollys Society, 1854), 13.

29. James R. Coggins, *John Smyth's Congregation* (Scottdale, Penn., 1649. Reprinted 1991.).

30. E. B. Whitley, *History of the British Baptists,* 2nd ed. (London: Kingsgate Press, 1932), 29–35.

31. H. Leon McBeth, *The Baptist Heritage* (Nashville: Broadman Press, 1987). A most valuable general study of four centuries of Baptist history. Also by the same author, *English Baptist Literature on Religious Liberty to 1689* (New York: Armo Press, 1980).

32. Joseph Ivimey, *History of the English Baptists, Vol. I* (London: Printed for the author, 1811), 179–80.

33. *Transactions,* Vol. I (Britain: Baptist Historical Society, 1908–1931), 242, 245.

34. *State Papers: Domestic Series, 1655–56,* 319.

35. G. F. S. Ellens, "The Ranters Ranting: Reflecting on a Ranting Counter Culture," *Church History*, Vol. 40, 91–107.

36. George Masse, "Puritan Radicalism and the Enlightenment," *Church History*, Vol. 29, 424–39.

37. William Haller and Godfrey Davies, eds., *The Leveller Tracts: 1647–1653* (Gloucester, Mass.: Peter Smith, 1964).

38. H. N. Brailsford, Christopher Hill, ed., *The Levellers and the English Revolution* (California, Stanford University Press, 1961), 85–86.

39. Eduard Bernstein, *Cromwell and Communism* (New York: Schocken Books, 1930). Emphasizes socialistic views and the civil wars as class conflicts.

40. See lecture by B. R. White, *Hanserd Knollys and Radical Dissent in the 17th Century* (London, Dr. William's Library, 1977), for a summary of Knollys's brief autobiography.

41. E. B. Underhill, *Confessions of Faith.*

42. Edward Bean Underhill, *Records of the Churches of Christ Gathered at Fenstanton, Warboys, and Hexham, 1644–1720* (London: Haddon Bros., 1854). See index for letters of these churches.

43. Thomas Edwards, *Gangraena*, Vol. III (1646), 12.

44. Helen Douglas-Irvine, *History of London* (New York: James Pott & Co., 1912), 227. A very readable source.

45. *State Papers: Domestic Series, 1655–56,* 319.

46. *Dictionary of National Biography*, Vol. XVI, 762.

47. Hanserd Knollys, *Exposition of the First Chapter of the Song of Solomon* (London, 1653). From the title page.

48. Knollys, *Exposition of the First Chapter of the Song of Solomon*, 56.

7. Trials and More Trials

1. Will Durant, *The Age of Reason Begins* (New York: MJF Books, 1961), 480.

2. K. Fischer, *Descartes and His School,* 212.

3. Will Durant, *Age of Louis XIV,* 224.

4. 2 Chronicles 24:21.

5. Cited in Josephy Ivimey, *A History of the English Baptists* (London, 1811), Vol. I, 189–90.

6. Lawrence Clarkson, *The Lost Sheep Found* (London, 1660), 10–19.

7. W. E. Foster, ed., *The Plundered Ministers of Lincolnshire: Extracts From Minutes of the Committee,* (Guildford: Billing and Sons).

8. *Life and Death,* 20.

9. Ashley Klaiber, *The Story of the Suffolk Baptists* (London: The Kingsgate Press, n.d.), 204.

10. E. I. Woodward, *History of England* (Harper & Row, 1962), 106.

11. Maurice Ashley, ed., *Cromwell* (New Jersey: Prentice Hall, 1969), 32–34.

12. Carlyle, *Cromwell,* Vol. II, 485, 589.

13. Charles H. Firth, *Oliver Cromwell and the Rule of the Puritans in England* (London: Putnam, 1901).

14. *State Papers: Domestic Series, 1652–53,* 240.

15. "Letters and Papers Relating to the Navy," *State Papers: Domestic Series, 1655–56,* 484.

16. Quoted in *Transactions of the Congregational Historical Society, Vol. III,* 1907–1908, T. G. Crippen, ed. (London: Published for the Society), 191–201.

17. G. Lyon Turner, "The Religious Condition in London in 1672," *Transactions of the Congregational Historical Society, Vol. III* (London: Published for the Society, 1907–1908), 200.

18. Gilbert Burnet, *History of My Own Time, Vol. I* (Oxford University Press, 1833), book 2, ch. 2.

19. Louise F. Brown, *The Political Activities of the Baptists and the Fifth Monarchy Men in England during the Interregnum* (London: Oxford University Press, 1912). Extensive endnotes with primary sources.

20. T. B. Howell, *A Complete Collection of State Trials VI* (London, 1816), 67–68, 106–17.

21. B. S. Capp, *The Fifth Monarchy Men* (Totowa, N.J.: Rowman and Littlefield, 1972), 102–03. A most authoritative and comprehensive work.

22. *Life and Death,* 25.

23. Arthur Griffiths, *The Chronicles of Newgate* (London: Chapman and Hall, 1884).

24. William Haller, *The Rise of Puritanism* (New York: Cambridge University Press, 1938), 229.

25. W. T. Whitley, *The Baptists of London* (1928).

26. *State Papers, 1661–62, Vol. XLI,* 87–98.

27. A. A. Reid, "Benjamin Keach, 1640," *The Baptist Quarterly,* Vol. X, #2 (April 1940), 71–72.

28. Ivimey, *History of the Baptists, Vol. I,* 339–55.

29. *Life and Death,* 27.

30. David Gilman, "An Outline of the History of Psalmody," *Baptist Quarterly Review* (London: Baptist Review Assoc., 1889), 166–74.

31. Quoted in Will Durant, *The Reformation* (New York: MJF Books, 1957), 419.

32. B. R. White, *Hanserd Knollys and Radical Dissent in the 17th Century* (London: Dr. Williams's Trust, 1977), 28. A lecture with extensive endnotes.

33. Katherine Sutton, *A Christian Woman's Experiences of the Glorious Working of God's True Grace* (Rotterdam, 1663).

34. Gordon Rupp, *Religion in England 1688–1791* (Oxford: Clarendon Press, 1986). A lively yet scholarly book.

35. Henry Waters, *Genealogical Gleanings in England, Vol. II* (Boston: New England Historical Society, 1901), 974.

36. Waters, *Genealogical Gleanings in Boston, Vol. II,* 1210–11. Also in *New England Genealogical and Historical Register,* Vol. 50, 423–24.

8. To Owe Nothing but Love

1. Edward Hyde, *The History of the Rebellion and Civil Wars in England Beginning in the Year 1641* (Oxford University Press. Reprint 1958.).

2. Thomas H. Lister, *Edward, First Earl of Clarendon, 3 Vol.* (London: Longman, Orne, Brown, Green, and Longmans, 1837–1838).

3. Ivimey, *History of the English Baptists*, 355.

4. Quoted in A. Reeve, *Cambridge* (New York: Hastings House, 1964), 64.

5. Henry Wheatley, ed., *The Diary of Samuel Pepys,* Vol. I (New York: Random House, 1946), 1113.

6. *Calendar of State Papers: Domestic Series 1666–67*, 95.

7. B. R. White, "William Kiffin: Baptist, Pioneer, and Citizen of London," *Baptist History and Heritage,* Vol. 2, #1, January 1967.

8. W. T. Whitley, *A History of the British Baptists,* rev. ed. (London: Kingsgate Press, 1932), 130–31.

9. Thomas Crosby, *History of the English Baptists,* Vol. III (London: John Robinson, 1738–1740), 4.

10. B. R. White, "William Kiffin," *Baptist History and Heritage,* 91–103

11. *Life and Death*, 32.

12. *Life and Death*, 34.

13. E. Crake, *Parish Registers of St. Giles, Scarthoe* (1926), 19.

14. James Culross, *Hanserd Knollys* (London: Alexander and Shepheard, 1895), 33.

15. Henry H. Harrison, ed., *Probate Records of the Province of New Hampshire, Vol. II,* State Paper Series, Vol. 3, 2 (Bristol, N.H.: R. W. Musgrove, 1914. Reprint, Heritage Books, 1989.).

16. *Life and Death*, 27.

17. Conrad Russell, *The Crises of Parliament: 1509–1600* (London: Oxford University Press, 1971). Well-organized and referenced. For discussion of courts, 49–55, 59–61.

18. *Life and Death*, 25.

19. *Calendar of State Papers, Nov. 1st, 1673 to Feb. 28, 1675,* F. H. Blackburne Daniell, ed. (London: Printed for His Majesty's Stationery Office by Mackie and Co. Ltd., 1904), 143.

20. *Calendar of State Papers: Domestic Series,* Vol. 16, 66–67.

21. Hanserd Knollys, *An Exposition of the Book of Revelations* (London, 1679).

22. Knollys, *An Exposition of the Book of Revelations*, 11.

23. Knollys, *The World That Now Is and the World That Is To Come* (London: Thomas Snowden, 1681).

24. H. W. Chapman, *Mary II, Queen of England* (London: Cape Publishing, 1953).

25. B. R. White, "The Twilight of Puritanism in the Years before and after 1688," *From Persecution to Toleration,* Ole Peter Grell, ed. (New York: Oxford University Press, 1991), 307–30.

26. David Benedict, *A General History of the Baptist Denomination in America. Vol. I* (Boston: Lincoln and Edmands, 1813), 585.

27. Joseph Ivimey, *A History of the English Baptists,* Vol. I (London, 1811–1830), 411.

28. *State Papers: Domestic Series,* July–September 1683, 196–97.

29. W. T. Whitley, "Bunhill Fields," *Baptist Quarterly*, Vol. 5, January 1931, 220–26.

30. Susan Easton Black, *Bunhill Fields: The Great Dissenter's Burial Ground* (Provo, Utah: Brigham Young University, 1990).

31. Knollys, "To the Church Whereof I Am Pastor," *Life and Death*.

Selected Bibliography

This selected bibliography reflects the diversity of sources used for this book and is included as a convenience for those who wish to pursue further study. It is not a complete list of all the records and references I have consulted. The chapter endnotes are more detailed and inclusive. The wide array of writings by Hanserd Knollys are too numerous to list here. His tiny book of forty-five pages which constituted his memoirs was published posthumously with an especially long title on its cover:

> *The Life and Death of that Old Disciple of Chriſt, and Eminent Minister of the Gospel, Mr. Hanserd Knollys, Who Dyed in the Ninety Third Year of his Age. Written by his own Hand to the year 1672. And continued in General, in an Epiſtle by Mr. Vvilliam Kiffin. To which is added, His laſt Legacy to the Church.* London, 1692.

Armitage, Thomas. *A History of the Baptists.* New York, 1887.

Ashley, Maurice, ed., *Cromwell.* New Jersey, 1969.

Aylmer, Geoffrey. *The Struggle for the Constitution: 1603—1689,* 2nd ed. New York, 1968.

Beresford, M. W. *The Lay Subsidies and the Poll Taxes.* Canterbury, 1963.

Bernstein, Eduard. *Cromwell and Communism.* New York, 1930.

Blackburne, F. H. Daniell, ed. *Calendar of State Papers, Nov. 1st, 1673 to Feb. 28, 1675.* London, 1904.

Boorstin, Daniel. *Hidden History.* New York, 1987.

Boulton, Nathaniel. *Documents and Records of the Province of New Hampshire: 1623—1686,* Vol. I. Concord, 1867.

Bowen, Catherine Drinker. *The Lion and the Throne: The Life and Times of Sir Edward Cole.* Boston, 1956.

Brachlow, Stephen, *The Communion of the Saints: Radical Puritan and Separatist Ecclesiology 1570—1625.* New York, 1988.

Bremer, Frances, ed. *Anne Hutchinson: Troubler of the Puritan Zion.* Huntington, New York, 1981.

Burrage, Champlin. *The English Dissenters Vol. I: 1550—1641.* New York, reissued 1967.

Capp, B. S. *The Fifth Monarchy Men.* Totowa, N.J., 1972.

Coggins, James R. *John Smyth's Congregation.* Ontario, 1991.

Cooper, Thomas. *Lincoln Episcopal Records 1571—1584,* C. W. Foster, ed. Lincoln, 1912.

Crosby, Thomas. *History of the English Baptists,* Vol. III. London, 1738—40.

Culross, James. *Hanserd Knollys: A Minister and Witness of Jesus Christ, 1598—1691.* London, 1895.

Dexter, Henry Martyn and Morton. *The England and Holland of the Pilgrims.* Baltimore, 1978.

Drake, Samuel G. *The History and Antiquities of Boston: 1630—1770.* Boston, 1856.

Duncan, Pope. *Hanserd Knollys: 17th Century Baptist.* Nashville, 1965.

Easton, Emily. *Roger Williams: Prophet and Pioneer.* Boston, 1930.

Edwards, Thomas. *Gangraena,* 4 vols. Facsimile ed. by M. M. Goldsmith & Ivan Roots, 1977.

Firth, Charles H. *Oliver Cromwell and the Rule of the Puritans in England*. London, reprinted, 1935.

Fissel, Mark Charles. *The Bishops' Wars: Charles I Campaigns Against Scotland, 1638–1640*. Cambridge, 1994.

Garrett, Christine. *The Marian Exiles*. Cambridge, 1938, 1966.

Gillett, Edward. *A History of Grimsby*. London, 1970.

Green, V. H. H. *Religion at Oxford and Cambridge*. London, 1964.

Haller, William and Godfrey Davies, ed. *The Leveller Tracts: 1647–1653*. Gloucester, 1964.

Heath, Peter. *The English Parish Clergy on the Eve of the Reformation*. London, 1969.

Hey, David. *The Oxford Guide to Family History*. Oxford, 1993.

Hill, Christopher. *Collected Essays*, Vol. II and III. Sussex, 1986.

Hodgett, Gerald. *Tudor Lincolnshire*. Lincoln, 1975.

Holmes, Clive. *Seventeenth Century Lincolnshire*. Lincoln, 1908.

Hyde, Edward. *The History of the Rebellion and Civil Wars in England Beginning in the Year 1641*. Oxford, 1702. Reprinted 1958.

Ivimey, Joseph. *History of the English Baptists*, 4 vols. London, 1811.

Kenyon, J. P. *Dictionary of British History*. Hertfordshire, 1994.

Klaiber, Ashley. *The Story of the Suffolk Baptists*. London, n.d.

Leckford, Thomas. *Plain Dealing or News from New England*, J. Hammond Trumbull, ed. New York, reprinted, 1970.

Lincoln, Bob. *The Rise of Grimsby*, Vol. I. London, 1913.

Marsh, Bower and Frederic A. Crisp. *Alumni Carthusiani: A Record of the Foundation Scholars of Charterhouse, 1614–1872*. 1913.

Matthew, David. *James I*. London, 1967.

Matthews, George, ed. *Abstracts of Probate Acts of the Prerogative Court of Canterbury*. 1926.

McLoughlin, William G. *Soul Liberty: The Baptist Struggle in New England, 1630–1833*. Providence, R.I., 1991.

Morgan, Edmund S. *The Puritan Dilemma*. Boston, 1958.

Neale, J. E. *Elizabeth and Her Parliaments 1584–1601*. New York, 1966.

Porter, H. C. *Reformation and Reaction in Tudor Cambridge*. 1958.

Rogers, Alan. *A History of Lincolnshire*. Chichester, 1985.

Roots, Ivan. *The Great Rebellion: 1642–1666*. London, 1966.

Rupp, Gordon. *Religion in England 1688–1791*. Oxford, 1986.

Russell, Conrad. *The Crisis of Parliaments: 1509–1660*. Oxford, 1971.

Sanborn, George F. and Melinda L. *Vital Records of Hampton, New Hampshire, Vol. I*. Boston, 1992.

Solt, Leo F. *Saints in Arms*. Stanford, Calif., 1959.

Taylor, Philip, ed. *The Origins of the English Civil War: Conspiracy, Crusade, or Class Conflict?* Boston, 1960.

Tolmie, Murray. *The Triumph of the Saints: The Separate Churches of London 1616–1649*. London, 1977.

Trevelyan, George. *England in the Age of Wycliffe*. London, 1906.

Tuchman, Barbara. *Practicing History: Selected Essays*. New York, 1982.

Underhill, Edward B. *Confessions of Faith and Other Public Documents*. London, 1854.

Underhill, Edward B. *Records of Churches of Christ . . . Fenstanton, Warboys, and Hexham, 1644–1720*. London, 1854.

Vaughan, Alden. *The Puritan Tradition in America 1620–1730.* New York, 1972.

Venn, John and J. A., eds. *Alumni Cantabigienses, Vol. 3.* Cambridge, 1924.

Wedgewood, C. V. *The Trial of Charles I.* London, 1964.

White, B. R. *The English Baptists of the 17th Century.* London, 1983.

White, B. R. *Hanserd Knollys and Radical Dissent in the 17th Century.* London, 1977.

Whitelock, Bulstrode. *Memorials of the English Affairs, Vol. II.* London, 1682.

Whitely, W. T. ed., *The Works of John Smyth Fellow of Christ's College 1594–1598, Vol. I.* Cambridge, 1915.

Whitley, W. T. *A History of the British Baptists,* Rev. ed. London, 1932.

Williams, Roger. *Bloody Tenent of Persecution.* Edward B. Underhill, ed. London, 1848.

Williams, Selma. *Divine Rebel: The Life of Anne Marbury Hutchinson.* New York, 1981.

Youings, Joyce. *The Dissolution of the Monasteries.* London, 1971.

Other Books Authored and Coauthored by Muriel James

Born to Win: Transactional Analysis with Gestalt Experiments (Addison-Wesley Publishing, 1971). Also in Chinese, Danish, Dutch, German, Parsi, Finnish, French, Greek, Hebrew, Italian, Japanese, Norwegian, Polish, Portuguese, Russian, Spanish, Turkish.

Winning with People: Group Exercises in Transactional Analysis (Addison-Wesley Publishing, 1973). Also in Spanish, Portuguese, Japanese, German.

Born to Love: Transactional Analysis in the Church (Addison-Wesley Publishing, 1973). Also in German, Norwegian.

What Do You Do with Them Now That You've Got Them? (Addison-Wesley Publishing, 1974). Also in Dutch, French, Japanese, Norwegian, Portuguese, Spanish.

The Power at the Bottom of the Well: Understanding the Church (Harper & Row Publishers, 1974). Also in German, Spanish.

The OK Boss (Addison-Wesley Publishing, 1973). Also in Danish, German, Italian, Japanese, Norwegian, Spanish.

The People Book: Transactional Analysis for Students (Addison-Wesley Publishing, 1973). Also in Spanish.

The Heart of Friendship (Harper & Row Publishers, 1976). Also in German.

Techniques in Psychotherapy for Psychotherapists and Counselors (Addison-Wesley Publishing, 1977).

A New Self: Self Therapy with Transactional Analysis (Addison-Wesley Publishing, 1977). Also in Parsi, Portuguese, Spanish.

Marriage Is for Loving (Addison-Wesley Publishing, 1979). Also in Japanese.

Breaking Free: Self-Reparenting for a New Self (Addison-Wesley Publishing, 1981). Also in Danish, Japanese, Portuguese, Spanish.

Winning Ways in Health Care (Addison-Wesley Publishing, 1981). Also in Japanese, Norwegian.

It's Never Too Late to Be Happy: The Psychology of Self-Reparenting (Addison-Wesley Publishing, 1985). Also in Danish, Portuguese.

The Better Boss in Multicultural Organizations (Published privately, 1991). Also in Japanese, Spanish.

Hearts on Fire: Romance and Achievement in the Lives of Great Women (Jeremy Tarcher Publisher, 1991).

Passion for Life: Psychology and the Human Spirit (Penguin, Dutton Publishers, 1991). Also in French.

Index

Page numbers in bold type indicate photo captions.

202

203